Beginni

Manchester University Press

Beginnings
Series editors: Peter Barry and Helen Carr

'**Beginnings**' is a series of books designed to give practical help to students beginning to tackle recent developments in English, Literary Studies and Cultural Studies. The books in the series

- demonstrate and encourage a questioning engagement with the new;
- give essential information about the context and history of each topic covered;
- show how to develop a practice which is up-to-date and informed by theory.

Each book focuses uncompromisingly upon the needs of its readers, who have the right to expect lucidity and clarity to be the distinctive feature of a book which includes the word 'beginning' in its title.

Each aims to lay a firm foundation of well understood initial principles as a basis for further study and is committed to explaining new aspects of the discipline without over-simplification, but in a manner appropriate to the needs of beginners.

Each book, finally, aims to be both an introduction and a contribution to the topic area it discusses.

Beginning realism

Steven Earnshaw

Manchester University Press
Manchester and New York
distributed in the United States exclusively
by Palgrave Macmillan

Published by Manchester University Press
Oxford Road, Manchester M13 9NR, UK
and Room 400, 175 Fifth Avenue, New York, NY 10010, USA
www.manchesteruniversitypress.co.uk

Distributed exclusively in the USA by
Palgrave, 175 Fifth Avenue, New York,
NY 10010, USA

Distributed exclusively in Canada by
UBC Press, University of British Columbia, 2029 West Mall,
Vancouver, BC, Canada V6T 1Z2

British Library Cataloguing-in-Publication Data
A catalogue record for this book is available from the British Library

Library of Congress Cataloging-in-Publication Data applied for

ISBN   978 0 7190 7220 8 *hardback*
ISBN   978 0 7190 7221 5 *paperback*

First published 2010

17 16 15 14 13 12 11 10 09 08   10 9 8 7 6 5 4 3 2 1

Typeset in Ehrhardt
by Action Publishing Technology Ltd, Gloucester
Printed in Great Britain
by Bell & Bain Ltd, Glasgow

For Beryl and Leslie Earnshaw

Contents

Acknowledgements

I am particularly grateful to Mike Harris for his observations, interventions and enthusiasm. I fear I have not addressed half the objections he raised, but perhaps they will do for another book. Many other colleagues have contributed substantially to my thinking about realism and pointed me in the right direction. It has been a real pleasure to share an interest in Mrs Oliphant with Lisa Hopkins, to argue about the finer points of *Middlemarch* and nineteenth-century realism with Jill LeBihan, Sue McPherson and Sarah Dredge, and to discuss the variety of fiction in the eighteenth century with Mary Peace. The treatment of modernism in relation to realism owes much to numerous conversations with Chris Hopkins and Mary Grover. John Milne has also proved an excellent sounding board – the fortune of having somebody on hand to discuss the accuracy of nineteenth-century nautical melodrama! And I was haunted by Jane Rogers's chance remark that Dickens is not a realist, for which I then had no adequate reply. Tom Rutter has probed away at my understanding of realism, and Ian Baker, with incisive charm, has prevented sloppy thinking on more than one occasion. Thanks to Keith Green, Alice Bell and Barbara MacMahon in helping out with language queries. I should also thank the anonymous readers of the original proposal for helping to shape the book, and the commissioning editor Matthew Frost, who showed considerable patience in waiting for the better book.

Liz, as ever, has provided the necessary sense of proportion and understanding – qualities much prized by the Realists.

Introduction

Ground rules

Realism should be easy. It is whatever is real, which we do not need to be told because we already know it: we live it every day of our lives. We all live in the real world, and nobody can tell us any different. We might need help with other 'isms' when studying literature or the arts – Romanticism, Surrealism, Modernism, Postmodernism, for instance, require some kind of explanation – but surely not an 'ism' which sounds as if it is based on our very existence. We may be aware that terms used to describe artistic practices have different meanings from their common usage, but 'realism' as an aesthetic idea surely cannot be too far removed from the way we would talk about something 'real' during the normal course of our lives: 'realism' is surely just the word 'real' made formal, a subject fit for study. What is the fuss about? Why on earth should anybody need to read a book about it?

The fact that realism should be, and often is presumed to be, 'easy', because we live in 'the real world' and therefore know what is real when see it, is one of the problems we face in trying to analyse it. We take for granted that we live in the real world, and in our everyday lives we judge things against what is 'real' all the time, only rarely stepping back to question this process. The 'real' is our 'default' position: fantasy, science fiction, unreal, implausible, surreal, gothic, nonsense – all these terms only work because they imply a relation to what we know to be real or true. Our judgement and attitude to what is real is, in the first instance, therefore mainly intuitive – we have a feel for what is real, and so we recognise instantly if something accords with what we believe to be true or real. If an event, fact, object or story falls outside of what we understand to be real we adjust our worldview in order to accommodate it, or we continue to 'not believe it' and assign it to 'yet to be verified' or 'just not true'. But how does this relate to realism as a concept used in literary criticism? Is the way we understand 'real' in everyday life simply transferred across to critical approaches to novels, plays and poems? Is literature 'realist' if it talks about a world we immediately recognise as 'real'? Is it 'realist' if we can nod our heads in agreement with novelists, dramatists or poets and congratulate them on having more or less faithfully copied a world we know or believe to be real?

The answer to this is probably 'yes', up to a point. If consciously, or not so consciously, we find ourselves saying, 'yes, that's just how it is', 'that's how it must have been' or 'that's true to life', we are probably within the bounds of traditionally realist literature. And if that is the case can there be much more in the way of interest or enlightenment to say about it? Our job as critics, analysts and commentators might then be to compare the work of literature with the world it represents, to look at how Dickens's *Hard Times* (1854) measures up to the reality of trade-union activity and life on the poverty line in Victorian England, for instance; or how Shelagh Delaney's play *A Taste of Honey* measures up to real working-class life in another northern town in England a hundred years later (1958). Identifying works as 'realist' immediately draws us into making these comparisons between the world depicted and the work that depicts it, a more-or-less game of 'spot the difference'. What this approach tends to obscure is the artistry – the myriad techniques – that the writer has to use in order to create a work that is realist, to create a world that seems real. It also glosses over the very deep assumptions we have – assumptions dependent upon culture, philosophy, science and ideology – which underpin our understanding of what is 'real' in the first place.

This book explores the artistry and aesthetics of realist literature, along with the assumptions (and criticisms) of realist literature. It explores the different ways in which theorists, critics and philosophers conceptualise 'realism', and it explores the different approaches we might bring to both the theories of realism and the analysis of texts, realist and otherwise. As we observe, when we talk of realism as a philosophical attitude, it is a particular way of seeing and understanding the world, and when we speak of 'literary realism', we are identifying a class of litera-ture that adheres to some version of this realist stance, and treats and presents its material accordingly. When we consider realism as a particular literary mode for representing the world, we see that it has its own techniques, presumptions, frameworks and limits, just as Romantic or modernist works do. In this sense, realist literature has conventions, it is not 'natural' in the way that it is sometimes taken to be. However, I argue in this book that a 'realist' sensibil-ity is the ground on which other modes of literature often exist.

The only thing, then, that is 'easy' about literary realism is that sometimes we find ourselves reading a type of literature that we find immediately comprehensible and familiar, or 'accessible'. How the literature works to achieve this is possibly more difficult to understand than other types of literature because we are so familiar with realist art that we do not notice how it manipulates its materials. We also see that what counts as 'real' and 'realist' is far from clear cut, and the very assumption that 'realist literature' is synonymous with 'accessible' or 'easy to read' is also open to question. For instance, Erich Auerbach's classic book on realism, *Mimesis*, first published in 1946, ends with a chapter on Virginia Woolf's *To the Lighthouse*, which he treats as ushering in a new type of realism. Yet Woolf's work is usually regarded, as are many other works of modernism, as being 'anti-realist' and falling within the 'difficult to read' bracket. We discuss this in Chapter 6, on modernism, but for now we shall stick with the more tradition-al views of realism before subjecting it to other critiques.

As a way of thinking about the complexity of realism let us consider a term that is often associated with it: 'verisimilitude'. This describes something that appears to be true or real, some-thing that has the appearance of truth or reality. We might therefore expect any work of literature that is realist to have the quality or character of 'verisimilitude', to have the appearance of truth or reality. The significant thing to note here is the qualifying phrase 'the appearance of'. In other words, the realist work of literature 'has the appearance of truth or reality', it is not *in itself* 'true' or 'real'. Another way of putting this is to say that realist literature, be it poem, play or novel, 'represents' the real, gives the impression of conveying what is real or drawing directly upon real life. It may even feel, as we read, that we are immersed in the real world as depicted – the characters are 'brought to life', it is as though we are really 'there'. These kinds of judgements are often used to determine the success or otherwise of realist literature: how much we 'lose' ourselves in the world of the text is an indication of how well the writer has convinced us of the reality of his or her creation, and this may be very much part of the pleasure a reader takes from the literature.

But to return to the central point, it is clear that what we are dealing with is the 'appearance of what is real' and the 'appearance of what is true', we are not dealing with 'the real' and 'the true' directly. Reality has been 'mediated' in some way by the writer, somebody has had to present 'the real' to us, or 're-present' it, 'create' or 'construct' it. These alternative ways of saying what the writer is doing – presentation, re-presentation, creation or construction – indicate that there is some dispute as to precisely what is going on when it comes to realist literature. As regards realism, if a writer has done the job well, we may easily forget that the subject matter has in fact been mediated, that it is a question of 'representation', that it is not *really* 'real' or 'true', it only *appears* to be. It could be argued that readers of realist novels do sometimes take events and characters in novels to be real world events and real world characters. People used to visit Little Nell's grave at St Bartholomew's church in the village of Tong, Shropshire, England, believing her to have been buried there ('supposed grave', I should say?). But we know these people were deluded because Little Nell is a fictional character in Dickens's *The Old Curiosity Shop* – and you and I both know the difference between 'the real' and the imaginary – we have a default knowledge or position of 'the real' from which we can quickly spot those who are deluded. And even if we, on occasion, find ourselves numbered among the deluded, there are the means for 'undeluding' us – reason, evidence, common sense – which, in the realist world, can readily be applied. (If you vehemently disagree with this common-sense notion of realism you might want to go directly to Chapter 10, on philosophy).

STOP and THINK

The assumption is often made that readers of realist works, particularly novels, believe themselves to be transported into the world described. Is this really the case? Do realist novels and plays make you feel more engaged than other modes of literature? Can you be equally immersed in gothic fiction, for instance?

You might also want to consider terms like 'realistic', mimesis, verisimilitude (and other related ideas). What differences are there between these ideas, or do you take them to be interchangeable?

Realism: capital 'R' and small 'r'

The term 'realism' tends to be used in two ways. The first use of the term identifies a literary-historical period, namely those years in the second half of the nineteenth century where there was significant production of a type of literature, which often identified itself as 'realist' (or 'naturalist'), or which can be regarded as such. It is synonymous with the novel genre, and the key figures here are writers such as George Eliot, Anthony Trollope and Elizabeth Gaskell in England, and Flaubert and Zola in France. When referring to this usage I will give Realism a capital 'R' in order to identify this literary-historical period, referring therefore to its literature and attendant aesthetic theorising. The second understanding of realism is a more general one, not too dissimilar from that which I have outlined above, whereby there is a tendency or aim in a work of literature to reproduce a faithful copy of the world, though the works are not necessarily just to be found in the literary-historical period of Realism, that is, not necessarily to be found in the second half of the nineteenth century. I hope that this distinction is helpful, and I will maintain it throughout the book. *Beginning Realism* is interested in both realism and Realism, and of course the two are related, that is, nineteenth-century Realism might be regarded as a special case of this more general realist tendency in art and literature, what I will call the realist impulse.

As it really is: the realist impulse

There is no one element that defines literary realism – it is a mixture of philosophical tendencies, aesthetic aims and literary techniques. Each of these elements is in the plural: there is no one philosophy, aim or technique that is definitive as 'realist', although I will suggest the main characteristics of each in relation to realism. The initial focus in this book is on the Realist novel of the second half of the nineteenth century, for this is usually what is understood by the term 'Realist' literature, and where it is most solidly and originally expressed. In other words, when there is discussion of Realism, as a self-conscious literary movement, it is to this particular period and this particular genre that commentary turns.

Nevertheless, one of the difficulties in discussing realism is that whatever is said to be distinctive about Realist novels may not be distinctive at all, and we end up with a variation on a long-standing theme, which may have been called by different names prior to the emergence of Realism. You may find yourself saying, for instance, 'yes, but you find that in Shakespeare', or, perhaps along with Margaret Anne Doody in *The Story of the Novel* (1996), you might find that the novel is far from 'novel' and has existed since Greek times, at least. A common, stated aim of the Realists was to represent the world 'as it really is', to 'hold a mirror up to reality'. This impulse is one of the things that unites the English and French Realist writers of the nineteenth century, for instance. Yet surely there has always been what might be called 'the realist impulse', the desire to faithfully render the world as it is? It is true, for instance, that this very same aim may be found in those writers and artists immediately prior to the nineteenth-century Realists, even in the Romanticism that preceded it and against which much Realist writing operated. Wordsworth in his Preface (1800) to the

Lyrical Ballads (1798) claims to offer a poetry that speaks in the 'real language of men', albeit men in a 'state of vivid sensation'; in the original advert for the collection Wordsworth asks readers to judge for themselves whether the book 'contains a natural delineation of human passions, human characters, and human incidents'. Both of these claims for the *Lyrical Ballads* would seem more in keeping with Romanticism's antithesis, Realism. Further, only a few years prior to Romanticism, Alexander Pope's aesthetic dictum from the first half of the eighteenth century would seem highly amenable to 'telling it as it really is':

> True wit is nature to advantage dress'd;
> What oft was thought, but ne'er so well express'd.

Pope acknowledges an ornamental mediation on behalf of art, but nature is the evident base, if slightly improved in representing it, perhaps.

Moving further back in literary history, readers and audiences may yet feel that the psychological accuracy to be found in some of Shakespeare's tragedies – Hamlet's ambivalence, Othello's jealousy, Lear's folly – is as real as anything to be found in some of the psychological detailing in nineteenth-century Realist fiction. Ultimately, we can find ourselves going back further and further, stopping perhaps at where another book on Realism/realism might start – Aristotle's *Poetics* and his discussion of 'mimesis'. The artistic desire to faithfully represent or reproduce the world 'as it is' appears to have been there for a long time, perhaps taking us back even beyond Aristotle to cave paintings and an urge to represent animals that were hunted and revered. So we need to consider what there is other than the realist impulse that combines to give us Realism. What I will argue is that there is a very particular combination of factors that produces Realism in the second half of the nineteenth century, with quite identifiable differences between England and France. Once we move out from this core to explore in greater detail how this is differentiated from other literature and art that precede and succeed it, we may yet find ourselves faced once again with the 'slipperiness' of Realism/realism, but at least we will have held on to something for a while before we part company in our understanding.

Classical literary 'Realism'

The term 'Realism' as an aesthetic category is relatively recent, and is first credited to its use in the field of painting in the nineteenth century. When Gustave Courbet entitled his solo exhibition in Paris in 1855 'Du Réalisme', one of the outcomes of the controversy around his exhibition was the founding of the journal, *Réalisme*, by Edmond Duranty (1856); and in 1857 Champfleury, a supporter of Courbet, 'brought out a volume of critical discussions entitled *Le Réalisme*. The term was launched, though its meaning was still to be defined' (Becker 1963: 7–8, and Fernand Desnoyers, 'On Realism', in Becker 1963: 80–9. See also Morris 2003: 63–5).

As will be shown, the origin of the term is French, and the impression remains that in England there was no comparable concerted debate on 'realism'. The mention of a 'realist school' appears as early as 1851 in *Fraser's Magazine*, nevertheless, and the first appearance in English of the term 'realism' is credited to G. H. Lewes in 1853 in the *Westminster Review* (Becker 1963: 7). The lack of significant theoretical work on realism in England is put down to a couple of reasons, both of which will have a bearing on the way we might think about English literary Realism later in this book, and which I will deal with briefly here.

The first reason is that the English novel has always keenly felt the realist impulse, and so its nineteenth-century incarnation seemed like a natural and gradual progression in the English novel tradition. From Defoe, through Richardson, Burney and Austen, for instance, the realist impulse is evident; and the works of Eliot, Trollope, Gaskell, Thackeray and Dickens continued this tradition. It was not necessary, therefore, to make a fuss over something that had been an ever-present feature of the English novel. The second reason sometimes given is that abstract theorising is not native to English writers and critics, but is something that those on the continent – the French and Germans – indulge in. An important corollary to the first reason is that, from a French point of view, and from some English viewpoints, as we will later see, the English tradition was too circumscribed by moral convention and literary decorum to ever be Realist in the manner of Zola or Flaubert. From this angle, there was no debate on Realism of comparable magnitude in England because the English novelists were simply not Realists after the Zola school – they were first and foremost middle-class moralists: in a word, 'bourgeois'. In comparison with the fervour surrounding French Realism, and the raw works emanating from that part of the world, the English realist impulse looked rather feeble, in hock to its tradition of gentility, and thus in no way Realist. This is the argument that Becker advances in *Documents of Modern Literary Realism*:

> As William Dean Howells wrote T. S. Perry in 1886, no one invent-ed it [realism]; rather it seems spontaneously to have come all at once and everywhere, except in England. As may be inferred from the selections presented in this volume the main battle over realism was waged in France, with subsidiary skirmishes in other countries in which French works were usually the bone of contention. (Becker 1963: 8)

Becker's volume is a major aid to research on Realism since it brings together many representative and seminal works on Realism from the nineteenth century, yet, as he avows here, he sees Realism as originating in France and spreading outwards around the world everywhere, except to England. The contrast between the English Realists and the French Realists is taken up through-out *Beginning Realism* since the fault-lines tell us much about the development and contours of the Realist aesthetic. According to Becker, the type of Realist novel produced by the French is not visible in England until the 1880s (1963: 15). As I show, George Gissing's novel *The Unclassed* (1884) attempts to import French-style Realism into the English novel in order to make it more 'Realist' than the English novel has hitherto been. However, the matter is more complicated than this brief sketch suggests: the 'unclassed' of Gissing's novel refers both to social classes, which have not been represented in English literature, but also a new kind of novel that wants to move beyond Realism. From the 1880s onwards, there is a new aesthetic pressure, which will become labelled 'modernism', and this complicates the acceptance of French-style Realism into the English novel and English litera-ture. Contrary to Becker's view, I suggest that to understand

Realism we need to view both the English and the French as contributors to different aspects of Realism.

Why is Realism important?

I would suggest that there are a number of reasons for studying literary realism. It is a significant feature in debates about the novel form; if 'the real' is our default orientation in the world, then an aesthetic which self-consciously embraces this tells us something about the way we understand self and world; modernist and postmodernist modes of literature depend heavily upon notions of 'the real' and an understanding of realism in order to construct their own aesthetics; politically motivated literature – for example humanist, socialist, feminist, postcolonial – has to come to terms with what mode of representation best suits its needs. As regards the latter, the argument is often along the lines that realism is itself representative of certain social interests, particularly 'bourgeois' (in the case of the novel and drama) or elitist (in the case of poetry).

STOP and THINK

If you have studied Realist novels, such as those of Dickens, Gaskell or Eliot, what assumptions did you bring to them? Did you study them in the same way as non-Realist novels? Do later realist works, for instance, Alan Sillitoe's *Saturday Night Sunday Morning*, strike you in the same way?

How did you know that these were examples of Realist writing?

Preliminary reading: a Realist mini-canon

There is a chicken-and-egg problem in writing a book about a term as contested as 'Realism'. I could list the features that characterise Realism, and then produce as evidence literature that has these characteristics. Alternatively, I could look at lots of possibly Realist work and identify what might be common features. There is a certain circularity to either of these methods. Another approach would take into account what latter-day commentators have said about Realism and produce a synthetic report, or I could push forward my own view on the basis of these, and then look at works which are supposed to be Realist and see if they match up. I could mix up these methodologies to produce an account that continually modified an initial understanding of Realism in response to research into Realist works.

I set out my stall at the beginning of Chapter 1, and make a very clear statement as to what I believe Realism to be. I then follow this through in more detail and relate it to Realist fiction (later chapters look at this with respect to poetry and drama from the period), largely using arguments as laid out in the nineteenth century, although highlighting objections (particularly in Chapter 3, 'Problems in defining the Realist novel') where appropriate. More formal consideration of theoretical and philosophical work on realism occurs in Chapter 7 on postmodernism, and subsequent chapters, and it would be possible to start there if you wanted to get involved more directly with secondary critical material on realism.

To make things manageable at the start, as well as helping to boost clarity, I have used a 'mini-canon' of Realist novels. In order to avoid a too-circular argument – that is, just choosing novels that support my statement – the novels, although all putatively 'Realist', never exhibit all the features that I define as typical of Realist writing. This is because there is no one novel which is 'the' Realist novel, only works which are Realist to a greater or lesser extent. Here is the set of novels I use in order to explore my preliminary definition of Realism:

> Elizabeth Gaskell, *Mary Barton* and *North and South*
> George Eliot, *The Mill on the Floss* and *Middlemarch*
> Charles Dickens, *Hard Times* and *Dombey and Son*
> Anthony Trollope, *The Warden* and *Barchester Towers*
> Émile Zola, *Germinal* and *L'Assommoir*
> William Makepeace Thackeray, *Vanity Fair*
> Mrs Oliphant, *Phoebe Junior* and *Hester*

Although there is much to discuss, I would just point out some of the more obvious points of contact between the novels, other than their proximity in dates of publication and operation within the Realist aesthetic. The Gaskell novels, *Hard Times* and *Germinal* all deal with a major thematic of the day, the relations between 'masters and workers', and allow for comparisons in their treatment of this. They all feature representation of a strike, for example. Eliot's *Middlemarch* could be 'the' Realist text, and it makes for an interesting contrast with a quite different execution of Realism in *The Mill on the Floss*. Trollope's work is what might be called 'standard realist', as might Oliphant's. Mrs Oliphant felt herself unfairly forever in the shadow of George Eliot, and so it is instructive to compare her work to Eliot's (as well as Trollope's – she is sometimes considered to be his female counterpart). *Vanity Fair* is significant for discussions of Realism yet, rather like Dickens, presents a number of problems for our definition. Zola's novels are clearly of a different order from the English novelists, so this provides a good point of contrast for English and French Realism, and *L'Assommoir* could also have a claim to be 'the' Realist novel, rather than *Middlemarch*. The other thing is that they are all great reads.

Further reading and works cited

Becker's Introduction to *Documents of Modern Literary Realism* is comprehensive, and the book itself provides an excellent collection of material from the nineteenth century related to Realism. Pam Morris's book *Realism* (2003) has plenty of detail about the schools of realism in the nineteenth century. I would also strongly recommend Lillian R. Furst's *All is True. The Claims and Strategies of Realist Fiction* (1995) and Elizabeth Deeds Ermarth, *Realism and Consensus in the English Novel* (1983). Furst's edited collection *Realism* (1992) has a judicious selection of important pronouncements on Realism. For an overview of the Victorian period, Philip Davis's *Victorians* (2002) stands out, and includes chapters on the Realist novelists.

Other books which treat realism are Peter Brooks, *Realist Vision* (2005), which looks at Realist novelists in the context of painting in the nineteenth century; George Levine, *The Realistic Imagination. English Fiction from Frankenstein to Lady Chatterley* (1981); J. P. Stern, *On Realism* (1973). A difficult book at times, I would nevertheless suggest Katherine Kearns's *Nineteenth-Century Realism. Through the Looking-Glass* (1996) for a provocative and thoroughly engaged treatment of Realism. René Wellek's 'The Concept of Realism in Literary Scholarship', *Neophilologus* 44 (1960), reprinted in *Concepts of Criticism*, ed. Stephen J. Nichols Jr (1963) remains a valuable contribution and overview.

Becker, G. J. (1963), *Documents of Modern Literary Realism*. Princeton: Princeton University Press.

Brooks, Peter (2005), *Realist Vision*. New Haven: Yale University Press.

Davis, Philip (2002), *The Oxford English Literary History Volume 8. 1830–1880. The Victorians*. Oxford: Oxford University Press.

Doody, Margaret Anne (1996), *The True Story of the Novel*. New Brunswick, NJ: Rutgers University Press.

Ermarth, Elizabeth Deeds (1983), *Realism and Consensus in the English Novel*. Princeton, NJ: Princeton University Press.

Furst, Lilian R. (ed.) (1992), *Realism*. Harlow, Essex: Longman.

Furst, Lilian R. (1995), *All is True. The Claims and Strategies of Realist Fiction*. Duke University Press.

Kearns, Katherine (1996), *Nineteenth-Century Realism. Through the Looking-Glass*. Cambridge: Cambridge University Press.

Levine, George (1981), *The Realistic Imagination. English Fiction from Frankenstein to Lady Chatterley*. Chicago and London: University of Chicago Press.

Morris, Pam (2003), *Realism*. London: Routledge.

Stern, J. P. (1973), *On Realism*. London: Routledge.

Wellek, René (1960), 'The Concept of Realism in Literary Scholarship', *Neophilologus* 44; reprinted in *Concepts of Criticism*, ed. Stephen J. Nichols Jr (1963), New Haven, Yale University Press.

Wordsworth, William (1798), 'Preface' (1800) to *Lyrical Ballads*.

1

The nineteenth-century Realist novel: two principles

Characteristics of the Realist novel

The Realist novel presents stories, characters and settings that are similar to those commonly found in the contemporary everyday world. This requires events to take place in the present or recent past, and the events themselves are usually organised in a linear, chronological sequence, and located in places familiar to author and audience either through direct observation or report. The characters and storylines are plausible, and in this they are therefore commonplace rather than out of the ordinary. The desire to portray contemporary everyday life entails and requires a breadth of social detail, and, as a consequence, the classes represented tend to be those categorised as working class and middle class, since these form the majority of the population. The medium of representation is prose fiction, and the prose itself is functional rather than poetic, accessible rather than elevated or ornate – it is the language of newspapers and Parliamentary reports, for instance, and aims to accurately represent the real life it draws upon.

Similarly, rendering of dialogue should be authentic and plausible. The subject matter for the Realist novel is whatever is to be found in everyday life, good and bad. The narrative point of view is characteristically omniscient. The novels often engage with social issues of the day, for instance, employment relations, or the place of women in society. Related to this, the Realist novel may thus offer some moral viewpoint, but there is a Realist sensibility that pressures this to be subordinate to neutrality and objectivity as the novel strives for accuracy in its representation. As part of the drive to be accurate, the representations are often given in detail. Characters, events, places, dialogue should all be 'true' in the sense of being 'verifiable', where that means being true to the experience of the readership, or to what it knows or believes to be true. The Realist world is one in which cause and effect explains everything, in that one event happens as a direct consequence of an event or events that have preceded it.

This is about as general – yet as specific – as I can make my definition of the nineteenth-century Realist novel. It is a description that nineteenth-century Realist novelists would recognise, even if they would not necessarily put it in such codified terms. The cluster of characteristics proffered here defines a body of literature that dominated the literary scene, both aesthetically and in terms of popularity, from the end of the 1840s to the close of the nineteenth century. In Europe it starts to be superseded aesthetically by modernism, most noticeably from the 1880s onwards, while Realism gathers momentum in the United States only towards the end of the nineteenth century. Realism has continued to be significant until the present day, and it could be argued that it boosted the previously more diffuse realist impulse to the point where realism has continued to be the most popular mode of artistic representation, in the visual arts as well as in literature, although critically the most maligned.

The remainder of this chapter looks at the above characteristics in more detail, as well as suggesting reasons why Realism dominates art in this period.

First principle: the faithful copy

There were numerous claims in the nineteenth century that the aim of art should be to represent the world faithfully, and this can be taken as the first principle of Realism. The reasons why artists, critics, philosophers and aestheticians make these claims are various, and the ways in which they believe the principle might be realised in and by art are various, but this first principle is dominant.

Stendhal's novel from 1830, *Le Rouge et Le Noir* (*Red and Black*), offers the quotation 'a novel is a mirror walking down the road', and this idea that the novel is an unmediated reflector of the real world gains a hold throughout the nineteenth century. Vissarion Grigorovich in 1835 talks of 'the poetry of reality' (where poetry is art in general): 'Its distinct character consists in the fact that it is true to reality; it does not create life anew, but reproduces it, and, like a convex glass, mirrors in itself, from one point of view, life's diverse phenomena, extracting from them those that are necessary to create a full, vivid, and organically unified picture' (in Becker 1963: 42). Grigorovich here notes some modification on the part of the mirror-artist – 'extraction' – but the essential Realist aim is the same, to mirror reality. It could be argued that the dominance of the mirror metaphor suggests a certain naivety, or lack of sophistication on the part of these writers, but while this may be true in some instances, in general I think that such a judgement is misplaced and does a disservice to the leading Realist novelists. Fernand Desnoyer's declamation, 'I demand for painting and for literature the same rights as mirrors have', certainly may seem to be an abuse of the language of rights, one that reflects the heated exchanges in French Realist debates, but more usually the mirror metaphor acts as a guiding aesthetic principle, rather than the mirror being an agent that somehow acts independently of the author in an unmediated manner. In George Eliot's first novel, *Adam Bede* (1859), the narrator takes stock of the novelist's role:

'This Rector of Broxton is little better than a pagan!' I hear one of my readers exclaim. 'How much more edifying it would have been if you had made him give Arthur some truly spiritual advice! You might have put into his mouth the most beautiful things – quite as good as reading a sermon.'

Certainly I could, if I held it the highest vocation of the novelist to represent things as they never have been and never will be. Then, of course, I might refashion life and character entirely after my own liking; I might select the most unexceptionable type of clergyman and put my own admirable opinions into his mouth on all occasions. But it happens, on the contrary, that my strongest effort is to avoid any such arbitrary picture, and to give a faithful account of men and

> things as they have mirrored themselves in my mind. The mirror is
> doubtless defective, the outlines will sometimes be disturbed, the
> reflection faint or confused; but I feel as much bound to tell you as
> precisely as I can what that reflection is, as if I were in the witness-
> box, narrating my experience on oath. (Eliot 1948: 178)

That the novelist does have a part to play in ordering material
taken from the real world is evident, but once again the guiding
idea is that the novel mirrors reality. The mirror may be in the
novelist's mind, and subject to defects, but it is the novelist's duty
to minimise this distortion. The guiding idea, for Eliot and others,
means that 'accuracy' of representation is at a premium, and that
the real world and the narrator's experience of it that will provide
the measure of this accuracy. We also get a sense of the common
expectations of art, which Eliot is working against in this period,
for example, that the novel should offer moral improvement on
what is to be found in the real world, and that it should aim for
what is beautiful.

As already suggested, there is an overriding impulse in Realist
art that moral viewpoints should be subordinated to the idea of
the neutral, reflecting mirror. It is clear here, therefore, that the
Realist novel should also avoid being didactic, a vehicle for the
author's sermonising. Again, we can see that the mirror metaphor
continues to act as a guiding principle for, after all, a mirror cannot
be expected to have its own opinions. On one level there are
obvious contradictions, since the narrator is claiming a mirror-like
neutrality and yet foregrounding the role of the novelist as an individual witness involved in narration, but this level is subordinate
to the overriding Realist tenets avowed here.

Not only does the principle of the faithful copy work as a
general guideline for novelists and their approach to novels, but it
becomes the measure of success for the Realist novelist, and the
measure of failure for others. Trollope, for instance, was not alone
in his dismissal of Dickens on the grounds that he grossly distorted reality. In Trollope's novel *The Warden* (1855) the Reverend
Septimus Harding receives money for looking after a group of
retired wool-carders who have fallen on hard times. The money
should arguably go directly to the men, but instead they only
receive a small amount of this income. The issue is taken up by

The Thunderer (a thinly-disguised version of *The Times*) and Harding finds himself in an unwelcome spotlight and the pawn of church politics. There is an entertaining passage in which Trollope recasts the narrative as it might appear in a serialised Dickens novel, *The Almshouse*. He does not name Dickens directly, but instead calls him Mr Popular Sentiment. Serialisation and Dickens's general style are criticised for encouraging only superficial engagement with the real nature of things: 'ridicule is found to be more convincing than argument, imaginary agonies touch more than true sorrows, and monthly novels convince, when learned quartos fail to do so. If the world is to be set right, the work will be done by shilling numbers' (Trollope 2004: 135). He goes on to imagine Dickens's recreation of the put-upon Mr Harding:

> The demon of the 'Almshouse' was the clerical owner of this comfortable abode. He was a man well stricken in years, but still strong to do evil: he was one who looked cruelly out of a hot, passionate, bloodshot eye; who had a huge red nose with a carbuncle, thick lips, and a great double, flabby chin, which swelled out into solid substance, like a turkey cock's comb, when sudden anger inspired him: he had a hot, furrowed, low brow, from which a few grizzled hairs were not yet rubbed off by the friction of his handkerchief: he wore a loose unstarched white handkerchief, black loose ill-made clothes, and huge loose shoes, adapted to many corns and various bunions: his husky voice told tales of much daily port wine, and his language was not so decorous as became a clergyman. Such was the master of Mr. Sentiment's 'Almshouse.' (Trollope 2004: 136)

Trollope's chastisement of Dickens is for his unfaithful copy of the real world, summed up as: 'his good poor people are so very good; his hard rich people so very hard; and the genuinely honest so very honest' (2004: 135). While Dickens himself was generally recognised as a literary giant, the increasing clamour for the 'faithful copy' led to criticism of his distortive style. Trollope is one of many authors acting as the Realist 'corrective' to the sensationalist, sentimental, melodramatic side of Dickens. And just as Trollope finds fault with Dickens's Realism, Mrs Oliphant finds fault with Trollope and others in her novel *Phoebe Junior* (1989). There is a point in the novel when Reginald is about to leave his father's house in order to take up the job of a warden (with fewer qualms than Harding – itself a testament to a certain realistic pragmatism which Mrs Oliphant mixes in with the Realist aesthetic) – and will be replaced by a paying pupil, Clarence Copperhead. Reginald says that a pupil is often trouble.

> 'A pupil is a nuisance. For instance, no man who has a family should ever take one. I know what things are said.'
>
> 'You mean about the daughters? That is true enough, there are always difficulties in the way; but you need not be afraid of Clarence Copperhead. He is not the fascinating pupil of a church-novel. There's nothing the least like the Heir of Redclyffe about him.'
>
> 'You are very well up in Miss Yonge's novels, Miss Beecham.'
>
> 'Yes,' said Phoebe; 'one reads Scott for Scotland (and a few other things), and one reads Miss Yonge for the church. Mr. Trollope is good for that too, but not so good. All that I know of clergymen's families I have got from her. I can recognize you quite well, and your sister, but the younger ones puzzle me; they are not in Miss Yonge; they are too much like other children, too naughty. I don't mean anything disagreeable. The babies in Miss Yonge are often very naughty too, but not the same.'

In addition then to the dig at Trollope, Mrs Oliphant has Phoebe view Reginald through the prism of Miss Yonge's church novels, and is puzzled by the lack of match between Miss Yonge's representation of children and 'real' children. Other than that, Phoebe tells Reginald that she knows what he is like, thanks to Miss Yonge: '"See how much I have got out of Miss Yonge. I know you as well as if I had known you all my life; a great deal better than I know Clarence Copperhead; but then, no person of genius has taken any trouble about him." / "I did not know I had been a hero of fiction," said Reginald, who had a great mind to be angry' (1989: 175).

Critics at the time noted the contradictions inherent in the Realist stance, and some of these contradictions would eventually lead to the undermining of Realism as the self-consciously dominant artistic mode, but for the moment let us accept Realism on its own terms and look at how novels carried out this mission to faithfully mirror everyday reality. We focus on just a few of the main considerations for the Realist novel – setting, description and characterisation – before turning to a second principle.

Setting

The subtitle of George Eliot's novel *Middlemarch* is *A Study of Provincial Life*, and this directs the reader to the fact that a certain type of social environment is the unifying feature and central focus of attention for the novel. This is quite typical for Realist writing, and not just because it provides a convenient method of bringing together what otherwise might be a disparate group of characters. The subtitle indicates that a certain type of behaviour – provincial life – is to be objectively observed. What we therefore have, if the title is anything to go by, is a scientific or naturalist approach to the study of human behaviour in a prescribed habitat. I deal with the 'study' part of the title later on when discussing the influence of science. It is enough to point out here that setting in the Realist novel is not merely incidental, providing colourful or recognisable backdrops for dramatic stories, but it often demonstrates the wholly interdependent connection between humans and their environments – determining character and behaviour in the way that an animal's character and behaviour are determined by its habitat.

In expanding upon the importance of place we see that it manifests itself in different ways. Eliot's use of a provincial setting is typical for English Realist novels. Gaskell's *Cranford* (1851) is another prime example. 'Provincial' in this usage means a preponderance of genteel society, 'bourgeois' life. The setting and the type of people to be found in that setting are co-dependent. Similarly, Trollope's *The Warden*, the first novel in the *Barchester Chronicles*, opens by giving us a sense of Barchester and what, therefore, we are likely to expect from such a place:

> The Rev. Septimus Harding was, a few years since, a beneficed clergyman residing in the cathedral town of —; let us call it Barchester. Were we to name Wells or Salisbury, Exeter, Hereford, or Gloucester, it might be presumed that something personal was intended; and as this tale will refer mainly to the cathedral dignitaries of the town in question, we are anxious that no personality may be suspected. Let us presume that Barchester is a quiet town in the West of England, more remarkable for the beauty of its cathedral and the antiquity of its monuments than for any commercial prosperity; that the west end of Barchester is the cathedral close, and

that the aristocracy of Barchester are the bishop, dean, and canons, with their respective wives and daughters. (Trollope 2004: 1)

Note how the narrator lists interchangeable cathedral towns from the west of England. This is a typical Realist gambit as regards place, suggesting that life in the fictional Barchester can be observed in any number of real towns in this area. The light-hearted determination to avoid any hint of 'personalising' allows it to offer up Barchester as generic, another study of everyday life, here set among the clergy, a more familiar social set then than now.

Next to a provincial location, the other typical setting for the Realist novel is an industrial town, and similar types of co-dependency between the characters and their environments are evident. *Mary Barton* opens with a description of the outskirts of the town, which has the partial effect of allowing us an overview of the location, and aiding objective consideration. When there is a fire at Carsons' mill the narration focuses on a specific area within the town that again reflects the importance of setting:

> Carsons' mill ran lengthways from east to west. Along it went one of the oldest thoroughfares in Manchester. Indeed, all that part of the town was comparatively old; it was there that the first cotton mills were built, and the crowded alleys and back streets of the neigh-bourhood made a fire there particularly to be dreaded. The staircase of the mill ascended from the entrance at the western end, which faced into a wide, dingy-looking street, consisting principally of public-houses, pawnbrokers' shops, rag and bone warehouses, and dirty provision shops. The other, the east end of the factory, fronted into a very narrow back street, not twenty feet wide, and miserably lighted and paved. Right against this end of the factory were the gable ends of the last house in the principal street – a house which from its size, its handsome stone facings, and the attempt at orna-ment in the front, had probably been once a gentleman's house; but now the light which streamed from its enlarged front windows made clear the interior of the splendidly fitted-up room, with its painted walls, its pillared recesses, its gilded and gorgeous fittings–up, its miserable squalid inmates. It was a gin palace. (Gaskell 2003: 50–1)

Once again we have a detailed physical description of a location, more integrated into the storyline than usual, and one which carries meaning beyond its ostensible description, for example, in the proximity of gin palace and factory. Phrases such as 'miserably lighted and paved' and 'dirty provision shops' are evaluative, and the repetition of 'miserable' in 'miserable squalid inmates' and 'miserably lighted' firmly links characters and environment in a typical Realist fashion. In such a passage adjectives such as 'miserable' and 'squalid' function equally as descriptions of the physical, mental and moral worlds of the inhabitants, a consequence of the belief in the interdependence of environment and human character.

Within the settings of city, town or village, and within particular areas (as above), we often then get descriptions of individual houses, again as evidence of the interdependence of character and environment, and also as part of the need to objectively describe the habitat in as much empirical detail as possible. For example, early on in *Mary Barton* we get a lengthy description of the Barton house:

Mrs. Barton produced the key of the door from her pocket; and on entering the house-place it seemed as if they were in total darkness, except one bright spot, which might be a cat's eye, or might be, what it was, a red-hot fire, smouldering under a large piece of coal, which John Barton immediately applied himself to break up, and the effect instantly produced was warm and glowing light in every corner of the room. To add to this (although the coarse yellow glare seemed lost in the ruddy glow from the fire), Mrs. Barton lighted a dip by sticking it in the fire, and having placed it satisfactorily in a tin candlestick, began to look further about her, on hospitable thoughts intent. The room was tolerably large, and possessed many conveniences. On the right of the door, as you entered, was a longish window, with a broad ledge. On each side of this, hung blue-and-white check curtains, which were now drawn, to shut in the friends met to enjoy themselves. Two geraniums, unpruned and leafy, which stood on the sill, formed a further defence from out-door pryers. In the corner between the window and the fireside was a cupboard, apparently full of plates and dishes, cups and saucers, and some more nondescript articles, for which one would have fancied their possessors could find no use – such as triangular pieces of glass to save carving knives and forks from dirtying table-cloths. However, it was evident Mrs. Barton was proud of her crockery and glass, for she left her cupboard door open, with a glance round of satisfaction and pleasure. On the opposite side to the door and window was the staircase, and two doors; one of which (the nearest to the fire) led into a sort of little back kitchen, where dirty work, such as washing up dishes, might be done, and whose shelves served as larder, and pantry, and storeroom, and all. The other door, which was considerably lower, opened into the coal-hole – the slanting closet under the stairs; from which, to the fire-place, there was a gay-coloured piece of oil-cloth laid. The place seemed almost crammed with furniture (sure sign of good times among the mills). Beneath the window was a dresser, with three deep drawers. Opposite the fire-place was a table, which I should call a Pembroke, only that it was made of deal, and I cannot tell how far such a name may be applied to such humble material. On it, resting against the wall, was a bright green japanned tea-tray, having a couple of scarlet lovers embracing in the middle. The fire-light danced merrily on this, and really (setting all taste but that of a child's aside) it gave a richness of colouring to that side of the room. It was in some measure propped up by a crimson tea-caddy, also of japan ware. A round table on one branching leg, really for use, stood in the corresponding corner to the cupboard; and, if you can picture all this, with a washy, but clean stencilled pattern on the walls, you can form some idea of John Barton's home. (Gaskell 2003, 14–15)

Although undoubtedly such a description asks us to understand the characters by their surroundings (see the discussion of 'metonymy' in Chapter 9 on language) – that is, the surroundings indicate what the characters are like – it is also part of the idea that we are observing these people in their usual habitat (or one of them – the other main one being the workplace), and that we need to know the habitat to know the person or people.

Of course, the degree to which habitat and character are co-dependent varies from novel to novel, and where a novel retains a strong sense of character as an autonomous agent largely free of environmental pressures, place does not figure so prominently. There is also the issue of class to be considered, since frequently it may seem that the working classes are victims of their circumstances, whereas the middle classes have greater opportunities and agency. However, the idea of generic provincial lives, as described above, also suggests that the bourgeoisie are equally susceptible to predominantly scientific or sociological observation.

Description

The distinction between 'description' and 'narrative' (story) is long established prior to the nineteenth century, and a novelist is always faced with finding a balance between keeping the audience's interest in the storyline(s) and offering descriptions of settings and characters which may serve to hold up the flow of narrative interest. The description above of the Barton household is very detailed. It certainly functions to establish character as well as setting, or rather, it functions to establish a character-type, that of the respectable working-class family in relatively prosperous circumstances. I have already suggested reasons why the novel establishes the character-type through a description of habitat, rather than perhaps simply saying something to the effect that John Barton was a hard-working, proud millhand with a headstrong daughter and a loving wife. Just as 'setting' is not 'incidental' in the Realist novel, nor is the predominance of 'description'. If we think of it in terms of 'description' versus 'story', 'description' would seem to take up more space in the Realist novel than the stories themselves might warrant. 'Description' – by which it is usually meant that 'there is a lot of description', or less generously, 'there is too much description' – is a major feature of the Realist novel. The Realist novel loves 'detail'.

STOP and THINK

Look again at the description of the room in the Barton house. What purpose does such detailed writing serve? Compare your thoughts with these possible responses:

- Detailed description accords with the Realist principle of the 'faithful copy': a mirror reflects everything, regardless of its significance.
- Hence, by offering such detail, the impression the reader

receives is that the narrative is mirror-like and reproduces a faithful copy of the real world.

- It also accords with the type of descriptions we might find in prose non-fiction for example, in a social report.
- Such 'reporting' on the real world, be it in the Realist novel or Parliamentary reports, is methodologically dependent upon scientific notions of empirical observation.
- This brings us back to a different version of 'the mirror' principle: empirical observation, with its aim of finding patterns and drawing conclusions, is not always certain what is and is not significant, hence it is important to have detailed description, so that nothing of possible significance is overlooked.
- Further, the attention to such physical objects implicitly suggests that what is important in our engagement with the world is its material aspect rather than any other relation (for example, spiritual).
- Related to this, the passage alerts the reader to a relation between economic prosperity and material objects – 'The place seemed almost crammed with furniture (sure sign of good times among the mills)' – suggesting that the world itself is constituted and to be understood through its physical manifestations.

This may seem rather a lot to read into one passage, and you may disagree with some of this, particularly perhaps the final two interpretations. However, I would ask that you stick with me for a little while longer as I try to support and elaborate upon some of these points. We will certainly be returning to 'setting' and 'description' throughout this book. However, you may feel that I should really have focused on some more obvious aspects of Realist novels, or novels in general: the characters or the stories the novels tell.

Characterisation

Just as there is a melding of the importance of setting with the importance of detailed description, there is a fusion of the use of detailed description with the techniques of characterisation, which is also typical of the Realist novel. Put more simply, just as we get detailed descriptions of setting and place, we get detailed descriptions of character.

In *Middlemarch* the narrator offers this observation: 'Our vanities differ as our noses do: all conceit is not the same conceit, but arise in correspondence with the minutiæ of mental make in which one of us differs from another' (chapter 15). It is at the level of psychological detail that we find significance. The way this observation is presented once more ties in with the attention to precise empirical detail that we have already observed as a general feature of the Realist novel, and is here directed at human nature. The interest at this particular point in the novel – an extended portrayal of the young Middlemarch doctor, Lydgate – would suggest that the novel is concerned with the eternal failings of human nature, a universal and consistent failing in humans no different from any other age. However, the important thing here is not that 'conceit' is a general characteristic of the human race, it is that the manner in which it is manifest is different with each person, and that this individuation is dependent upon 'the minutiæ of mental make'. In other words, if we are interested in individuals, we need to get at the very precise detail of the mental world that each person contains or inhabits.

This attention to the great detail of 'mental make', to what constitutes each individual's psychology, is part of the same drive for 'accuracy', for the faithful copying of the world as it is, with which we started this chapter. Not only do we get lengthy descriptions of social setting in the Realist novel but we also get lengthy character descriptions, many of which offer the 'minutiae' of the characters' minds. The method of characterisation is thus to present in detail the thoughts and thought-processes of individuals, rather than just offering sketches of what someone thought, or a summary of what otherwise in a Realist novel is described at length. The detailed description we find in the Realist novel is a tool in the drive to produce a faithful copy of the world, and it is applied to both the social world and the psychological aspects of characters in that world.

There is an immediate objection to be made, I think, which I will address here, since it will gain in importance as we proceed in our discussion. While it might be conceded that, on the one hand, detailed descriptions of the physical world fit in with notions of empirical observation and the importance of materialism, and fit in with the idea of the Realist novel 'mirroring' a reality that any number of people might observe and agree upon, on the other hand the representing of the inner mental world of people is hardly consistent with the 'mirror' metaphor. You can see objects and people in a mirror, but what is in somebody's mind is hardly an observable physical phenomenon, and so can hardly be 'mirrored' in the way that furniture and dress can.

I would respond by saying that this is not an objection to be found in nineteenth-century thinking. Art has always presumed to know the thoughts and mental worlds of others; the sense that individual psychology might be 'unknowable' or 'hidden', in the sense that it cannot be known or seen in the way that physical phenomena can, is not really an issue for the nineteenth-century Realists. Instead, it is part of art's general endeavour to render characters and their mental worlds, and it can be said that the novel has always shown a great interest in this from *Robinson Crusoe* onwards. Although there is much more to say on 'the minutiae' of individual psychology, for now I will leave this possible objection as one that cannot be readily assumed to be a nineteenth-century one.

This objection aside, I would argue that when Eliot's narrator is interested in the minutiae of Lydgate's mental profile, it is not as an end in itself, and nor is attention to mental landscapes the primary goal in other Realist novels. The psychological detail is important because it explains social behaviour, not because there is a fixation on aberrant mental states or on mental states in themselves, as becomes the case in modernist literature, for example. One of the great achievements of the Realist novel is its ability to offer detailed pictures of the mental lives of individuals as they are enmeshed in social networks. Again, it is the use of minute 'detail' which is different here from previous art infused with the realist impulse and having some psychological interest. As an example, early in Eliot's novel *The Mill on the Floss* the narration devotes a whole chapter to explaining why Mr Riley recommends a particular tutor, Mr Stelling, for Mr Tulliver's son Tom. In terms of the overall storyline, such detailing appears disproportionate, and it would not make much difference if the narrator showed Riley to be motivated by self-interest and left it there. But, as if the narrator needs to defend such precision in representing the factors leading up to Mr Riley's recommendation, the chapter concludes:

> If Mr. Riley had shrunk from giving a recommendation that was not based on valid evidence, he would not have helped Mr. Stelling to a paying pupil, and that would not have been so well for the reverend gentleman. Consider, too, that all the pleasant little dim ideas and complacencies – of standing well with Timpson, of dispensing advice when he was asked for it, of impressing his friend Tulliver with additional respect, of saying something, and saying it emphatically, with other inappreciably minute ingredients that went along with the warm hearth and the brandy-and-water to make up Mr. Riley's consciousness on this occasion, would have been a mere blank. (Eliot 2003: 30)

It is not just that the novel is giving a particular kind of detailed attention to what is in essence a rather trivial, everyday event (giving advice). The novel at this juncture is making a point about the way we engage with the world and the way we understand it. When it talks of 'inappreciably minute ingredients' it draws attention to the complexity involved in such a commonplace action and, just as with Gaskell's detailed description of the Barton household, it tells the reader that this is how the world is constituted, how it is to be described, and how it is to be understood. It is the job of the good empirical observer (Realist novelist) to get down to such fine detail in order to understand how the social world works. Detail is not, therefore, just a consequence of making the world appear 'concrete', that is, a rhetorical effect to make it seem 'real' to the reader, it is a consequence of a belief that what is significant about the human world, in its social, physical and mental dimensions, is to be found in the minutiae of everyday existence. This partly explains why Realist prose is characteristically 'unpoetic', if we take the traditional view of poetry as a 'compression' or 'crystallisation' of the world, as a highly selective and unusual use of language. It also partly explains why nineteenth-century novels are so large, and perhaps why there is a happy coincidence between the 'three-decker' publication and the Realist novel. The three-decker novel has to be filled with matter;

the Realist novel requires enough space for its social and psychological minutiae.

Second principle: the here and now

As part of the general characteristics of the Realist novel, I suggested at the start of this chapter that settings, characters, and storylines are to be taken from the contemporary world. Again, while we can identify this general characteristic we should note that there are various reasons as to why 'the contemporary' is overwhelmingly important. These various reasons combine and unite behind a belief in the primacy of the 'here and now' during the Realist period. The emphasis on the contemporary, like the emphasis on mirroring reality, is not without problems, of course, but again we will deal with this general feature in the manner that the Realists found it to be necessary before looking later on at the difficulties.

The factors contributing to the emphasis on contemporary reality are:

1 the consequences of industrialisation
2 humanism
3 the growing authority of science
4 the development of the social sciences.

The interrelations and overlaps between these factors are extremely complex. I will simplify here, and offer a more nuanced assessment when we look at the Realist novels in detail. I would also warn that, taken individually, these factors do not in themselves account for the belief that the Realist novel has to deal with the contemporary. Do not forget as well that the first principle – the faithful copying of reality – might in itself imply that the writer is obliged to deal with the contemporary, so the factors listed below are both a consequence and reinforcement of this first principle. They will also start to touch on 'why' Realism occurs when it does within literary history.

Industrialisation

The rapid increase in the urban population in England in the nineteenth century, as the economy moved to what is termed 'industrial capitalism', might on first appearance only seem to offer subject matter for Realism, and thereby be rather incidental to discussion of a Realist aesthetic. Put another way, the interest in the contemporary on the part of Realism will obviously find itself dealing with industrialisation in some form or other, simply because it is a major feature of nineteenth-century life – but does that make it intrinsic to what Realism is, or contribute to Realism's interest in the contemporary world in the first place?

If we look at our mini-canon of Realist novels, 'industrialisation' certainly does not appear to be essential. Although Gaskell's novels are often directly focused on 'industrialisation' (*Mary Barton*, *North and South*), just as Dickens's *Hard Times* is, many Realist novels deal with contemporary life in provincial settings and thus have very little to do with industrialised Britain: Eliot's *Middlemarch*, Mrs Oliphant's novels *Hester* and *Phoebe Junior*, Trollope's Barchester novels. George Eliot's *The Mill on the Floss* has a rural setting. A large chunk of Thackeray's *Vanity Fair* is set in the Regency period (1811–20) with no intimations of the industrialised age. Zola's *L'Assommoir* and *Germinal* do, on the other hand, concentrate on the working classes and working conditions, and with a strong sense that we are here dealing with life under capitalism, although in quite different settings, Paris and a mining village respectively. However, if not directly dealing with 'industrialisation', I think that the sense of 'urgency', the idea that art should concern itself with the 'here and now', is still partly a consequence of the pressure of industrialisation, brought on by the fact that the world is changing very quickly in the nineteenth century and bringing with it a need to reflect society as it operates within such speedy change.

Obviously, art and literature have felt obliged to represent change in previous periods, but here it is allied to the tenet of representing the world as it appears, rather than through the generic filters of satire or idealism. Sometimes, the Realist attachment to the contemporary may be socially motivated – to raise awareness of terrible working and living conditions – at other times simply partaking in the dominant aesthetic of Realism or the fashion for Realist literature. But the second point to make is that there is (arguably) a correlation between Realism's focus on representing the physical world, and industrial capitalism's interest in 'things', in producing them and acquiring them.

The key term here is 'materialism', both as an economic ideology – an attachment to production and acquisition – and as a philosophy, that the world is constituted solely as a 'material' entity. The Realist novel is then seen to embody this materialist age because it is interested in describing the real world and the relations that pertain in the real world between objects and people (or environment and people – see above). Nineteenth-century critics of the Realist novel often argued that the genre was obsessed with the material world, at the expense of the spiritual, and that the dominance of the Realist novel was a consequence of the materialist age. It was an aspect of the Realist novel to be criticised precisely because it seemed complicit with materialism, in the two senses of the word described above: that is, complicit with materialism as the consequence of capitalist endeavour and materialist because it was antagonistic towards the spiritual side of life. So the consequences of industrialisation give a social urgency to art which the Realist novel is able to accommodate, or sees itself particularly suited to. In its treatment of the world as primarily a material entity the Realist novel is part of an age characterised by materialism. The preponderance of detailed descriptions of settings and objects, as outlined above, often taken to be typical of Realist writing (and a more general realist art that follows the Realist period) would certainly seem to follow from an age increasingly interested in the material world, which is, in turn, inevitably *this* material world, that is, the contemporary world.

Renaissance humanism

Industrialisation is firmly associated with economic, social and cultural developments in the nineteenth century, and, although open to argument, it seems plausible that there is a correlation between the emergence of the Realist novel and its interest in the contemporary material world. There are other factors in the emergence of Realism that are longer-standing and thus make it more

difficult to argue for equally strong correlations between the existence of the Realist novel and such influences. 'Humanism' is one
such possible long-term influence. Its origins in European
thought and culture are usually located at the end of the four-
teenth century, part of the Renaissance, and defined by: a belief in
man as essentially endowed with reason; a belief that man is
autonomous; a belief in the idea that there is a universal ethics,
which can be discovered through the use of reason; a belief in
social progress through mankind's rational endeavour (I retain the
use of 'man' and 'mankind' to reflect the language of humanism).
Conversely, humanism is antagonistic to religious belief and belief
in the supernatural. Humanism would therefore seem to go hand
in hand with a perceived decline in religious authority, and to run
alongside the growing authority of science and scientific method.
As you can see, humanism encompasses a very broad set of related
ideas. In comparison with the discussion of industrialisation
above, the relationship between the influence of humanism on the
Realist novel, and in particular in this section on the Realist
novel's insistence on attending to 'the here and now', would seem
vague at best. Suffice to say, I am not describing a one-to-one
causal relationship between humanism and the Realist novel's
focus on 'the contemporary'. Instead, I am suggesting that
humanism in many of its aspects encourages and allows the Realist
novel form to take centre stage, particularly in its preference for
scientific and rational explanations of the world as it is physically
manifested and constituted.

I have stressed that Realism and the realist impulse are intent on
recording the world as it is. In itself, and significantly, this does not
preclude a religious worldview. Alexander Pope, in his *Essay on
Man*, opens Epistle II with the following lines: 'Know, then,
thyself, presume not God to scan; / The proper study of mankind
is man'. Pope urges the reader and society at large to confine itself
to looking at the material world because it is human arrogance or
folly to believe we could study God. This exhortation to stay with
the world around us could easily be claimed as part of the realist
impulse, but is in fact part of a wider crisis in religious faith in the
eighteenth century. Pope's argument is that it is the very world
around us – nature – which is God's work, and to which we

belong, so to confine ourselves to 'the study of mankind' is not a realist injunction in this case but rather the consequence of a reassertion of faith in the face of growing doubts.

The outcome may be the same, of course, in terms of representing the study of mankind, but the fact that humanism stresses the idea that humans have innate reason, and through reason can determine universal laws, such as those governing ethical behaviour, certainly entails that any art subscribing to the humanist outlook will turn itself to mankind as it is 'in itself', rather than viewing mankind as the temporal and physical manifestation of some aspect of eternity and divinity. This does not necessitate that the study should therefore be of mankind as it exists 'now', in the contemporary world, and Renaissance Humanism indeed is characterised by its insistence on the benefit of studying Classical literature and art, among other things. Nevertheless, the fact that humanism is a turning away from 'the supernatural' certainly has, as one of its consequences, an exclusive turning towards what is visible. There is a certain inevitability, perhaps, that such interest in the visible world leads to an interest in the contemporary world in its physical manifestation. The role of humanism in the emergence of Realism is part of a long-term shift in sensibility, spanning centuries and, of course, Realism is not its only consequence. Another consequence of this longer-term outlook, however, is that it enables science to gain as an authority on how the world is constituted, and this too feeds into the emergence of Realism, although sometimes in ways which contradict humanist tenets, as we shall see.

The next subsection is on 'science'. This is both part of the 'short-term' set of influences in the nineteenth century, in the manner of what was said about the influence of industrialisation on the Realist novel, and part of the longer-term influences, such as humanism.

Science
One of the main distinctions of nineteenth-century Realism from the more general realist impulse is the importance it gives to the scientific view of the world, a perspective not readily or widely available to the realist impulse of previous centuries. Its

importance is that it contributes to how the novel genre as a whole
– a genre that is a newcomer relative to poetry and drama – is to be
conceptualised.

Belief in the value of the scientific methods of experiment and
observation comes to the fore in the nineteenth century. The rise
in the authority of science is partly due to its successes since the
Renaissance in explaining the world in terms of physical laws, and
partly due to the corresponding decline in religious faith and religious authority, as described above under 'humanism'. The
growing dominance of a scientific worldview at the expense of a
spiritual or religious one generates much debate in the nineteenth
century, with Darwin's *Origin of Species* (1859) something of a
tipping point in favour of science. The 'scientific viewpoint' is not
uniform, however, and although it often underpins the Realist
novel, it does so in different ways. I should also point out that just
because a writer states a particular theoretical viewpoint, it does
not necessarily mean that the artistic works produced adhere to it.
The two main scientific approaches might be characterised as
naturalist and experimental. These approaches themselves can
either be part of a broadly humanist outlook, which regards man as
different from the animals, or non-humanist in that they regard
mankind as simply another species of animal. It should also be
clear from what I am saying here that Realist novels self-
consciously or implicitly defer to the authority of science and its
accompanying methodologies.

Naturalist science

The naturalist, non-humanist viewpoint treats man in exactly the
same way as it would view any other creature from the natural
world. In an article on Balzac in 1858, Hyppolite Taine, a high-
profile champion of Realist literature in France, commented:

> In the eyes of the naturalist man is not a reasoning creature who is
> independent, superior, healthy in himself, capable of achieving
> truth and virtue by his own efforts, but a simple force, of the same
> order as other creatures, receiving from circumstance his degree and
> his direction. He likes man for himself; that is why at all levels, in all
> occupations he likes him; provided that he sees him in action, he is
> satisfied. He is as glad to dissect an octopus as an elephant; he is as

eager to analyze a doorkeeper as a minister of state. (in Becker 1963: 106)

Taine also quotes Balzac's Preface to *La Comédie humaine* in which Balzac 'sets forth his intention to write the *natural history* of man'. This non-humanist, naturalist view of man as no different from octopuses and elephants certainly suggests that behind the Realist novel is a pressure to represent mankind in the manner that the naturalist renders his descriptions of animals, through their common features of physiognomy and behaviour, and through their engagement with their habitats. Implicit in such an influence has to be the idea that such observations can only be carried out on what is actually observable in the real world – what is physically manifest and recordable. How far a particular Realist novelist or novel goes down the route of adopting and adapting the language of the naturalist is a different matter, but it is certainly another factor in shaping the Realist novel as a form interested in the contemporary world as it exists.

This naturalist, non-humanist approach may seem harsh and extreme if the Realist novels you are familiar with are of the English variety, where feelings of empathy and sympathy are often present as a counterbalance to a 'dog-eat-dog' naturalism. The works of Dickens, Trollope, Oliphant, Eliot and Gaskell certainly adhere to a view of humanity that draws upon sympathy and empathy. When the later novels, such as those of Hardy, Gissing and Moore take on more of the French naturalist approach, the idea that the human race is characterised by fellow feeling is diminished in comparison to that of the immediately preceding generations.

Experimental science
The scientific method that was most attractive to the Realist novel was that of drawing conclusions from observation. This comfortably accords with the 'mirror' metaphor that so frequently underpins the Realist aim to provide a faithful copy of the world, and such an attachment is evident in the novels and in the critical writing of the time about Realism. Another scientific method that the Realist novel sometimes laid claim to was that of 'experiment'. Such a claim is harder to substantiate, and again it is worth bearing

in mind that there is often a disjunction between a theoretical assertion and the artistic works that follow, or indeed, precede it. Nevertheless, it is further demonstration of the ways in which science impinges upon thinking about the Realist novel and the manner in which it should or might conduct itself.

In his essay 'The Experimental Novel' (1880) Zola notes that science relies on two things: observation and experiment. We have seen above how observation is proclaimed as a tenet of the Realist novel's aesthetic, but the idea of 'experiment' in relation to the Realist novel might seem more tenuous. Zola is insistent upon his use of science, and argues that what he is doing is simply translating the work of Claude Bernard's *Introduction to the Study of Experimental Medicine*: 'This book by a scientist of decisive authority will provide me with a solid base', and: 'Usually it will be sufficient for me to replace the word "doctor" by the word "novelist" in order to make my thought clear and to bring to it the rigor of scientific truth' (in Becker 1963: 162).

Zola picks up on the idea of an experiment as 'a provoked observation', and develops the idea that the novelist sets up the necessary conditions for the experiment by putting all his characters and situations in place and then seeing what happens, just as the experimental scientist might, to test a hypothesis:

> The observer in him [the novelist] presents data as he has observed them, determines the point of departure, establishes the solid ground on which his characters will stand and his phenomena take place. Then the experimenter appears and institutes the experiment, that is, sets the characters of a particular story in motion, in order to show that the series of events therein will be those demanded by the determinism of the phenomena under study. It is almost always an experiment 'in order to see,' as Claude Bernard puts it. The novelist starts out in search of a truth. (Becker 1963: 166)

As I have suggested, in practice it may be hard to substantiate such claims in the novels themselves, since this proposes a working method for the Realist novelist which may end up in producing novels that could equally be said to derive from 'observational' method. It does call for a logic of narrative development, one that plausibly stems from the mix of character, heredity and environment, at least in Zola's formulation. However, to say that this is the equivalent of a scientific experiment where elements are flung together and the results are recorded, as if all the novelist does is choose characters and setting but then has nothing to do with the story, would seem to be rather far-fetched. It is certainly of a different kind of application to the novel-writing process than the idea of simple scientific observation.

Social science

Sometimes overlapping with this view of humankind as an animal to be approached in the same manner as any other species, is the view that society can be (should be) seen as the dynamic of group behaviour rather than that of individuals. The nineteenth century sees the emergence of the social sciences and sociology, and under such an overview individuals are merely representatives of more general types. Realist novelists often took their cue from a society and culture increasingly interested in viewing humans as social groups, behaving in ways that were patterned, mainly through the effects of environment and custom, and to a lesser extent, heredity. Science itself often depends upon mathematical modelling, and the interest in viewing society 'statistically' is another feature of this turn to science. *Hard Times*, in many ways a Realist novel that is uncomfortable with the tenets of Realism, takes issue with the statistical view of humanity and society, but the fact that it does so vociferously through Gradgrind's utilitarian philosophy is indicative of the prevalence of the statistical approach to mankind.

George Eliot's comments in her review essay 'The Natural History of German Life' (1856) for the *Westminster Review* exemplify the Realist novelist's turn towards the natural history model described above, and the nineteenth-century trend towards quasi-scientific observation of social groups. Both of these approaches are coupled with a concern for social issues which, as we have already seen, is a feature of the Realist novel:

> If any man of sufficient moral and intellectual breadth, whose obser-
> vations would not be vitiated by a foregone conclusion, or by a
> professional point of view, would devote himself to studying the
> natural history of our social classes, especially of the small shop-
> keepers, artisans, and peasantry, – the degree in which they are
> influenced by local conditions, their maxims and habits, the points

of view from which they regard their religious teachers, and the
degree in which they are influenced by religious doctrines, the
interaction of the various classes on each other, and what are the
tendencies in their position towards disintegration or towards development, – and if, after all this study, he would give us the result of
his observations in a book well nourished with specific facts, his
work would be a valuable aid to the social and political reformer.
(Eliot 1856: 56)

The way in which Eliot talks of the observation of social classes
in terms of environmental influence and how they interact
certainly accords with Zola's views (and see below, 'Objection').
More importance is perhaps given here to things such as tradition and the influence of religion but, broadly speaking, there
is a shared vision for what should be the method or interest of
the writer and observer. The end of the quotation suggests a
social use for such work, and this is not something that Zola
would necessarily advocate (even if some of the novels did in
effect serve this purpose). The comments here certainly accord
with the fact that *Middlemarch* is called 'A Study of Provincial
Life', and again I would suggest consideration of that very subtitle, which frames the novel as a naturalist's observation of a
defined social group.

Summary of chapter

I have argued that the Realist novel's overriding principle is 'a
faithful copy of reality'. This finds expression in metaphors such
as those of 'the mirror', and in the deference to the methods of
science, particularly those of observation. The second principle is
that it should deal with the contemporary 'here and now'. The
reasons for this are varied, partly to do with the growing significance and influence of science and (quasi)-scientific approaches
against a background of decline in the authority of religion and
religious discourse; partly to do with industrialisation; partly to do
with the Realist novel itself becoming fashionable. Again, I should
reiterate that no one characteristic in itself defines, or is to be
found only in, the Realist novel, and so just as 'pressing social
issue' does not in itself define the Realist novel, nor does 'contem-

porary', but they do certainly loom large in any understanding of what defines the Realist novel.

The next chapter looks in greater detail at the characteristics of the Realist novel now that we have dealt with two of its dominant principles.

Works cited and further reading

Becker, G. J. (ed.) (1963), *Documents of Modern Literary Realism*. Princeton: Princeton University Press.

Desnoyers, Fernand (1963), 'On Realism', in Becker, *Documents of Modern Literary Realism*.

Dickens, Charles (1982), *Hard Times*. Harmondsworth: Penguin.

Eliot, George (1856), 'The Natural History of German Life', *Westminster Review*; July and October; New Series; Vol. X, LION Full-Text Database.

Eliot, George (1948), *Adam Bede*. New York: Holt, Rinehart and Winston.

Eliot, George (1965), *Middlemarch. A Study of Provincial Life*. London: Penguin.

Eliot, George (2003), *The Mill on the Floss*. London: Penguin.

Gaskell, Elizabeth (2003), *Mary Barton*. London: Penguin.

Oliphant, Mrs (1989), *Phoebe Junior*. London: Virago.

Taine, Hyppolyte (1963), 'The World of Balzac', in Becker, *Documents of Modern Literary Realism*.

Trollope, Anthony (2004), *The Warden*. London: Penguin.

Zola, Émile (1963), 'The Experimental Novel', in Becker, *Documents of Modern Literary Realism*.

2

The nineteenth-century Realist novel: particulars

At the start of Chapter 1 I set out some general features of the Realist novel, and then concentrated on what I suggested were two overriding concerns – 'the faithful copy' and 'the here and now' – along with some discussion of the motivations and consequences for these two principles. I now look at some of those other features that the Realist novel exhibits and which underpin the Realist aesthetic.

If I were to set out these characteristics in a rather abstract, analytical manner, it would soon become apparent, if it is not already, that there is no novel which is 'the Realist novel'. That is, Realist novels are Realist to a greater or lesser degree when set alongside what is deemed typical of the Realist novel. This is not a circular argument – 'Realism' exists as a term because at a particular historical period there were a number of prominent artists, writers and critics arguing for this named aesthetic and philosophical approach, and this was related to (and drawn from) the art, writing and criticism which these writers and artists produced. The reason why there is no archetypal Realist novel is that it has a broad range of characteristics drawing on diverse sources. My approach is to continue to refer to novels in our mini-canon in order to allow consistent comparisons, rather than ranging across a wider selection where the illustration of such characteristics becomes more diffuse and arbitrary. In doing so, I will be referring back to the ideas in Chapter 1, and dealing with some further characteristics of the Realist novel mentioned at the start of that chapter. The first, and one of the most important aspects, is plausibility.

Plausibility

In the drive towards 'the faithful copy' it is plausibility that Realists are concerned with more than anything else. The term 'mimesis', which the expression 'faithful copy' certainly suggests, is more appropriate for painting and sculpture, since visual correlations offer more direct comparisons between the object and its representation. Writing cannot be said to be mimetic in the same way, since a written description of grapes will not fool birds into eating a single word, whereas a realistic visual representation might elicit a peck at the picture.

STOP and THINK

The Realist novel is a faithful copy of the real world, and yet does not copy the real world in the sense that it reflects real events. If it did so, it would be (ideally, and for the sake of argument) history, or journalism, or court proceedings, or diaries, or log-books, or journals. In what sense then does it copy the world? What features does it attempt to faithfully represent? For example, in what way can a fictional character be a faithful copy if the copy is not a direct representation of an actual existing individual?

If we took a critical or hostile view of the aims of the Realist novel we could quickly dismiss its claims as follows: the novel is 'fiction' and cannot therefore be this all-important 'faithful copy'. Do you hold to this view?

Plausibility, character and *Dombey and Son*

Dickens's work is particularly interesting with respect to representing character, since he offers a mixture of old-style, pre-Realist characters who embody particular vices or virtues, and a more nineteenth-century Realist view where the characters are types drawn from the observable social world. In *Dombey and Son* (1848), for instance, Dombey verges on a caricature of 'pride', and many critics found his transformation to that of a more humble, sympathetic human character at the end of the novel to be rather implausible. This was Dickens's response in his Preface to the 1867 edition of the novel: 'Mr. Dombey undergoes no violent change, either in this book, or in real life' (Dickens: 1970: 43). What can he possibly mean by claiming that his presentation of Dombey is both accurate in the novel and an accurate representation of an actual, existing Dombey, that is, an accurate account of a (the?) Dombey in the real world?

A modern-day critic might have difficulty with Dickens's conflation of his fictional character with that of a real-life human being, but a Victorian audience is reading Realist literature in a particular way which is differently sophisticated. The invitation to its readership to compare the accuracy of the novel with the world that the audience inhabits allows an author to claim a reality for his or her fictional creations. This is very much part of nineteenth-century Realism and, it could be argued, a feature of realism in general. Critics may object that this makes no logical sense – Dombey does not exist (did not exist) as an actual living human being – but it clearly makes aesthetic and logical sense to readers of Realist novels. It is not that the nineteenth-century readership is naive; it is reading in a way whereby 'plausibility' is part of the Realist aesthetic, and whereby the judgement of the novel depends upon 'plausibility' for its Realism. Dombey is both fictional and actual, an existing individual because he is a type of person recognisable to the reader. That is the assumption that Dickens makes as an author. The fact that contemporary critics of the novel found Dombey's conversion to be implausible demonstrates that they too are reading within this Realist framework. Plausibility is everything here because it is the starting point from which authors, readers and critics can assess the success in Realist terms of the novel. Dickens is furious because he believes he has indeed created a plausible character in Dombey, and the assumption on everybody's part is that 'plausibility' is possible. This in turn depends upon the implicit idea that there is a contract between the author and the audience which seeks to establish what is 'true' in the sense of what is 'plausibly true' rather than what is physically or historically true. 'Plausibility' is not to be found 'in the text', nor in the individual's assertion of the truth of the portrayal, it exists in the relationship between author, novel and audience.

I have here used 'character' as an example of where plausibility needs to be exhibited in a Realist novel, but virtually every feature of the Realist novel must aspire to the condition of plausibility, for example, setting, dialogue and plot. We saw in the previous chapter how setting is established as 'typical', and hence 'plausible'. Let us look at plot, a particularly tricky issue in discussion of Realism.

Story versus plot

Novels have narratives. Or stories. Or plots. Life consists of narratives and stories, but does it have plots?

We may be able to offer opinions on the accuracy of representations of typical settings, characters and dialogue, but what are we measuring the stories against? 'Plot' would seem to describe the deliberate artifice of the writer or dramatist in constructing a novel or play. To have a plot, therefore, would appear to intrinsically work against the Realist aesthetic since 'plot' is not part of the real world, and belongs purely to the realm of narrative art. A plot cannot be a faithful copy in the way that character, dialogue and setting can.

In general, the 'plausibility' rule continues to operate. The Realist novel strives to move away from classical plot structures, such as marriage in 'comedy', and starts to take its structure from everyday 'typical' (common, ordinary) stories that do not have moral, sensational or genre underpinnings. One of the subsequent charges against Realist writing was that it was 'dull', precisely because things that might appear uncommonly dramatic had been removed. For the Realist writer, stories should be drawn from everyday life, they should not be 'exceptional', they should exhibit typicality. But what is a typical story?

The answer to this, or the manner of responding to this, is no different from any of the other typicalities required for plausibility – it is a judgement on the part of the novelist, which in turn is open to approval or otherwise by the novelist's readers. It is a feature of Realist novels that the stories must appear as 'stories' that could occur in the real world, and conversely, the Realist novels must 'hide' the artifice of their 'plotting'. Again, a hostile interpretation of Realism would argue that this way of talking about the Realist novel does not hold up, and this antagonistic view would argue that a novel's 'story' is nothing other than its 'plot', the two cannot be separated. But the Realist reader is content if in his or her judgement 'typicality' and 'plausibility' are maintained at the level of the narrative's trajectory, because as soon as 'plotting' becomes apparent the novel's Realism is undermined.

Gaskell's novels *North and South* and *Mary Barton* are interesting cases since they have aspects of both the typical, Realist 'story' and the non-Realist, dramatic 'plot'. Both have workers' strikes as fairly central. Are strikes typical events? For the time period we are talking about, relatively speaking, they are. A Realist writer is always faced with the problem of making the typical interesting, since by its very nature what is typical is also 'common' and 'ordinary' and thus, in a way, dull, as mentioned above. A strike in the mid-Victorian period is both typical and interesting, so not unsurprisingly it can form the basis for a Realist novel. For instance, other Realist novels discussed here besides Gaskell focus on strikes: Zola's *Germinal* and Dickens's *Hard Times*.

In *North and South* the strike offers the central points of narrative interest, played out through the lives of the factory owner Thornfield, the middle-class heroine Margaret Hale, and the workers. Since a strike is inherently dramatic it allows for more typical, detailed elements of working-class life and middle-class life to be incorporated while still maintaining the more exciting strike story. Yet *North and South* does have narrative elements which the reader may feel are out of step with its other more plausible aspects. Margaret's status as a virtuous woman is compromised when Thornton sees her with an unknown man. None of these things appear, when written down like this, as particularly implausible perhaps, but the novel at this juncture stands out as dependent upon the Victorian non-Realist craving for sensational storylines. The unknown man is her elder brother, Frederick, a fugitive who has been living in Spain following his participation in a British navy mutiny. The first suggestion that Margaret may be a 'fallen woman', and the marine interest and disgrace involving Frederick, are typical sensationalist fodder. You may disagree that this counts as implausible, but for me this part of the novel certainly seems like (melo)dramatic plot rather than Realist story. You may disagree, but that is part of the way in which we talk about Realist texts: if we quarrel about how plausible something is or is not it is because we care about this aspect of it and because Realist novels are premised upon our engagement with plausibility. We want plausibility at the level of narrative as well as character and setting. More than this, the engagement with plausibility is engagement with the world outside the novel, whether it is for an audience contemporaneous with its publication, or an audience like ourselves, placing the novel in its social, historical and cultural context, and even perhaps comparing it with what is plausible now.

As with *North and South*, Gaskell's earlier novel *Mary Barton* has a strike as a central narrative plank, and plays out 'masters and workers' through its central characters. *Mary Barton*'s implausible aspects are rather more obvious than those in *North and South*. At what point does this novel's plausible 'story' become implausible 'plot'? We have already established that the strike itself presents no problems for plausibility. The depiction of John Barton as an angry striker, whose anger is exacerbated by the loss of his wife, is also plausible. He takes opium to counter hunger and the misery of his life. That is plausible as well because the novel impresses upon the reader that this is typical behaviour for men in this predicament. So far, so plausible. Mary falls in love with the factory owner's son, Henry Carson, and he strings her along with no intention of marrying her. That is plausible. The strikers get together and draw straws to see who should kill Henry Carson – are we starting to stray into the implausible here? John Barton draws the short straw and kills Henry Carson. It is at this point, I would suggest, that we have non-Realist plot rather than the foregoing Realist storylines. It is not that this plot could never be drawn from a real-life story, it is that it loses its typicality and shades into the implausible – it would be a rather rare set of events.

In addition to this evident 'plotting', Jem Wilson becomes the prime suspect in Henry Carson's murder because it is well known that he has nursed his unrequited love for Mary throughout the novel and thus bears a grudge against Henry. Mary is convinced that Jem is innocent, and uncovers evidence to that effect, thanks to her aunt Esther, a 'fallen woman' – and a scrap of paper. These are the elements of melodrama, not Realist fiction. There is further melodrama when Mary has to chase a boat and bring back somebody who can prove Jem's innocence, just as Jem is about to be convicted for murder by the court. There are certain similarities between this part of the plotline and that of a very popular Victorian melodrama, *Black-Eyed Susan* (of which more in Chapter 5, on drama). We have moved away from the elements of Realist narrative into non-Realist territory. *North and South* has fewer non-Realist elements than *Mary Barton*. Again, such matters are on a sliding scale rather than cut and dried.

Causality

A story, broadly speaking and with the Realist aesthetic in mind, is a sequence of connected events unfolding over time. Since part of this aesthetic is an attachment to the scientific view of the world as one that is understandable in terms of cause and effect, it naturally follows, in theory at least, that the Realist novel is one that adheres to the idea that events are understandable according to laws of causality. There may be differences of opinion as to where the causes are to be located – biology, genetics, environment, psychology – but the underlying belief is that events are explicable according to deterministic laws that observers – be they scientists or novelists – can uncover. You may think that the reliance on cause and effect explanations hardly requires scientific authority to validate it, but it needs to be remembered that the nineteenth century is an era when religious authority can still countermand everyday experience with a supernatural explanation.

Although some advocates of Realism pushed for an absolute determinism, particularly some of those in the Zola camp, in general, we are once more talking about a sliding scale of determinism rather than an idea that every human action has a simple determining cause. The role and scope of determinism in Realism's reliance on causality is open to debate, however. A view of Realism that places Zola and the French Realists at the centre of any definition of Realism will also claim that scientific determinism is central to the Realist aesthetic, and that is because such a notion of Realism represents human behaviour as very close to animal behaviour. Nevertheless, the English Realists could also express determinist sentiments. *Hard Times* makes a very clear case for the kind of life that is possible and actually led by people constrained to factory life and constrained to be 'hands'. They are completely determined by their environment at this level, just like animals. Eliot, in *The Mill on the Floss*, is also capable of making similarly determinist statements. This is how the narrator describes Mr Tulliver's reaction to losing his all-important lawsuit: 'There are certain animals to which tenacity of position is a law of life – they can never flourish again after a single wrench: and there are certain human beings to whom predominance is a law of life and who can only sustain humiliation so long as they can refuse to believe in it, and, in their own conception, predominate still' (Eliot: 2003: 207). Even at the end of *Middlemarch* the narrator observes: 'For there is no creature whose inward being is so strong that it is not greatly determined by what lies outside it' (Eliot: 1965: 896).

However, I think the emphasis on determinism is a rather stereotypical view of the science of the time and scientists had a wider view of the role of facts and observation than one of identifying simplistic determinisms. It does partly depend upon which area of science the underpinning scientific model is drawn from, and then to what extent the novelist attempts to replicate this in the novel. The discussion of 'detail' in Chapter 1 and the manner in which Eliot, for instance, argues for the aggregation of many different, often barely perceptible influences on human behaviour suggests a quite different view of causality from that of a more reductive determinism. Eliot and other Realist novelists use scientific method(s) of observation, recording and inference to order their understanding of human behaviour, but human behaviour itself is usually understood to be different from that of animal behaviour when it is granted extended consideration.

Looking at it from an opposite point of view, one of the features of non-Realist novels is that they are not obliged to adhere to plausibility in things such as storylines or causality. A novel like

Wuthering Heights refuses causality in its overriding aesthetic when Heathcliff goes missing from the scene for some years, a time period which is left unexplained to the characters and to the readers, thereby playing up the mysterious element rather than explicating (and perhaps, so the argument would go, taming) Heathcliff and his actions. Compare this to *Middlemarch*, where there are the related motifs of 'web' and 'tissue'. If Lydgate were presented with Heathcliff as a case study, he would want to find 'those invisible thoroughfares which are the first lurking-places of anguish, mania, and crime' (Eliot: 1965: 194), his assumption being that we can uncover and explain all causes of behaviour. *Middlemarch* is the kind of novel which can supply those explanations, *Wuthering Heights* the kind of novel which has no obligation to.

There is another reason why causality is important, and that is because it reflects the belief that the world is understandable, and that it is understandable because it conforms to behaviour the laws of which can be discovered. Related to this, of course, are notions of 'reason' – the universe is rational. In turn, all of these are important in order to support a moral universe in the absence of a controlling deity, or any deity at all.

I have placed 'causality' under the heading of 'Plausibility' since in Realist texts story events and character actions need to conform to this principle. It is possible to argue, contra to the Realist assumption asserted here, that not everything in life is explicable according to deterministic laws, be they physical, social or psychological, and therefore the Realist novel's attachment to a determinable causality is in itself implausible. However, we are dealing with a historical time period where there is a growing belief that things are explicable in one causal way or another, and a belief that we can get at these various causes through scientific method. Conversely, the one explanation increasingly untenable is that 'God moves in mysterious ways' because the more reasonable response is that science will eventually explain all of the mysteries of this universe, and this places the emphasis firmly on understanding the laws of that physical universe.

Time

Intertwined with the unfolding of a story or stories, and the cause-and-effect explanations accompanying them, is the belief that we experience time in a linear fashion; one event follows another as a consequence of a previous event or events. You may feel that this is rather obvious, rather like the idea of cause and effect, in which case you are probably a common-sense realist (see Chapter 10 Philosophy, science, and the ends of realism). However, we will see later in our discussions of modernism and postmodernism that there are ways of viewing time other than as linear, so the fact that it operates in this manner in Realist novels is a characteristic, although one that is obviously not exclusive to Realism.

To recall the opening to *Middlemarch*: 'Who that cares much to know the history of man, and how the mysterious mixture behaves under the varying experiments of Time.' The Victorians' own perceptions of time had to change thanks to the revelations of geology, which showed earth to be much older than the six thousand years that biblical scholars had previously asserted. It was this lengthening of earthly (temporal) time that was to make Darwin's theory of evolution both possible and plausible, and which simultaneously heightened awareness and appreciation of the 'here and now' in opposition to religion's emphasis on 'eternal' time. Realist novels subscribe to the 'here and now' of time and to the appreciation of it as the only kind of time that there is. It is another factor, I would suggest, in the prevalence of 'detail', in the recording of the particularity of the everyday – for what else is there to contemplate if there is no eternal hereafter? This passage from *Middlemarch* certainly suggests that Eliot's appreciation of time is one that owes much to an idea of geologically-styled time played out over the life of each individual:

> The two men were pitying each other, but it was only Will who guessed the extent of his companion's trouble. When Lydgate spoke with desperate resignation of going to settle in London, and said with a faint smile, 'We shall have you again, old fellow,' Will felt inexpressibly mournful, and said nothing. Rosamond had that morning entreated him to urge this step on Lydgate; and it seemed to him as if he were beholding in a magic panorama a future where he himself was sliding into that pleasureless yielding to the small

solicitations of circumstance, which is a commoner history of perdition than any single momentous bargain. (Eliot 1965: 840–1)

Again, it is the sense that it is time slowly acting on human lives which is key. There is a passage in *The Mill on the Floss* which also stresses the slowness of time as integral to each individual human life, and thus to each individual human story. It is this notion of Realist 'story' time which acts against the 'paciness' of plots and 'plot' time. In this passage Mr Tulliver's son Tom attempts to face up to the consequences of his family's ruin in wake of his father's failed lawsuit:

It was intolerable to think of being poor and looked down upon all one's life. He would provide for his mother and sister, and make every one say that he was a man of high character. He leaped over the years in this way, and in the haste of strong purpose and strong desire, did not see how they would be made up of slow days, hours, and minutes. (Eliot: 2003: 237)

Tom is sixteen years old at this point, and imagines himself the saviour of the family: he 'plots' this heroic action. The narrator stands as the Realist corrective, deliberately stating that this is not how life is, and that this is not how time works in the unfolding of human affairs.

Endings

Even if we accept that some stories are more plausible than others in Realist novels, and that these novels endeavour to conceal the impression of 'plotting' in favour of a natural unfolding of typical events that follow on from, and naturally interconnect with, each other, there remains the problem of 'endings'. There may be arguments over whether there are plots in life or not, but apart from death there are no natural ends. And since the Realist novel is interested in groups of people rather more than in a particular individual, unless a provincial town is wiped out or London or Paris disappears, an ending is a contrivance and thus contrary to some of our key Realist elements – endings are not to be found in the real world because life in general always goes on, even when it stops for an individual.

Tragedy: the hero dies. Comedy: characters get married. The

Realist novel must move away from these conventional, classical structures and their derivatives as part of its drive towards the faithful copy of reality. Victorian novels in general are often stereotyped – probably accurately – as ending in marriage, inheritance or emigration, and Realist novels are sometimes no different. They want the same sense of completion, or 'closure' as it is often called, with all the psychological benefits closure suggests. How then does this square with the description of the Realist novel so far? It is not that marriage, inheritance or emigration are uncommon in the nineteenth century, so the problem is not typicality or plausibility. The problem is narrative convenience – why 'end' here? If the Realist novel looks to give us a faithful copy of reality why not at least suggest that conventional endings, and indeed closure itself, are false representations?

Trollope's *The Warden*, with its main story of the morally compromised Mr Harding, ends when his daughter marries, and adds to an impression that a traditional comedic structure holds it together. *North and South* ends with the marriage proposal from Thornfield to Margaret. *Mary Barton* ends with the marriage of Jem and Mary, and emigration to Canada. The problem here is that the novels are structured according to tradition and convenience rather than by any pressure to be Realist. For those readers looking for pertinent social comment, as might be expected of these social or industrial novels, to resolve all the issues surrounding a strike with a marriage is disappointing and 'weak', for it reinstates the status quo rather than challenging social inequity. There is a sense in which to fall back on a traditional ending relegates the core material of the socially-concerned Realist novel to the status of backdrop.

The question of narrative structure in relation to Realist novels, particularly endings, is therefore quite problematic. However, I think that many Realist novels do endeavour to find ways out of the stereotypical, inherited narrative conventions, and when they do not do this the impression is that they somehow weaken their Realist intent. The complaints against the finale of *North and South* indicate that readers feel a sense of betrayal, that it has stepped outside of Margaret's character, and that it is simply too neat a finish for a Realist novel. However, it is perhaps not the fact of the marriage but rather the very subservient manner in which Margaret accepts which is the problem. It is just a bad ending rather than a case of not being Realist. But it does fit in with the Victorian ideal that happiness is to be found in domestic harmony, and that marriage remains the social ideal to be aspired to above all else, and so its 'Victorianness' here subdues its 'Realism'. *Dombey and Son* ends with the marriage of Florence and Walter, and the subsequent reconciliation of Florence with her father. Do these happy endings remedy the miseries they have uncovered? Hardly, but they do offer the reader a feeling of well-being which has not been in evidence throughout the preceding chapters. The fact that Realist novels have 'happy' endings demonstrates the strength of the classical plot conventions.

Nevertheless, some Realist novels do not conveniently and conventionally 'end', and thus are more in keeping with the aims of Realism. I particularly like the ending of two of Mrs Oliphant's novels, *Hester* (1884) and *Phoebe Junior* (1876). At the end of *Hester* the narrator says: 'And as for Hester, all that can be said for her is that there are two men whom she may choose between, and marry either if she pleases – good men both, who will never wring her heart. Old Mrs. Morgan desires one match, Mrs. John another. What can a young woman desire more than to have such a possibility of choice?' (Oliphant 1984: 495). It is predictably concerned with marriage, yet the conventional idea of romance has been discarded since the men 'will never wring her heart', and remains 'open' because Hester's story is not concluded, and the heroine remains 'empowered' both because she has not chosen and because she will not make a choice based (solely) on her affections. *Phoebe Junior* ends more traditionally, with the marriage of Phoebe and a quick glance at how her life works out after this. The difference is that from the traditional romantic-love point of view she marries the wrong man: she marries for worldly interest rather than for love. By rejecting romantic love in favour of something more pragmatic and realistic, the novel undercuts the conventional romance plot in favour of a Realist's story.

Middlemarch, which has multiple storylines, ends by offering a 'where are they now?' for all the main characters. Lydgate dies relatively young – for no particular reason: it is not a moral judgement, for instance, or a death on the understanding that God has called in a life. The novel does, however, have its own belief in how lives are shaped by the 'limits' of that life, which are both environmental and personal. Prefacing the final commentary, the narrator claims: 'Every limit is a beginning as well as an ending. Who can quit young lives after being long in company with them, and not desire to know what befell them in their after-years?' It is a natural curiosity to see how people's lives turn out, and that is perhaps the only 'natural' storyline in keeping with Realism's plausibility of time, character, causality and ending.

One final comment on this section is a variation on a theme. There is a moment in Thackeray's *Vanity Fair* (first published in 1848) which is quite remarkable. I quote John Carey's introduction to the Penguin Classics edition since he states the case for the importance of the event in relation to the Realist novel:

> at the midpoint of the whole novel, comes the most shattering sentence in English literature: 'Darkness came down on the field and city; and Amelia was praying for George, who was lying on his face, dead, with a bullet through his heart.' Nothing has prepared us for this. To remove a major character so casually, in a mere subordinate clause, was unprecedented – sudden, callous, unreasonable and shocking, like real death. (Thackeray 2003: xiii)

This is how *Vanity Fair* severs its ties with conventional endings, by having it happen in the middle of the novel. The above lines end the chapter, but rather than follow this up with a chapter that meditates on the significance of the event, or details the devastation on all those around George, it simply moves on and moves elsewhere. Although it is true that *Vanity Fair* is framed in a particular satirical way that is suggestive of an earlier generic structure (the characters are the narrator's 'puppets'), in another way the novel has already done away with a conventional and convenient ending with George's mid-novel demise.

Narrative point of view

Chapter 29 of *Middlemarch* begins:

> One morning, some weeks after her arrival at Lowick, Dorothea –
> but why always Dorothea? Was her point of view the only possible
> one with regard to this marriage? I protest against all our interest, all
> our effort at understanding being given to the young skins that look
> blooming in spite of trouble; for these too will get faded, and will
> know the older and more eating griefs which we are helping to
> neglect.

The nineteenth-century Realist novel is committed to presenting
a faithful copy of reality, but who's doing the looking? Typically
the Realist novel is delivered to us through the eyes of a third-
person omniscient narrator. The theoretical justification for this,
either at the time (nineteenth century) or after the fact (later
commentators on Realism), is that the scientific objectivity aspired
to by Realism is concomitant with the idea of a neutral observer
with all the information to hand from which to identify patterns
and causality, and from which to draw conclusions. The narratorial equivalent of the nineteenth-century scientist is therefore the
omniscient third-person narrator. The passage above from
Middlemarch opens up discussion of the narrative point of view
and its relation to how we understand the world.

The initial basic point is the simple one: the narrative is just
about to launch into a description of the issue of marriage from
Dorothea's point of view and then pauses to consider the methodology. Why should it always be the point of view of the young
people? What about view of those with more experience? It is a
simple point, but it immediately opens up a can of worms. Where
will such viewpoints end? If we are obliged to gather all possible
views in order to be as objective as possible, are we not setting
ourselves an impossible task? Is not the implication thus that
objectivity itself is called into question, and, consequently,
Realism? Is this a question the Victorians could ask themselves, or
is it the introduction of a scepticism towards the possibility of
objectivity that postdates Realism's heyday?

George Eliot is certainly aware of the difficulties surrounding
objectivity. We have already partly seen an answer to this in the

discussion of the mirror metaphor. The mirror may be defective if the mirror is indeed the author's mind, but that does not mean we give up on the attempt at accurate representation. There is a passage in *The Mill on the Floss* when the young boisterous Tom Tulliver cannot help but admire the drawing of a pony and cart made by his detested co-student Phil. Tom asks him how he has achieved such success. The answer is continual practice – to continue to strive for accuracy, and not give up on it as an impossibility: "'You've only to look well at things, and draw them over and over again. What you do wrong once, you can alter the next time'" (Eliot 2003: 171). It sounds like another statement on behalf of those engaged in the Realist project.

Nevertheless, the matter is not so easily settled. Eliot offers another mirror-image metaphor in *Middlemarch* which suggests that subjectivity overrides any potential objective perspective. In this famous passage the narrator describes the pier glass (a type of mirror) as a highly polished metal surface which, on close inspection, is seen to consist of numerous tiny scratches flying off in all directions without rhyme or reason. Shine a light on the surface, however, and the scratches gather themselves into circular patterns. The narrator makes the analogy between the light bringing order to random scratches and the tendency of each individual's ego to make sense of otherwise random events. George Eliot is thus certainly aware that subjectivity can provide gross distortions of reality, often with serious consequences for our choices and lives. If this is the case, to return to our earlier reasoning, does it not undermine the possibility of an objective point of view? Who could possibly have sufficient overview untainted by egotistical ordering? The powerful pier-glass analogy is surely enough to declare all striving for objectivity a futile exercise?

The answer, I think, is a mix of the continual striving for accuracy, as illustrated in the *Mill on the Floss* example, and a simultaneous questioning of the accuracy of the picture, as at the beginning of Chapter 29 of *Middlemarch*. The fact that the narrator steps back from the scene to question the narrative progression is part of this self-correcting facility. 'Omniscient' in this sense is misleading since the narrator, while appearing to assume a position of ultimate authority and knowledge on all matters that come into view, simultaneously questions the accuracy of the pictures and the method by which the representations are arrived at. For some readers and critics this reasoning may seem specious and the declared goal of objectivity delusional, but the shared understanding for those involved in the Realist project is that this questioning attitude and awareness on the part of the trusted authority is sufficient for the needs of Realism. A more radical questioning of objectivity and the possibility of objectivity moves the discussion outside of Realism, since Realism, as suggested, depends upon this implied contract, that is, it depends upon the idea that the world is comprehensible through a collective, questioning endeavour.

These are just opening comments, for the term 'omniscient narrator', as if this narrative perspective now offers a bird's-eye view only previously available to God, does not really give us the whole picture about how narrative perspective works in the Realist novel. A closer look will reveal how it incorporates and reinforces many of the previous ideas discussed about Realism.

The trustworthy narrator

The above passage from *Middlemarch* in which the narrator holds up the narrative achieves another thing in relation to the narrative point of view – it functions to draw the reader into a trusting relationship with the narrator. Such overt self-questioning is a strategy that helps the reader to believe in the teller, and hence in the tale. We trust the narrator. In order to achieve such trust it is not uncommon for the narrator to deny omniscience, because to gain trust one of the essential things is that the narrator should appear as somebody no different from a reader. A wholly omniscient narrator would therefore be highly implausible since no one individual can really lay claim to omniscience.

Dickens, Eliot and Trollope all set up narrative voices designed to gain the trust of the reader. We can call this the 'Dear Reader' tactic – it assumes familiarity on the part of the narrator, as if he or she is addressing us directly, 'telling us a story', and will thus include certain features that make this seem realistic. For example, we get this at the beginning of Chapter 3 of Trollope's *Barchester*

Towers: 'This narrative is supposed to commence immediately after the installation of Dr Proudie. I will not describe the cere- mony, as I do not precisely understand its nature. I am ignorant whether a bishop be chaired like a member of Parliament' (Trollope 2003: 15). Trust is engendered because the narrator appears to have a slightly restricted view of events and knowledge of what is happening, both specifically and in the usual run of things. However, this lack of knowledge is not extensive enough to bring the narrative itself into question. We trust narrators all the more because they appear to be honest in describing their own limitations.

Of course, this technique is not confined to Realist novels and can be used in any genre to make a story seem more plausible, but it does feature in the Realist novel in this particular way as a link between the author, narrator, novel, reader and real world. It is a guarantee of 'the real' and of Realism, which reinforces the acceptance of the inherent relationship between the real world outside the novel and the novel itself, whereas the trustworthy narrator of a horror novel or gothic tale is there for a different reason, something more akin to leading the reader by degree into a world or worlds that are not otherwise plausible. The reader in the non-Realist novel is not being asked to correlate the related events with the plausible, typical world that constitutes the real world and so 'trustworthiness' is useful for reasons other than those implicit in Realist texts.

The impersonal narrator

The personalised, 'Dear Reader' narrator, functioning as if the author is speaking to us directly, is a feature of the English Realist novel. This intervention by the narrator in Charles Kingsley's *Yeast* (1851) shows to what extent there is an assumed complicity in the telling and hearing of the story:

> Lancelot, in the meantime, shrank from meeting Argemone; and was quite glad of the weakness which kept him upstairs. Whether he was afraid of her – whether he was ashamed of himself or of his crutches, I cannot tell, but I daresay, reader, you are getting tired of all this soul-dissecting. So we will have a bit of action again, for the sake of variety, if for nothing better. (Chapter III)

On the other side of the channel, however, there was a strong argument that the narrator should be impersonal and invisible. Taine insisted: 'now a narrative ought to set down the facts, all the facts, in detail but they should be set down completely bare. The author must not intervene and interject a tirade every twenty lines, as Balzac did. He should disappear' (June 1854 in a letter, quoted in Becker 1963, note on pp. 94–5). I say 'narrator', but you will see that Taine talks of the author. For novelists and readers at the time the narrator is assumed to be a version of the author. Again, this is part of the narrator's 'trustworthiness', which is guaranteed by the author's. Although current literary and critical theory is highly suspicious of the idea that the narrator in a novel is somehow the author and therefore represents the author's opinions, the belief was widespread in the period and undoubtedly part of the Realist aesthetic.

However, this is actually problematic for Realism. In itself the belief stems most directly from the Romantic idea that the work of art is an expression of the soul and genius of the artist, and the Victorian audience certainly believes that there is an intimate connection between the life and beliefs of the author and those of a third-person omniscient narrator. While it serves to guarantee the trustworthiness of the work of art, through the implied connections between narrator and author, for other writers at the time it runs counter to the goal of objectivity that Realism usually aspires to, as this letter from Flaubert makes clear: 'Art ought ... to rise above personal feelings and nervous susceptibilities! It is time to give it the precision of the physical sciences, by means of a pitiless method!'; and in another letter to Mademoiselle Leroyer: 'The novel has been nothing but the exposition of the personality of the author, and indeed I would say this of all literature in general, with the exception of two or three men perhaps. However, the moral sciences must take a new path and proceed, as do the physical sciences, in an atmosphere of impartiality' (Letters To Mademoiselle Leroyer de Chantepie, 18 March 1857, and 12 December, 1857, in Becker 1963: 95).

There are then two competing models for the third-person narrator in Realist novels. One relies on the bond between author, novel and reader in a shared intimacy within a shared world. This is the author as participant in the world of the reader and the novel, through the voice of the narrator. The second model is that of the cold-eyed scientist, merely observing phenomena without comment. The fact that there are at least two contradictory models for the narrator is an example of writers working within the Realist aesthetic but having different interpretations as to how best to implement its aims. This leads us on to a discussion of a related aspect of narrative transmission within Realism, 'Sympathy and empathy'.

Sympathy and empathy

> Being observed,
> When observation is not sympathy,
> Is just being tortured . . .
>   (Elizabeth Barrett Browning, *Aurora Leigh*, II, 866–8)

We have seen that the Realist aesthetic, particularly the English variety, depends upon a configuration of author, narrator, novel and audience, which draws all into a shared universe, and the main emotional and conceptual tenor through which this is done is 'sympathy' and 'empathy'. Modes such as satire and gothic do not require these emotional responses, but the Realism of Gaskell and Oliphant does – they want to engage hearts and minds. Thus, while analysing 'texts' often draws us to look on them as logical propositions, including a kind of aesthetic logic, a text which is working towards a manipulation of sympathy for characters and issues may subordinate such 'logic' to other means. The quotation at the head of this section succinctly frames the problem. The increasing emphasis on 'observation' as the means to scientifically understanding the physical and natural worlds entails a subject–object relationship. When taken in the scientific sense, this is 'objective' in that the role of the subject – the observer – should not interfere with the observation. Such objectivity was meant to transfer across to the social sciences, to observations of man as a social animal. This is observation without sympathy. To view with sympathy is to place the observer, the subject, in a distorting manner to the object, it is to take up a particular, subjec-tive role with regards to what is observed.

Yet the nineteenth-century English Realists did not necessarily see 'objective' realism as an end in itself, whereas the Zola school of realism certainly did (in theory) aim for the objective, scientific stance as an ultimate goal. It partly accounts for the difference in reading a novel like *L'Assommoir*, where, for instance, the descent into misery and oblivion of Gervaise and Coupeau is charted without any sympathetic narrative commentary. When Gervaise's shop, and her management of it, starts to go into decline the narrator remarks: 'Little by little she was letting everything go to pot' and the narration studiously avoids any attempt to directly elicit our sympathy (Zola 1998: 277). It is therefore not just the way that material is presented within any given text, but the kind of relationship established between the reader and the novel via the narrative perspective. The reader of a Realist novel is placed in the role of observer – the report on reality is offered for his or her inspection. The attitude of the English Realists who engage in social commentary is that the role of the reader is one of a sympathetic observer; that of Zola would appear to be, 'here is the material, make of it what you will'. While some critics will quite reasonably argue that the very selection of the material guides the reader to a sympathetic gaze – how can readers not look upon the plight of the miners in *Germinal*, or the inhabitants of *L'Assommoir* but with sympathy? – the narrators in these novels do not themselves offer the viewpoint. If there is sympathy it is at the level of a narrative perspective distinct from that of the narrator.

In this latter type of realism there is more 'showing' than 'telling': Zola presents us with pictures of desperate situations and environments, but with little in the way of narratorial commentary to direct the reader's sympathies. There are no speeches on behalf of the working classes or destitute, which trump all other viewpoints, as we get in Gaskell and Dickens. Dickens is vital in the development of this aspect of Realism since his novels so clearly attempt to draw the reader into worlds of poverty and deprivation while maintaining sympathy. The non-Realist nature of it is down to the fact that the mode is predominantly sentimental, a manipulation of the reader's emotional response, which distorts the accuracy of the representations. What Dickens perhaps does not offer, as do those other writers following, is the intellectual apprehension of these matters. His one attempt in *Hard Times* to achieve something approaching the work of these other Realist novelists seems to admit its own defeat in the repeated phrase of the central character, Stephen Blackpool – 'it's all a muddle'.

You may be wondering why I have headed the section 'Sympathy' and 'Empathy'. The distinction, although not hard and fast, is that 'empathy' suggests much more of an identification with the person or persons represented, as if the person asked to empathise is in the character's shoes or experiencing as the characters experience, often being able to draw on one's own similar experiences to effect such empathy. With sympathy there is less expectation of this kind of identification; there is a recognition of the plight of the characters but no sense of personal identification with it. When reading Realist texts it is interesting to see where along a sympathy–empathy line readers are being asked to place themselves, and this leads us into discussion of the implied reader.

The implied reader

The perspectives of sympathy and empathy partly depend upon how the novels establish a relationship with readers. Again, I am talking about the assumptions of Realist novels in the context of the nineteenth-century audience. Here is an interesting opening from George Gissing's first published novel, *Workers in the Dawn* (1880). The chapter is titled 'Market Night':

> Walk with me, reader, into Whitecross Street. It is Saturday night, the market-night of the poor; also the one evening in the week which the weary toilers of our great city can devote to ease and recreation in the sweet assurance of a morrow unenslaved. Let us see how they spend this 'Truce of God;' our opportunities will be of the best in the district we are entering.
>
> As we suddenly turn northwards out of the dim and quiet regions of Barbican, we are at first confused by the glare of lights and the hubbub of cries. Pressing through an ever-moving crowd, we find ourselves in a long and narrow street, forming, from end to end, one busy market. Besides the ordinary shops, amongst which the conspicuous fronts of the butchers' and the grocers' predominate, the street is lined along either pavement with rows of stalls and booths, each illuminated with flaring naphtha-lamps, the flames of which shoot up fiercely at each stronger gust of wind, filling the air

around with a sickly odour, and throwing a weird light upon the multitudinous faces. Behind the lights stand men, women and children, each hallooing in every variety of intense key – from the shrillest conceivable piping to a thunderous roar, which well-nigh deafens one – the prices and the merits of their wares. The fronts of the houses, as we glance up towards the deep blackness overhead, have a decayed, filthy, often an evil, look; and here and there, on either side, is a low, yawning archway, or a passage some four feet wide, leading presumably to human habitations. Let us press through the throng to the mouth of one of these and look in, as long as the reeking odour will permit us. Straining the eyes into horrible darkness, we behold a blind alley, the unspeakable abominations of which are dimly suggested by a gas-lamp flickering at the further end. Here and there through a window glimmers a reddish light, forcing one to believe that people actually do live here; otherwise the alley is deserted, and the footstep echoes as we tread cautiously up the narrow slum. If we look up, we perceive that strong beams are fixed across between the fronts of the houses – sure sign of the rottenness which everywhere prevails. Listen! That was the shrill screaming of an infant which came from one of the nearest dens. Yes, children are born here, and men and women die. Let us devoutly hope that the deaths exceed the births.

The level of detail is typically Realist, as is the subject matter, and the narrator adopts the 'Dear Reader' stance. The overriding tone is one of pity – here is a place where humans are condemned to live. The point of view is that of the moral observer and we can see, in typical metonymic fashion, how Gissing reads the lives of the inhabitants solely from the environment (see Chapter 9 on language for a detailed discussion of this feature of Realism). How does it position the reader, and who, then, is the implied reader?

The 'descent' into the 'hell' of the living poor is typical of Realist novels. The first assumption here is that the reader is not one of these people and has no experience of these things at first hand. The opening invites the reader to share the experience of the observer who is about to be enlightened, and the ensuing descriptions are meant to evoke our sympathy through the somewhat gothic horror of 'horrible darkness' and 'unspeakable abominations'. The narrator is keen for us to really step inside this world: 'Listen! That was the shrill screaming of an infant which came from one of the nearest dens. Yes, children are born here, and men and women die.' The reader is intended to enter the novel with a sympathetic outlook, with the narrator acting as the guide, a mediator between the reader's more privileged world and this world of deprivation.

This much is obvious – that the implied reader in the Realist novel is of a higher social status, middle-class (or perhaps respectable working class) and asked to look on the characters as people living and breathing within a fictional representation of a part of the real world. This implied reader has an effect on the way that the material is represented. There are broadly two types of presentation to the reader with respect to this, dependent upon the class of persons being presented. The world of the middle classes is assumed to be the shared one of the novel and does not require a guide, whereas the world of the working classes is presented as an unknown world – the northern working classes, for instance, in Gaskell, or the London poor as here in Gissing – where every detail has to be laid out. A detailed description of an already-familiar typical household has a different effect from a similarly detailed but unknown type of household.

Mary Barton is a good source for the relationship between author and reader. There are often authorial interjections which are not too dissimilar from the assumptions of Gissing's opening: 'There were desperate fathers; there were bitter-tongued mothers (O God! what wonder!).' This again invites the reader into observing the same world from the same position as the narrator, and more importantly, asks the reader to respond emotionally to the events at the same time as the narrator. The emotional engagement is simultaneously a moral one, often shading into moral persuasion: 'The vices of the poor sometimes astound us HERE; but when the secrets of all hearts shall be made known, their virtues will astound us in far greater degree. Of this I am certain' (Gaskell 2003: 58).

It also suggests that the implied reader is to be actively engaged, to stand alongside the narrator in judging events. We have seen that *Mary Barton* involves the reader at an emotional and moral level – this is the dialogue of sympathy – and a novel like *Middlemarch*, which does not so baldly attempt to affect the reader's emotions yet still solicits a generosity of spirit for the various plights of its antagonists, is one of sympathetic dialogue with the reader. How far the implied reader is to be intellectually engaged in Realist fiction is a different matter. Sympathy and empathy perhaps predominate because the assumption is that these are the more fundamental levels with which we are engaged in the world, so that the bond between the physical world that we experience and the represented world of the Realist novel is strongest when it is constructed emotionally rather than intellectually and abstractly. Gissing's opening clearly wants a rather visceral emotional reaction, as do the novels of Dickens and Gaskell.

Eliot more often than not inclines to a more 'reasoned' emotional response. In fact, in Gaskell there is the general disavowal of understanding political economy in *Mary Barton*, with the implication that such an understanding can only be factored in once we have understood the world emotionally. There is a certain disingenuousness here because some of the speeches and narrative commentary show a particular economic understanding, and such a strategy perhaps also reflects the 'flawed' narrator approach. Nevertheless, the narrator further undermines intellectual enquiry as the means of understanding when she states: 'Even philanthropists who had studied the subject, were forced to own themselves perplexed in their endeavour to ascertain the real causes of the misery; the whole matter was of so complicated a nature, that it became next to impossible to understand it thoroughly' (Gaskell 2003: 84–5). Thus, if it exceeds the capacity of the best minds to understand how such a state of affairs has come about, it might be best to focus on the actual misery and see how that might be relieved, in addition to the greater sympathetic and empathic understanding the novel seeks to engender between owners and workers.

Subject matter

Theoretically, if the aim of Realism is to faithfully represent the observable world there is nothing that should not come within its domain. However, this is clearly not the case and, as we have already seen, it is the lives of the middle classes and the working classes as seen from a middle-class perspective which form the bulk of material for the Realist novel. So, while in theory the Realist novel can and perhaps should cover anything and everything of contemporary life, the evidence suggests that this was not so. Indeed, part of the argument suggesting that the English novel, especially before 1870, was not 'Realist' is that its subject matter and treatment were confined to, and constrained by, its genteel audience. If the implied (and actual) English readership is middle class it is, of necessity, 'polite' and genteel and does not wish to have thrust before it what is unpleasant. If unpleasantness is to be shown, for example the lives of the destitute, it must be done tastefully. This does not sound like Realism at all.

In general, this characterisation has some validity, and most English Realist novels observe the unwritten laws of gentility, knowing that if they had wished to upset their audience they would not have found a publisher. So one of the limits of the English Realist novel is that of a decorum which is both social and literary. For some writers this is not a problem since they may share the sensibility of the audience as to what is suitable subject matter for literature. For others, and Gissing was one of them, it is an unwarrantable censorship. Sometimes a writer will present material which falls outside what is 'proper', but inevitably the narrator will apologise and seek forgiveness, arguing that it is necessary for one reason or another.

Although the narrators in Realist novels do not usually assert that they are constrained to represent according to what is decorous, the narrator in *Vanity Fair* sees this as a hypocrisy. In highlighting this the novel operates very much in the manner of an eighteenth-century voice exposing society's hypocrisies, rather than the typical narrative voice of the Realist novel, but in doing so it tangentially highlights the limits of the English Realist novel.

At the beginning of Chapter 64 the narrator is faced with giving us the details of Becky Sharp's life when she falls on hard times as an adventuress. The narrator teases the reader: 'We must pass over a part of Mrs. Rebecca Crawley's biography with that lightness and delicacy which the world demands – the moral world, that has, perhaps, no particular objection to vice, but an insuperable repugnance to hearing vice called by its proper name.' Although it is framed – as so much of *Vanity Fair* is – in a way which suggests a readership complicit in the hypocrisy exposed (something that the Realist narrator rarely does) – the point is clear: everybody knows what goes on but is too polite to spell it out: 'a polite public will no more bear to read an authentic description of vice than a truly refined English or American female will permit the word breeches to be pronounced in her chaste hearing'. In one way Thackeray observes the rules, as he suggests here, by alluding to them rather than describing them: 'And so, when Becky is out of the way, be sure that she is not particularly well employed, and that the less that is said about her doings is in fact the better. / If we were to give a full account of her proceedings during a couple of years that followed after the Curzon Street catastrophe, there might be some reason for people to say this book was improper.' And I think it fair to say that the English Realist novel in general takes this route.

Theoretically its aim is to represent all that there is in the affairs of the world, but in reality it is circumscribed by literary and social decorum. There is plenty in *Vanity Fair* which asks us to consider it as a Realist novel, but when we get to Becky's very low life the omniscient narrator affects not to know the details of it, in contrast to the immense detailing elsewhere in the novel: 'She was, in fact, no better than a vagabond upon this earth. When she got her money she gambled; when she had gambled it she was put to shifts to live; who knows how or by what means she succeeded?' (Thackeray 2003: 758). The narrator moves on, and in a manner which once more draws on decorum (although also in the context of a certain hypocrisy) concludes: 'what shall we say, we who have moved among some of the finest company of Vanity Fair, of this refuse and sediment of rascals? If we play, let it be with clean cards, and not with this dirty pack' (759). This decorous constraint changes after the 1870s, but until then, while it is hardly 'the drawing room' which is the sole focus of the English Realist novel, it is still the case that subject matter is constrained to whatever is acceptable there. So while 'everyday life' among the middle and working classes provides the bulk of subject matter for the Realist novel, certain aspects of it remain taboo, particularly material of a sexual nature.

Contrast this with Zola's works, where there appear to be no such constraints. Reading his work alongside the English Realists readily shows up the difference. For instance, in *Germinal* there is a scene in which the wives of the striking miners take out their anger on the exploitative grocer by castrating him; in *L'Assommoir* Gervaise openly lives in a *ménage à trois* with Coupeau and Lantier. The neighbourhood is scandalised but Gervaise becomes immune to this social approbation:

> Amid this general outrage Gervaise went placidly about her busi-
> ness, weary and half asleep. At first she'd felt dreadfully guilty and
> shameless and had been disgusted with herself. On leaving Lantier's
> room she'd wash her hands and, with a wet rag, scrub her shoulders
> hard enough to abrade the skin, as if to clean off the filth. If
> Coupeau tried to fool about she'd get angry and rush off shivering to
> the back of the shop to dress; nor would she allow the hatter to touch
> her when her husband had just kissed her. She'd have liked to
> change her skin when she changed men. But, slowly, she became
> inured. It was too tiring to wash every time. (Zola 1998: 274)

It is very difficult to imagine Gaskell, Eliot or Dickens able to offer such a psycho-sexual perspective on one of their characters. Anything that relates to improper sexual behaviour is simply glossed over, as the passage from *Vanity Fair* indicates. Note here also how the narrative voice does not take up that of the moral outrage of the neighbourhood, and moves into Gervaise's perspective, thus completely refusing to offer any moral guidance for the reader. Again, it is not a method of narration that the English Realists could or would adopt, and such events and situations in themselves would seem inconceivable as suitable material for an English Realist novel prior to the 1870s. Even though the sugges-tion in *Vanity Fair* is that Becky Sharp openly exploits her sexuality for financial gain and to fund her gambling habit, it is nonetheless decorous in its preference for allusion over detail.

In *Mary Barton* one of the worst events caused by a strike is when acid is thrown in a strike breaker's face. The event is told third-hand, and with the intention of showing how John Barton's innate sympathy is activated despite peer-group pressure to hold firm against strike breakers. The English Realists always frame what contentious material there is; the French Realists appear to be under no obligation to compromise either the subject matter or their treatment of it. We return to the question of 'subject matter' again in Chapter 3 where it is viewed in a more problematic light.

Proportion

George Eliot, in her essay 'Silly Novels by Lady Novelists', says this:

> A really cultured woman, like a really cultured man, is all the simpler and the less obtrusive for her knowledge; it has made her see herself and her opinions in something like just proportions; she does not make it a pedestal from which she flatters herself that she commands a complete view of men and things, but makes it a point of observation from which to form a right estimate of herself. (Eliot 1856)

The idea of proportion thus brings together a number of elements that we have already discussed: point of view, knowledge, accuracy, class. To bring all of these things in correct alignment it is necessary to have a sense of proportion. It is partly a consequence of features such as 'plausibility', 'everyday' and 'typical' which brings in the idea that things must be in proportion to each other. If not, then things start to look distorted or abnormal and begin to fall outside of the dictates of the Realist aesthetic. The Realist writer must therefore maintain a sense of proportion in all things, particularly in subject matter and in the representation of the inner world of a character and the social world to which he or she belongs. Too much unmediated character 'consciousness', for instance, militates against putting things in just proportion. Hence the novels of Henry James, which overlap with the Realist period, are deemed to be on the fringes of what might be regarded as Realist (now and then) because of the way in which reality is delivered up through highly detailed consciousnesses. This serves to highlight that detail in itself is not enough to define Realism; it is different types of detail – physical, social, psychological – which in proportion underpin Realist writing. To be disproportionate is to violate the rules of typicality and reason. The 'right' view is the one that has everything in just proportion.

As with other features of Realism, this would immediately appear to beg the question, how is the right proportion to be judged? Again, the answer is that it is a dynamic set up between the author, the novel and the readership, and is something to be monitored and engaged with. Zola receives criticism precisely because the amount of space he devotes to detailing the lives of the lower classes is not a true reflection of how life is. It is too narrow; its focus is on the seedier side of life to the exclusion of all other typical ways of life. Although the representation of the antagonism between middle classes and working classes in *Mary Barton* and *North and South* could be argued to stem from the necessity to set up an inherently dramatic scenario, it also establishes a just ratio between the classes. Similarly, *Middlemarch* attempts a just ratio between types within a large social band. *L'Assommoir*, on the other hand, deliberately refuses to show anything beyond the specific lower working-class district.

The question of proportion is thus particularly evident when it comes to dealing with 'low' subject matter and characters. Henry James's review of Zola's *Nana* is typical, and shows up that despite the differences he identifies between Zola and the English Realists, the point upon which the matter rests is indeed some notion of just 'proportion'. Although James in this review is generally favourable towards Zola's naturalism, he argues that Zola's novel *Nana* fails to live up to the Realist project because the characters are invariably of one type. James finds that what Zola lacks is 'taste', by which he appears to mean something like 'proportion' rather than 'decorum'. In broaching this topic he notes the difference between what the English and French reading publics will accept. The French storyteller has much greater freedom to deal with all aspects of reality, and this certainly has many benefits. Unfortunately, without English 'taste' – an understanding of what is proportionate – it has led to a different kind of conventionality, but conventionality all the same.

The fact that, despite the constraints, the English system has produced writers such as Thackeray, Dickens and George Eliot is to be admired, even if it seems anomalous to the advocates of naturalism – although James also notes that the French have little to say about these writers (in Becker 1963: 240–3). In other words, 'just proportion' is deemed to be part of the Realist aesthetic, but beyond that it is subject to the contingencies of cultural and literary expectations. Once the later English Realist novelists like Gissing and Hardy enter the scene, they too will be prey to criticisms of the kind levelled at Zola, for concentrating on subject matter that in itself is either taboo or that the representation of it is excessive and a breach of 'taste' because it is 'disproportionate'. It is another way of understanding the desire for 'correct' vision that Realism strives for.

STOP and THINK

This chapter and the preceding chapters have made a strong case for what constitutes the Realist novel. In passing, they have looked at some of the objections to Realism, but usually overcome these with arguments that have been advanced by promoters of Realism. However, you may have lingering doubts as to the validity of some of these assertions. You might want to list two or three of these to see if they are answered in the next chapter, which looks more directly at problems associated with some of the principles and particulars I have put forward as belonging to Realism. These objections may be either to my own characterisation of what Realism is, or objections to the claims and intentions of the Realist novels and writers. It may also be an objection to the gap between Realist rhetoric surrounding the novels and the novels themselves.

Works cited and further reading

Becker, G. J. (ed.) (1963), *Documents of Modern Literary Realism*. Princeton, New Jersey: Princeton University Press.

Brontë, Emily (1981), *Wuthering Heights*. Oxford: Oxford University Press.

Dickens, Charles (1970), *Dombey and Son*. London: Penguin.

Eliot, George (1856), 'Silly Novels by Lady Novelists', *Westminster Review*; July and October.

Flaubert, Gustave on realism and art. Material collected in Becker 1963.

Gaskell, Elizabeth (2003), *Mary Barton*. London: Penguin.

Gissing, George (1880), *Workers in the Dawn*. Available in e-text, http://lang.nagoya–u.ac.jp/~matsuoka/GG-Dawn.html. Last accessed 13 August 2008.

James, Henry (1880), Review of *Nana*, in *The Parisian*, 26 February, in Becker 1963.

Kingsley, Charles (1851), *Yeast*. BiblioBazaar, 2007.

Levine, George (2001), 'George Eliot and the Art of Realism', Introduction to *The Cambridge Companion to George Eliot*. Cambridge: Cambridge University Press.

Thackeray, William Makepeace (2003), *Vanity Fair: A Novel without a Hero*. London: Penguin.

Williams, Raymond (1970), 'Introduction' to Penguin Classics edition of *Dombey and Son*.

Zola, Émile (1998), *L'Assommoir*. Oxford: Oxford University Press.

3

Problems in defining the Realist novel

Some of the objections to Realism are variations on a theme, and others, such as those found in the second half of the twentieth century and the beginning of the twenty-first, are new(ish). The objections might be quite specific, for example, the way that critics and theorists talk about the type of language or prose style that characterises Realism, or at a much broader level, for example, objections to the claim that reality can be faithfully copied. Other objections take a different tack, such as the idea that Realism itself is nothing new, that it is no different from other periods when the realist impulse predominated. Yet another objection might be that the way I have gone about classifying novels as Realist and then drawing out the Realist elements is a circular argument. The objections are therefore many and contribute to the ongoing assessment that 'realism' is a slippery term that might be best avoided.

Nevertheless, in the previous chapters I have attempted to show that a shared set of concerns and beliefs around the middle of the nineteenth century led to literary Realism, that is, a term that identifies a group of characteristic elements in works of literature. This chapter deals with a number of the objections that are raised in discussions of Realism, both from the Realist period and from twentieth- and twenty-first century criticisms. Although the chapter has sub-headings suggestive of quite discrete issues, there is a great deal of interdependency and overlap, which I would ask you to bear in mind throughout this chapter. Objections to the more diffuse term 'realism' are dealt with in Chapter 10 on philosophy.

The novel genre

The argument thus far has been that there is a set of beliefs and works in the nineteenth century which we identify as constituting Realism, and that the literary form most associated with it is the novel. The problem here is that some of the features identified in Chapters 1 and 2 as part of the Realist novel could be said to be typical of the novel as a whole prior to the 1840s.

It is important to remember that the novel genre is still a new and emerging form in the nineteenth century and that Realist writers do not have to contend with arguments about what a novel traditionally is and what it should do in the same way that dramatists and poets are obliged to. The dominant narrative for the emergence of the novel form is that it starts to take shape in the eighteenth century with writers such as Defoe, Richardson, Fielding, Sterne and Smollett. Cervantes' *Don Quixote* exists as a major precursor, and the work of Fanny Burney, and then Jane Austen at the start of the nineteenth century, help to steer it into a more settled order, which becomes the Realist novel. Other types of novel, such as the gothic, in the latter half of the eighteenth century and the beginning of the nineteenth, and Scott's historical novels, offer other dimensions which the Realist novel genre is free to draw on. Such a narrative privileges the Realist novel as the full realisation of a genre that had previously existed in embryo form, such that 'novel' becomes synonymous with 'Realist novel' unless otherwise specified by sub-genres such as crime novel, science-fiction, gothic or postmodern, for example.

There are various objections to this. The very term 'novel' as described in this way is open to criticism since some of those writers in the eighteenth century commonly now regarded as novelists may not even have called themselves novelists at the time. Since there was no eighteenth-century consensus on what the novel form was, it can appear doubly anachronistic to label such eighteenth-century novelists as 'Realists' as well. However, it would seem unhelpful to deny that a work is part of the novel genre because the term where it existed did not adhere to later usage. It is not the argument of this book that 'the novel' is synonymous with 'Realist' novel, and it is perhaps easier to see the profile of the Realist novel if it is regarded as one particular manifestation of a broader category 'novel', even if a predominant one as regards 'serious literary fiction'.

Nevertheless, this does not answer the objection that many of the features identified as constitutive of the Realist novel are to be found in earlier novels. My view is that while the Realist novel is a narrowing down of some of the potential and variety of fictional prose narrative in the eighteenth century, it is a very full exploitation of some of its properties in other directions that, at the same time, were congenial to the aims of the Realist aesthetic in the nineteenth century. The novel's relative newness as a genre in comparison to poetry and drama also meant that it was more adaptable to new pressures. Drama in much of the nineteenth century appeared moribund, and poetry, again through much of the nineteenth century, was closely identified with the Romanticism that Realism had deliberately set itself against. Critics could argue that what the Realist novelists were doing – particularly the French variety – was not 'art', but they could not argue that it was not 'the novel', since the boundaries of the novel were being more firmly fixed as they wrote (albeit temporarily, as it turned out) through its adherence to Realist tenets.

Realism was the means by which the novel consolidated its position as a serious literary genre, selecting certain features from previous manifestations of fictional prose narrative which variously announced that they were 'history of ...', 'letters of ...', 'gothic novel', 'romance' or Fielding's description of *Joseph Andrews* (1742) as an 'epic poem in prose'. With the more or less firm criteria of Realism in the nineteenth century there was an agenda for what could and should be incorporated into 'the novel', and hence what the novel genre itself should be. Even Dickens, genius as he was acknowledged to be, could be deemed as a flawed novelist because certain aspects of his writing did not conform to the Realist aesthetic. It is the dominance of the Realist aesthetic in relation to the still fluid novel form that leads to the sometime equivalence of the novel and realism/Realism. More specifically, however, let us look at some of the shared features of the Realist novel and earlier novels.

The thing to remember is that the Realist novel does not happen overnight, and the Realist novel itself exhibits experimentation with form, albeit less extreme than that of some of the eighteenth-century novels. The gauche quality of the narratorial interjections in *Mary Barton* and its reliance on defensive footnotes for its use of dialect terms in speech indicate just how new some of this is for its target audience. Nor should it be forgotten that Dickens offers an interesting narrative experiment in *Bleak House*, which alternates between first- and third-person narrative point of view. Even so, why is Samuel Richardson's *Pamela* not a Realist novel, or Henry Fielding's *Tom Jones*, or Fanny Burney's *Evelina*, or the novels of Jane Austen, other than the fact that they were published outside of the putative Realist period? And is it not also the case that we find these novels attempting 'faithful copies of reality' that represent contemporary or near-contemporary time periods?

The ready answer is that these novels do exhibit certain characteristics of the Realist novel, and that arguments about the novel form in the eighteenth century were for a certain representation of everyday, ordinary life, but rarely if ever will one eighteenth-century novel contain anything like the cluster of elements that we identified as Realism and discussed in the preceding chapters. Richardson's *Pamela* (1740), for instance, offers detailed description and has a central character who is from the lower classes. These are recognisable features of the Realist novel. However, the setting is confined to an upper-class house, and the plot-structure is heavily reliant on the fairy stories 'Beauty and the Beast' and 'Cinderella'. There is a fair amount of psychological detailing of Pamela, but the novel's roots as a moral conduct book mean that the whole is subordinate to this. Set alongside the Realist novel, there is simply too much which does not 'fit' our description of it.

Richardson's later novel *Clarissa* (1748), on the other hand, would appear to answer some of these objections. There is an ostensible moral in that Clarissa's death can be seen as a consequence of setting herself against her parent's wishes, but this fades into the background when we consider the detail and length of the novel. However, one third of the book concerns itself with Clarissa's plans for the afterlife: the focus on one character in this manner takes the novel out of the realm of 'Realism' since it lacks the sense of 'proportion' necessary. Neither this nor any of the other exclusory notes I have made on 'pre-Realist' novels is meant to suggest that the novels are failures or that they lack certain Realist characteristics, it is just that they do not have a predominance of the aims, objectives, techniques and execution of Realist novels. In other words, they are successful in other ways while exhibiting certain features which contribute to the emergence of the Realist novel, itself a particular, if dominant, type of novel.

As to other novels: *Tom Jones* has a plot that is self-consciously full of artifice and has little interest in the inner worlds of its characters; Fanny Burney's *Evelina* is basically romance, as are the works of Jane Austen, and none of them approaches 'human society' as the object of scientific or sociological scrutiny, no matter how socially observant and accurate they may be. These novels and novelists certainly feature in any history of the novel and the emergence of the Realist novel, and offer techniques that the Realist novelist uses, but it would be hard to argue that the aims, objectives and execution of these novels and novelists are predominantly the same as those of the Realist novelists we have been discussing.

STOP and THINK

It is no surprise that the novel form became the predominant medium for the nineteenth-century Realist aesthetic. The following is from Clara Reeve's *The Progress of Romance* (1785), part of the eighteenth-century attempt to define the novel form:

The Romance is an heroic fable, which treats of fabulous persons and things. – The Novel is a picture of real life and manners, and of the time in which it is written. The Romance in lofty and elevated language, describes what never happened nor is likely to happen. – The Novel gives a familiar relation of such things, as pass every day before our eyes, such as may happen to our friend, or to ourselves; and the perfection of it, is to represent every scene, in so easy and natural a manner, and to make

them appear so probable, as to deceive us into a persuasion (at least while we are reading) that all is real, until
we are affected by the joys or distresses, of the persons
in the story, as if they were our own. (in Allott 1959: 47)

How close is the resemblance between this and the Realist
aesthetic described in previous chapters? What differences
are there? Is it that the theory is present but the successful
execution must wait until the nineteenth century? One way to
answer this would be to find eighteenth-century novels that
read like those of Eliot, Gaskell and Zola. Are there such
novels?

Language

There is an assumption that realism depends upon a readily accessible language, and that concomitantly language is itself
transparent: that is, the written word refers unproblematically to
things and ideas. A criticism of this, mainly from the second half
of the twentieth century onwards but with strong roots in the
century's start, is that language is far from having the capacity to
be 'neutral' and 'objective', and that such apparently transparent,
accessible writing is part of the Realist's/realist's technique and
trickery. That is, Realists give the impression that words and
language can give unmediated access to reality whereas in fact
language either inherently distorts the world it describes, or at a
more extreme level it is asserted that language creates the world
for us. In this latter view we are trapped in the 'prison-house' of
language, and it is language itself which prevents us from getting
at the real world, whatever that world might be.

I discuss this in more detail in Chapter 8 on theorists, but I
would here point out that some Realist writers at the time were
fully aware of the difficulties presented by 'language', even if they
did not express it in quite the same way as theorists from the next
century did. George Eliot in her review essay 'The Natural
History of German Life' is very attentive to such difficulties. The
essay begins with the way that a single word like 'railway' can
conjure up different associations in two people who have quite

different experiences or knowledge of the railway (and this in itself has consequences for the way we order society, and the way we go about producing accurate representations in art; in Becker 1963: 51–2), but she also points out that if we were finally to reach a language that was immediately intelligible to all, one where 'railway' would mean the same thing to all people, this is a language that might well do for science but it would be completely devoid of 'life'. Language, then, for Eliot, is inherently difficult, and only with the greatest care can it begin to offer something approaching accuracy (69–70).

Again, this is the Realist aesthetic as a shared, consensual enterprise, calling for attention to accuracy of representation. Just because language is problematic that is no reason to throw up our hands and declare that 'faithful copies' are impossible, it just means that we should try harder. Some twentieth- and twenty-first-century views maintain that this central premise of Realism (and realism) is theoretically untenable, and argue instead that language creates our world(s) rather than describes it. There is a fuller discussion of this in Chapter 10 on philosophy, but the general Realist/realist response then and now is the 'common-sense' view that there is a real world and the language we use can and does tell us what it is like, the accuracy of which depends upon the skill of the artist.

Selection

One of the characteristic aims of Realism is that anything is fit material for art, because 'all is true', as Balzac has it in his Preface to *Old Goriot*. Put another way, a mirror does not choose what it reflects, it shows everything that it captures. However, a logical criticism of this analogy as it applies to Realist literature is that of course writers select and manipulate their material, and if they are selecting and shaping then this is hardly the equivalent of a mirror.

Perhaps a better word here is 'focus': what does the writer choose to focus on? It certainly may be that a writer, wedded to the idea of realism in its more strongly mimetic form, wants to give the impression of not having selected and that he or she is, to all intents and purposes, acting like a mirror. He or she may use techniques which accumulate and aggregate objects, ideas and associations in the writing; and this is because all of the observable world within the purview of characters and narrator is being recorded regardless of any other selection criteria. One of the reasons that detailed description is so prevalent in Realist novels is no doubt this idea that everything has to be caught in the narrative picture. However, while sometimes giving the impression that they are holding up a mirror, Realist writers and artists are still nevertheless aware of their role in constructing the picture. This is how George Lewes describes the issue of selection in his *Principles of Success in Literature*:

> Those who suppose that familiarity with scenes or characters enables a painter or a novelist to 'copy' them with artistic effect, forget the well-known fact that the vast majority of men are painfully incompetent to avail themselves of this familiarity, and cannot form vivid pictures even to themselves of scenes in which they pass their daily lives; and if they could imagine these, they would need the delicate selective instinct to guide them in the admission and omission of details, as well as in the grouping of the images. Let any one try to 'copy' the wife or brother he knows so well, – to make a human image which shall speak and act so as to impress strangers with a belief in its truth, – and he will then see that the much-despised reliance on actual experience is not the mechanical procedure it is believed to be. (Lewes 1865)

The 'faithful copy' remains the key theme, but according to Lewes artists and writers must have a talent for selection that makes the faithful copy work. It may be objected that this does not make logical sense – how can a mirror require skill? – but, rather like Eliot's notion that an absolutely intelligible language would lack 'life', the absolutely mechanical reproduction would also fail to capture and copy the world we all recognise. Selection is crucial in making the work of art or novel successful in its Realism. There is no pretence here that somehow the Realist project is anything other than artifice. The answer to the objection that Realist novels must 'select' and cannot, therefore, live up to the 'mirror' analogy is one that acknowledges art as a medium of representation, but does not find this an obstacle to providing 'faithful copies'.

Visible and invisible

I have constantly stressed that Realism is characterised by an observable 'here and now', and have given some of the reasons as to why this is the case. In discussing the contrast between Zola and the English Realists I have highlighted that Zola appears to present an observable world without overtly directing the reader, whereas the English Realists often have the narrator assume the role of a wise, moral authority able to pass judgements and correct the reader's own moral vision while eliciting sympathy or empathy, or both. There is an assumption behind this latter approach that the narrator, and implicitly the author, sees further than the reader. Moreover, what the narrator/author 'sees' is perhaps what the reader is blind to. This suggests that the English Realist novels are revealing something 'hidden'. Yet how can this be, if Realism's aim, following a more scientific approach, is only to record and represent what is observable? Just as it might be objected that Realism's claim to be a mirror is logically undermined by the problem of 'selection', its claim to present the observable world appears to be undermined when we look at the novels themselves and the amount of credit given to what is not observable. In this instance it looks as if the Realists do not practise what they preach. The evidence would suggest that the Realists continue to adhere to a belief in an invisible world of some sort, which in itself veers once more to a belief in the 'beyond' or the unseen, a belief most usually found in a religious worldview, a worldview that we have argued in the preceding chapters is not part of Realism, but also perhaps a 'beyond' that is intrinsic to humanism.

The truth of the matter is that the works of Realism are some-times imbued with religious notions, or ethical views which depend upon largely 'invisible' qualities such as sympathy. I put 'invisible' in quotation marks here because these things, while not 'visible', are often held by the novels to be self-evident truths. Viewed in this way, the principle of 'faithful copy' is not contra-dicted since if the author believes that there is God or sympathy in the world, then a faithful copy must represent this. There is no consensus on this among the Realist writers. Again, the naturalist school of thought is more rigid in its belief that only the observable physical world can and should be represented, and hence these supposed Realist writers are not Realist at all. Some of the English Realists certainly believed in powers and life beyond the observable world. This is one of the moot points raised when considering this objection to Realist novels. Perhaps the best response here is to acknowledge that there is sometimes a disjunction between Realist theory and Realist practice, although those novelists who fall into this bracket (Gaskell, for instance) would not see any problem here.

I will reiterate what is at stake: the visible world, ostensibly the world of Realism, consists at the most fundamental level of time and space. The underlying Realist doctrine is that life on earth is nothing other than this human experience of space and time. This experience is the beginning and end for us, this is the one and only life, and whatever there is in the world is in the here-and-now visible world. The visible world is the world itself, it does not point to a hidden world or evidence another world. As a consequence, whatever is 'true' can only be discovered in the contemporary spatio-temporal world. Perhaps the most fitting conclusion to draw in response to this objection is that the Realist interest in the observable, 'here-and-now' world remains paramount, but some Realist novelists retain a view of the world which accepts a 'beyond' of one kind or another, and that while this may affect the overall meaning that we might attribute to a novel, the greater part of the novel material is not taken up with these matters. For instance, we get this in Mrs Oliphant's *Hester*, which suggests a Wordsworthian notion of a force that runs through everything:

> A sort of instinctive consciousness that something was going to happen seemed in the air about her. All was still, and everything going on in its calm habitual way. There were not even any heavings and groanings, like those that warn the surrounding country before a volcano bursts forth. Nevertheless, this girl, who had been so long a spectator, pushed aside from the action about her, but with the keen sight of injured pride and wounded feeling, seeing the secret thread of meaning that ran through everything, felt premonitions, she could not tell how, in the heated air, and through the domestic calm. (Oliphant 1984: 340–1)

I pick up this theme again in Chapter 4, since it is poetry that often lays claim to 'the spiritual' and the symbolic mode of representation, as opposed to the visible commonplaces of the Realist novel. However, it does lead us into a related issue concerned with the Realist novel, and that is 'the bigger picture'. Just as Hester appears drawn to understand the mystery of life, so Realist novelists often go beyond the supposed boundaries of the observable, physical world to reveal meanings not directly evidenced here.

The bigger picture

The passage above from *Hester* is not the only place where this novel hints at a more philosophical view of things. However, for the most part the novel does not meditate upon the nature of existence. Compare this to the way that Eliot's narrators frequently make comments suggestive of a deeper understanding than that of the characters. The insight offered in the *Hester* passage stays with the character, it is not expanded to make a more general point. This is partly why novels such as those of Oliphant seem less ambitious and have fewer 'serious' intentions than a work by Eliot – in whose shadow Oliphant forever felt herself. It is part of the scheme of *Middlemarch* to explore just how we do relate ourselves and our lives to 'the bigger picture', and is a theme that runs through Eliot's other work. A passage from her *The Impressions of Theophrastus Such* demonstrates the drive to get at the widest significance of human behaviour:

> The most arrant denier must admit that a man often furthers larger ends than he is conscious of, and that while he is transacting his particular affairs with the narrow pertinacity of a respectable ant, he subserves an economy larger than any purpose of his own. Society is happily not dependent for the growth of fellowship on the small minority already endowed with comprehensive sympathy: any molecule of the body politic working towards his own interest in an orderly way gets his understanding more or less penetrated with the fact that his interest is included in that of a large number. (Eliot 1880: 109)

Eliot suggests that all individuals are part of a larger whole that they cannot see. It is not too much of a leap to realise that it is precisely the kind of novel Eliot writes with *Middlemarch* that allows readers to get this view of the way in which individual affairs are caught up in larger connected systems: society, economy, the body politic. In *Middlemarch* there is a particular passage where we seem to get the perfect description of how Realism should work as an active enquiry that gives us both the individual world and the larger intellectual vision. Farebrother has heard the occasional comment that Lydgate is living beyond his means. When he meets up with Lydgate he notes that Lydgate is distracted, even though he talks constantly about his theories: 'but he had none of those definite things to say or to show which give the way-marks of a patient uninterrupted pursuit, such as he used himself to insist on, saying that "there must be a systole and dia-stole in all inquiry," and that "a man's mind must be continually expanding and shrinking between the whole human horizon and the horizon of an object-glass"' (Eliot 1965: 690). It is not just the connections between people that *Middlemarch* undertakes to represent, but it constantly asks us how we might conceive of the connections themselves as well, that we need to be mindful of micro-worlds and their possible relations to, and constitution of, the whole world.

The objection that might be raised to all this is that 'the bigger picture' is nothing other than the opinions or philosophy of the author, and this has no place in constructing a Realist novel, which should really just present what is there in the world (to return to the mirror idea). Eliot's kind of Realism always has an eye on how everything fits together: it is a to-ing and fro-ing between the everyday and the bigger picture, the hidden connections – the tissues, the causes – that construct the world as it is, and which we are in a position to verify from our own experience of the world. The stricter (naturalist) view argues against this and says that the kind of commentary Eliot's narrative voice provides hardly counts as a faithful copy, since the novel is being used as a vehicle for Eliot's explicit ideas about society. Again, the problem is that 'faithful copy' has a number of fault lines. Eliot observes the tissues that connect society and 'copies' them as part of her accurate picture, but these 'tissues' are invisible, and other writers may not agree on them, or may believe that the connections between people are of a different order. Gaskell does not permeate her description of human relations with such a web, but does put forward a similar belief in the efficacy of sympathy.

Zola simply 'presents' the material without too much omniscient commentary, and this may seem more in keeping with the Realist remit of only presenting what is observable, yet it could also be objected even here that the belief in the primary effects of environment and heredity on individuals is hardly a neutral copying of reality, as it purports to be, but represents Zola's philosophy. After all, one of the ideas behind the whole *Rougon-Macquart* sequence of which *Germinal* is a part is that alcoholism is passed on from one generation to the next. This view may have had a certain orthodoxy in Zola's day, but it is certainly not 'observable' as something genetic.

Another instance in which we might claim a covert authorial philosophy or viewpoint in Zola is the opening to *Germinal*. It describes Étienne's approach to the mining village Le Voreux: 'The pit, with its squat brick buildings crammed into the bottom of the valley, raised its chimney like a threatening beast, crouching ready to gobble you up' (Zola 1998: 7). The image of the pit as a force feeding off mankind is certainly how Étienne views it, as the reader will come to understand, but it is not clear here where the implicit judgement lies: is it with the narrative perspective or with the character. Zola rejected any claims that he was putting forward the miners' case, yet this novel was always taken as such by the miners themselves. The very selection and presentation of material, ostensibly neutral, nevertheless appears to add up to a quite definite social critique on Zola's part and thus comparable to that of the English Realists.

Mimesis

I have avoided saying too much about mimesis, even though this term is often used in conjunction with discussions of Realism. In Potolsky's book *Mimesis* (2006), for instance, 'realism' is regarded as one of three types of mimesis. In general, there is an assumption that if something is Realist it must be mimetic, that is, it must be a copy of an original that in some way stands in for the original.

In the visual arts the idea is relatively straightforward: the idea, for instance, that a bird could be fooled into pecking at a picture of grapes believing them to be physical realities. But I have already mentioned, in passing, that writing cannot be mimetic in this sense. It certainly can reproduce 'writing' in a mimetic way, for example, the use of letters in novels, or the supposed discovery of the manuscript that has been translated, which mimics what is the case in the 'real' writing world. Richardson's *Pamela* is presented to the reader as a series of letters which have been put before readers by the Editor, and so readers are 'fooled' into believing that the letters are 'real' in the way that the bird believes the grapes are real. However, as I have already pointed out, the contract established between the reader, the novel, and the narrator/author in Realism is one which often readily acknowledges fictionality, so that there is no attempt to 'fool' at this level of understanding.

The accuracy of the picture/representation in a Realist novel is to be judged on its plausibility of subject-matter and execution. It is not, therefore, a matter of mimesis. This is not central to Realism at all. A Realist novel might on occasion suggest that something is 'really real' rather than 'fictionally real' – a novel such as *North and South* reminds the reader of the reality of events from which the novel is drawing upon – but it does not, in the main, attempt to deceive the reader into believing its own tale has the same ontological status of an actual happening. Conversely, it should also be pointed out that aspects of a work of art might be highly mimetic in the above sense, yet the work of art itself as a whole is in no way Realist. For instance, the pre-Raphaelite painters, who were contemporary with the Realists and shared some similar aims, were drawn to executing their works to a remarkable degree of mimetic accuracy. The grass on Millais's painting 'Ferdinand lured by Ariel' (1849) for instance, is extraordinary, striking the viewer as 'hyperreal' in its visual impact and detail. Yet Ariel is floating at the side of the character's face in a garment fringed by ghostly faces: the manner of representation for the scenery is mimetic, but the subject matter is not.

Although we are starting to stray into philosophical questions of what constitutes the 'real world' and how fictional worlds relate to it – a topic dealt with more fully in the Chapter 10 – I suggest here a way of at least making one distinction that I hope will be helpful in relation to Realism and mimesis.

There are two types of 'real' involved in Realism's narrative mimesis. The first is what we might call 'the real real', alluded to above, whereby the story itself is presented as one that has actually happened and which the narrator has some knowledge of. The opening chapter to *The Mill on the Floss* operates in this way:

> How lovely the little river is, with its dark changing wavelets! It seems to me like a living companion while I wander along the bank, and listen to its low, placid voice, as to the voice of one who is deaf and loving. I remember those large dipping willows. I remember the stone bridge.
>
> And this is Dorlcote Mill. I must stand a minute or two here on the bridge and look at it, though the clouds are threatening, and it is far on in the afternoon. (Eliot 2003: 9)

This establishes the location as real, since the narrator vouchsafes for it in a way which places it on the same plane as the world of the reader. This equivalence of the novel's world with the reader's world is suggested by this narrative stance, and re-enforced as the novel progresses with narratorial observations that serve to draw the reader in to the narrator's world. A little further on from the above passage and the narrator vouchsafes for the reality of the story itself:

> Ah, my arms are really benumbed. I have been pressing my elbows on the arms of my chair, and dreaming that I was standing on the bridge in front of Dorlcote Mill, as it looked one February afternoon many years ago. Before I dozed off, I was going to tell you what Mr. and Mrs. Tulliver were talking about, as they sat by the bright fire in the left-hand parlour, on that very afternoon I have been dreaming of. (Eliot 2003: 11)

Not only is the locale established as real, but the idea that the narrator is present in front of us telling us a story in an oral fashion is maintained, along with the reality of the story itself. The technique is not specific to Realism, and can be found in any number of genres where giving the impression of 'the real real' is important – horror fiction, for example – but it ties in with the aims of Realism in a different way.

The second way in which this kind of mimesis works – 'the fictional real' – is the one which has been mostly implied by discussions thus far. Resemblance between places and characters in the fiction and in the real world are based on 'plausibility' rather than 'actuality'. It is this second type of mimesis, I think, which is more crucial to Realism since it draws on a different principle, one more in keeping with the scientific tenor of the times as regards typicality and consensus. The first type of mimesis does not need to bear in mind much that relates to Realist principles, and is analogous to the grapes that fool the birds. The second type asks for a sophisticated relationship between author, novel and reader. Although it is possible to make too much of the difference, it is worth noting that Eliot uses the first type for *The Mill on the Floss*, but the second type for *Middlemarch* when her ideas regarding Realist issues are perhaps more fully developed. There is little to be gained intellectually by presenting a novel as offering a 'really real' story, whereas the 'fictionally real' narratives require the different level of engagement that we have frequently argued for in Realist literature.

'Realistic'

The discussion of mimesis leads on to consideration of a related term that is often conflated with Realism: 'realistic'. It would seem uncontentious to suggest that if something is Realist we would expect it to be realistic. Is it possible that something could be Realist and not realistic, or realistic but not Realist?

The answer is 'yes' to both those questions, but it depends what you mean by 'realistic' and at what level the term is applied. The grass in Millais's painting mentioned above is realistic, but the painting is not Realist. Aspects of science fiction and fantasy may be 'realistic', for example, the psychological portrayals of characters may be realistic, but the genres are by definition not Realist (or realist). A novel could be premised on the idea that there is no meaning in the world, that the world is full of chaos and that our brains operate in irrational and chaotic ways. The novel itself might reproduce this at the level of structure and content and lay claim to being 'realistic' because it is faithfully copying the world as its author sees it. In fact, these were precisely the arguments put forward by those novelists now classified as part of the modernist movement (for example, Virginia Woolf and James Joyce) who became dissatisfied with Realism and argued that Realism provided unfaithful copies of reality. The modernists argued that they were more 'realistic' than the Realists at (predominantly) psychological levels. However, this is not Realism that the novelists are arguing for – this is mimesis, for Realism is underpinned by ideas of reason, consensus and explicability. So what may seem like nit-picking with respect to the term 'realistic' (and the term 'mimesis') is a way of more clearly seeing what is involved in the definition of Realism.

Individuals, types and stereotypes

The following quotation from the opening to *Middlemarch* indicates an interest in the relationship between time, its effect on character, and the idea of a human nature:

> Who that cares much to know the history of man, and how the mysterious mixture behaves under the varying experiments of Time, has not dwelt, at least briefly, on the life of Saint Theresa, has not smiled with some gentleness at the thought of the little girl walking forth one morning hand-in-hand with her still smaller brother, to go and seek martyrdom in the country of the Moors? Out they toddled from rugged Avila, wide-eyed and helpless-looking as two fawns, but with human hearts, already beating to a national idea; until domestic reality met them in the shape of uncles, and turned them back from their great resolve. (Eliot 1965: 25)

There is a complex set of ideas informing this, the very first paragraph of Eliot's novel. It opens with its broad theme, that of observing the 'history of man' 'under the varying experiments of time'. This does indeed seem close to what has been said previously about the move away from a religious context to one which sees man on his own terms, a creature subject to the force of Time. The connection between 'experiments' and 'knowledge' would seem to be drawn from a scientific approach – what is the effect of the force 'Time' on the object 'Man'? The framework for the novel does indeed seem to be drawn from the world of science, observation and experiment. Further, the emphasis on 'domestic reality' suggests Realism's primary engagement with the everyday world. So much, then, is Realist.

But hang on – who is Saint Teresa? The opening continues the theme and suggests that Dorothea, one of the central characters, is a latter-day Saint Teresa. This would seem to contradict the idea of dealing with 'the contemporary' as the most important frame of reference, and instead to refer to the more classical or humanist idea that there is an invariable human nature. Eliot may be hauling in natural history, but here it seems a cover for a quite traditional view of universal character-types recognisable beneath superficial social and historical circumstances. The introduction of domestic reality is, likewise, a human constant. The novel's commitment to the Realist tenet of contemporary life and specific typicality would appear to be undermined since Dorothea's typicality is nothing other than one of a transnational, transcultural and transhistorical kind.

The use of 'typicality' and 'types' within realism becomes more of an issue after our period of Realism, for in Realism itself there is a convergence of viewing society sociologically, statistically, and with the representation of 'average' (statistically 'mean') characters in novels. These 'types' are not (or are not meant to be) stock figures from history, myth or literature, but real representations of contemporary, socially-recognisable types. Fielding's claims that his characters are just as likely to be found in Greek literature as in his novels is a view that argues for unchangeable human nature, that is, a human nature impervious to environment and heredity (although the latter is complicated by ideas relating to class, perhaps). Opposing this view, Realists claim that they are reflecting the world that actually exists, that is visible and observable and quantifiable. For a reader, Dorothea in *Middlemarch* may seem a vivid, individuated character, an individual even, but Eliot casts her in the role as typical of many similar women, 'Saint Teresas', quietly suffering in nineteenth-century England. Although the equation with Saint Teresa suggests another eternal character, Eliot recasts the idea of the single, heroic, historic figure into one whereby there are recognisable – sociological – figures. This accords with Eliot's interest in 'natural history'. In these terms,

Dorothea belongs to a particular species, but it does seem that there is a tension here between the eternal verities a humanist ethic suggests, and the more locally specific natural historian's view. The problem is that in aiming for 'typicality' to enhance claims of 'plausibility' a character cannot be too unique. It is not that such people do not exist, but that to focus on them would be to distort a just picture of the world as it is.

However, Realism's claim to present the world as it is would perhaps lead us to expect that the literature does not use 'types' at all. This is where humanist ideas tend to underwrite the Realist aesthetic, since the argument is that there is a specific human nature which is not tied to time or place. There is an inherent conflict then in the aims of Realism when it also draws on humanism, at once aiming to show how character and environment are interdependent, yet that human nature is immutable. How is this to be answered?

At some levels the two views are just not compatible, although for the most part Realist authors subscribe to the humanist ethos regardless of these possible contradictions. The description here applies more to the English school of Realism, where its tendency to moral frameworks entails a dependency upon ethics derived either from religion or humanism, whereas Zola's novels, and later English novels, eschew any notion of an ameliorative ethical world. Nevertheless, none of this answers a more general objection to Realism's use of 'types'. George Gissing's second novel *The Unclassed* (1884) addresses the issue of social groups that are omitted from Realist novels. Although the novel suggests that it continues to be an aim of Realism in general to represent those who have escaped representation within the genre, in doing so the novel itself reinforces the idea that Realism proceeds by using types – classes and groups of people rather than individuals – and this presupposes that the 'world as it is' is open to sociological and natural historical observation as a means to understanding human behaviour. The natural historian and the sociologist do not necessarily have to subscribe to or agree on what defines 'human character', and can define it in a way which does not conform to the humanist's transhistorical notion of 'the human'. Nevertheless, to use 'types' is to open up Realism to a charge of inconsistency as regards representing 'the world as it is'. In part, it goes back to the objection to Realism's assumption about the self-evident visibility of certain features in the world. It is typical of the Realist novel to draw precisely on naturalist, historical, sociological and statistical approaches to society, but Realism's underlying presumption here is that these approaches simply render what is 'visible', whereas it could be argued that the frameworks for focusing on society and individuals always distort or construct what it is that is observed.

There are two other problems with the use of types. The first is that they may actually be stereotypes, and the second is that they may stand for or be representative of something else, in the manner that a symbol is a mode of representation antithetical to plain-speaking Realism.

The problem with type as stereotype is that the character becomes shorthand for a particular group or idea, and that they thus function in the way that stereotypes do, and so again undermine the claim of Realism to objective observation. A stereotype, while possibly containing some truth, largely depends upon traditional or conventional perceptions, so an author can hardly claim to have represented something from direct observation. Those characters of Dickens which appear to the reader as caricatures are functioning in such a manner.

The second problem, that of the character type standing in for something else other than itself, suggests that the type is operating in a symbolic mode, again something which is antithetical to the general aims of Realism. There appears to be a general distaste for symbolic material in Realism, and this is one of Realism's features and the reason why it is usually regarded as 'prosaic' rather than 'poetic', aside from the formal definition of prose as opposed to poetry. Symbols by their very nature argue for a world that is not visible, that is, not readily or self-evidently present. Symbolic art also requires its audience to be educated into the meanings, such that any understanding is conventional rather than based upon observation. There is a comic passage in *Middlemarch* which mocks such art. Will Ladislaw is executing a picture of Aquinas, using Casaubon as the model, and here Mr Brooke gives his assessment of the achievement to Casaubon: 'There you are to the life: a deep subtle sort of thinker with his fore-finger on the page, while Saint Bonaventure or somebody else, rather fat and florid, is looking up at the Trinity. Everything is symbolical, you know – the higher style of art: I like that up to a certain point, but not too far – it's rather straining to keep up with, you know' (Eliot 1965: 364).

The fact that it is Mr Brooke who punctures the idea of symbolical art suggests that distrust of symbolic art is perhaps not quite as clear cut as we might expect in a Realist novel, and we only have to remember the way in which certain images in *Middlemarch* operate – webs and tissues for instance – to see that Realist novels themselves rely upon a certain symbolic ordering. Philip Davis in *The Victorians* (2002) talks of the way in which Realist novels use 'natural symbols'. A natural symbol is something that stands 'for *more* than itself without ever ceasing to *be* itself', and this seems to be a good way to think about 'type' as 'symbol', but also the way in which 'types' function in general in Realist novels, where characters point to something larger than themselves without ceasing to be themselves.

The question of 'types' reoccurs in the work of Georg Lukács, a twentieth-century champion of Realism/realism, and we return to this in Chapter 8, on theorists.

Blind spots: fallen women

An objection to Realism, or perhaps an identifiable fault in Realism, is that what purports to be an accurate representation of the real world, a 'faithful copy', is nothing other than the reproduction of cultural norms. The most obvious example would be the way in which Eliot in the opening to *Middlemarch* quoted above talks of 'the history of man', thereby apparently dismissing the history of half the world's population, an irony compounded by the fact that the narrator's historical example is indeed a woman. Although some might argue that the use of 'man' for 'mankind' does not in itself exclude women, and that it was par for the course for anything prior to the twentieth century, it is still common for novels of the period to present certain aspects of gender difference as having a basis in nature. From our point of view these aspects (or some of them) seem to be nothing other than cultural constructs, the prejudices of that age. As with gender, so with class, and it can be demoralising in both these cases to see otherwise quite intelligent pieces of work seemingly complicit with such injustices. This would not normally be a problem, perhaps, since it is no trouble to recognise that it is inevitable that society at different times has different values, and our own age will itself have its own considerable blind spots. However, the issue of blind spots is a problem for Realism since Realism's assumption is that it can present material from a neutral, objective, omniscient point of view. I use the figure of 'the fallen woman' as she appears in Realist novels to illustrate the objection.

Nineteenth-century literature abounds with the figure of 'the fallen woman'. Typically a fallen woman is a prostitute, or a woman who has had sexual relations outside of marriage. Realist novels would often include such a figure and treat them reasonably sympathetically. In doing so they would fulfil the aims of Realism: not flinching in the face of unwelcome social truths; representing all parts of society, including those not acceptable to polite society; extending sympathy to everyone, regardless of social position. Gaskell's *Mary Barton* has Esther, and the focus of her novel *Ruth* (1853) is the fate of a seduced woman; Dickens's *Bleak House* has Lady Dedlock as a woman with a past; *Dombey and Son* (1846–48) has Edith Granger, and his *David Copperfield* (1850) has Marta; Elizabeth Barrett Browning's verse-novel *Aurora Leigh* has Marian Erle. A staple of Victorian melodrama, the Realist novel is legitimately able to spice up its tale or attempt to treat this social outcast seriously and sympathetically, as in *Mary Barton* and *Ruth*, respectively.

The problem, however, is in the very term 'fallen woman'. Although many of these works attempt to portray fallen women with great sensitivity and an open mind, the woman's life and fate is predetermined by the 'rhetoric of fallenness' (Amanda Anderson, *Tainted Souls*) and by the prevailing moral disapproval. If you are fallen, all you can do in this fixed schema is die or repent, and rather than challenging this schema, the works, sympathetic as they are, uphold the term 'fallen woman' as the correct way to see women who do not conform to the socially acceptable view of women's sexual behaviour. Esther, Ruth, Lady

Dedlock and Marta all die. 'Repentance' or redemption can only come through having the soul of an angel. At the end of W. S. Gilbert's melodrama *Charity* (1874) Mrs Van Brugh, the woman with a past, has to do years of penitence in helping other fallen women, becoming angelic in the process in order to gain a modicum of respectability. Even then at the end when the servant Ruth (another fallen woman) kneeling says, 'My mistress, my pure and perfect mistress, my angel from heaven, we will never part again', Mrs Van Brugh replies:

> We will never part again, Ruth. Under the guidance of our loving friend, we will sail to the new land, where, humbly as becomes penitents, cheerfully as becomes those who have hope, earnestly as becomes those who speak out of the fulness of their experience, we will teach lessons of loving-kindness, patience, faith, forbearance, hope, and charity.

Even though Gilbert wraps up Mrs Van Brugh in this homily it was not enough to prevent Victorian disgust at the subject matter, and the play closed within a week. Readers similarly found the subject matter of Gaskell's *Ruth* 'unfit'. There were sympathetic readers such as Elizabeth Barrett Browning and Charlotte Brontë, and they certainly complained about the death of Ruth as unwarranted, but even here the assumption was that Ruth does not deserve to die because her soul is spotless, an assumption that depends upon the limited options for the 'fallen woman' script. As Amanda Anderson says: 'The inevitable downwards trajectory of the fallen woman was a commonplace narrative' – 'the "harlot's progress"' – and only occasionally challenged by reformers as 'an unrealistic, specifically literary depiction' (Anderson 1993: 12).

Again, Gissing's novel *The Unclassed* (1884) attempts to look beyond the distortion of literary depictions in its portrayal of the prostitute Ida Starr, and this is part of the novel's whole project to represent those social groups that have fallen outside of accurate representation. Yet even here, at the end, Ida is shown as nearing angelic status as she does good social works in those areas in which she had once been so familiar. In Pinero's *The Second Mrs Tanqueray* (1894) we still have not escaped the rhetoric of fallenness since here is another instance of the fallen woman dying, and this despite the telling way in which the play reveals the double standards operating with respect to men's and women's sexual behaviour, something also evident in Gilbert's *Charity*.

The objection here, then, is that Realism may proclaim that it can represent 'everything' that passes before it in an open, object- ive manner, even something like prostitution or other unacceptable sexual behaviour but, in practice, it cannot really escape the same cultural and social blinkers that it sets itself up to address. A comparison with *L'Assommoir* is again instructive as to what the English Realists might have achieved had they wished to, or if the public had allowed them to. Gervaise is a fallen woman from the start, according to the English scheme of things, but in Zola's novel there is a non-judgemental tracing of her life whereby her miserable end is not put down to any sexual impropriety. The sensual nature of Gervaise's life is always through Gervaise's point of view, and although social disapproval is often shown by other characters, there is no one prevailing opinion. This leads us to a discussion of point of view, which, as you will have noticed, has often been raised as problematic for Realism.

STOP and THINK

I have used the figure of the fallen woman to illustrate a cultural blind-spot in Realist works. A more mundane way of thinking about what Realist writing misses out is to consider what you do during a normal day and how much of this simply does not find its way into novels of this period. One obvious commonplace event is going to the toilet, but how often do Realists note this? To what extent does this reveal a disjunction between what the Realists claim theoretically and what they put into practice? Does it matter that Realism fails to describe these and other bodily processes at the same level of detail as it describes mental life, furniture or social behaviour?

Point of view

I have set the English Realists against the Zola school in such a
way that the latter appears to offer the objective, neutral viewpoint
that Realism craves, whereas the former are compromised by
'unscientific' moral imperatives. The conclusion that has often
been drawn is that the English Realists fall short of the theoretical
aims of Realism, partly because what is socially acceptable severely constrains any attempts at 'faithful copies', and partly because
the novels themselves are structured around the moral education
of characters and readers, a feature of the novel since at least
Richardson and Fielding. But let us take a step back: is it really the
case that the way in which Zola arranges the view for us is
predominantly scientific, whereas the English Realists are
compromised by the expectations of middle-class morality?

There is a passage in *Middlemarch* where Mr Brooke is about to
visit a cottage, 'Freemen's End', where the farmer Dagley lives. It
is this kind of poor homestead that would be 'picturesque' under
normal circumstances, but because Brooke has Dorothea's speech
in mind about the kind of poverty such 'picturesqueness' masks,
he becomes aware of its shortcomings.

> Mr. Brooke got down at a farmyard-gate, and Dorothea drove on. It
> is wonderful how much uglier things will look when we only suspect
> that we are blamed for them. Even our own persons in the glass are
> apt to change their aspect for us after we have heard some frank
> remark on their less admirable points; and on the other hand it is
> astonishing how pleasantly conscience takes our encroachments on
> those who never complain or have nobody to complain for them.
> Dagley's homestead never before looked so dismal to Mr. Brooke as
> it did today, with his mind thus sore about the fault-finding of the
> 'Trumpet,' echoed by Sir James.
>
> It is true that an observer, under that softening influence of the
> fine arts which makes other people's hardships picturesque, might
> have been delighted with this homestead called Freeman's End: the
> old house had dormer-windows in the dark red roof, two of the chim-
> neys were choked with ivy, the large porch was blocked up with
> bundles of sticks, and half the windows were closed with grey worm-
> eaten shutters about which the jasmine-boughs grew in wild
> luxuriance; the mouldering garden wall with hollyhocks peeping

over it was a perfect study of highly mingled subdued colour, and there was an aged goat (kept doubtless on interesting superstitious grounds) lying against the open back-kitchen door. The mossy thatch of the cow-shed, the broken grey barn-doors, the pauper labourers in ragged breeches who had nearly finished unloading a wagon of corn into the barn ready for early thrashing; the scanty dairy of cows being tethered for milking and leaving one half of the shed in brown emptiness; the very pigs and white ducks seeming to wander about the uneven neglected yard as if in low spirits from feeding on a too meagre quality of rinsings, – all these objects under the quiet light of a sky marbled with high clouds would have made a sort of picture which we have all paused over as a 'charming bit,' touching other sensibilities than those which are stirred by the depression of the agricultural interest, with the sad lack of farming capital, as seen constantly in the newspapers of that time. But these troublesome associations were just now strongly present to Mr. Brooke, and spoiled the scene for him. Mr. Dagley himself made a figure in the landscape, carrying a pitchfork and wearing his milking-hat – a very old beaver flattened in front. (Eliot 1965: 428–9)

Here is the *Middlemarch* narrator once more showing how our vision may be distorted under the influence of the comments of others, by our mood and by our state of mind, and how we might therefore go about correcting it by being alert to it. Hence, this is another means by which we can be more accurate. It demonstrates, moreover, that in the endeavour to see things 'clearly', we can be helped by the views of others. The point I would make here is that the apparent lack of neutrality in the *Middlemarch* narrator (and the narrative viewpoint for the English Realists) is one that largely accepts this fault. Although these novels might still imply that the correct view is one of a middle-class being challenged from within, coming to a sense of correct view is a collaborative enterprise which the dialogic contract established between novelist, narrative viewpoint, novel and reader engages in. The narrative viewpoint of the Zola school – presenting the material without apparent comment – makes no such attempt. The argument here would be that Zola's method – methodology even – lacks the attempt to 'understand' that is a prerequisite of the endeavours of science, social science and the humanities. 'Showing' is not 'understanding'.

Defining the Realist novel

I commented earlier that novels are Realist to a greater or lesser extent. Logically, then, there must be a novel which is more Realist than others and which I should be able to identify. I think there are two possible ways to answer this: there is the novel which most represents all of the features of Realism, and there is the novel which is most typical of the Realist novel. The first is perhaps *Middlemarch*, the second could be represented by any number of novels. The initial question – what is the most Realist novel? – and the way in which it could be possibly answered, take us into the difficulties of the process of defining Realism and the Realist novel, and the way in which this book has set about its task.

The Realist novel: *Middlemarch*

If a novel is Realist to a greater or lesser extent, then *Middlemarch* would appear to be closest to a notion of 'the' Realist novel: it draws upon natural science for its methodology and aims to produce a faithful copy of the world; it focuses on everyday lives in detail, and conversely eschews dramatic incident; it offers a panoramic view of society, a society which is itself 'provincial' and therefore precisely 'in the middle' or typical of English life. The provincial life observed is taken from the contemporary world of living memory. Its characters, like its setting, are familiar, and described in close detail. Its prose style is not poetic; the multiple narratives proceed chronologically with events following one another in complex cause-and-effect fashion. The world is this world and this world alone, and behaviour, both psychological and social, is entirely explicable in terms of individual character, tradition and environment. *Middlemarch* is also to be recommended because it self-consciously treats these very characteristics and deals with them as a critic or philosopher interested in the topic of Realism might do. The novel also offers a very sympathetic treatment of all its main characters, including that of Casaubon, the dry-as-dust, ugly scholar who blights a young girl's life. The novel even finds a sympathetic end for Bulstrode, a thoroughgoing hypocrite. In this management of the narratives and characters the novel is humane, and indeed seems permeated by an attractive humanism. *Middlemarch* is not, therefore, just close to an arche-typal Realist novel, it is the acme of the Realist novel's achievement. For some, of course, that makes it the greatest achievement of the novel genre. *Middlemarch* thus counts for a lot, and so we must have it in our Realist mini-canon.

There are two questions or criticisms which arise from the manner in which I have summarised *Middlemarch*:

1   'How Realist is *Middlemarch*?'
2   'Isn't the argument circular – Realism is defined according to all the features present in *Middlemarch*, and then these features are used to define Realism?'

How Realist is *Middlemarch*?

I have itemised above the Realist credentials for *Middlemarch*. However, there are certain features of the novel which mitigate its supposed Realism, other than those objections usually levelled at the English Realists. The main objection is that because it so self-consciously takes up the questions raised by Realism, questions surrounding plausibility, accuracy, the nature of representation, the nature of science and approaches to society, the novel is more a working out of philosophical thought than we might expect from a novel – it is closer to a 'novel of ideas' than just being a Realist novel.

There can only be a tentative response to this. It certainly is full of ideas, to the extent that some commentators have seen this novel as taking the place of philosophy. Whether it is the job of a (Realist) novel to construct itself on the basis of philosophical ideas to be worked through is another matter, but for some readers and critics it makes *Middlemarch* appear less of a novel than it might otherwise be, and therefore, in a way, less of a Realist novel, especially where the latter idea carries with it something of the notion of a story which maintains the realist illusion. To keep breaking into the stories with narratorial observation and philo-sophic musings somehow makes it seem less Realist.

The other response is that because the novel appears to interro-gate just about everything that the English Realist novel could conceivably cover at the time, it is atypical. Again, this is true. It is *the* Realist text in a particular way, and other Realist novels certainly do not exhibit this comprehensiveness or interest in all the aspects of Realism that we have discussed. It holds a central position in discussions of Realism, but for these reasons cannot be held to be a typical Realist novel.

Circularity of argument

There is a difference between a circular argument, and using a method which shuttles backwards and forward between ideas about Realism and (possibly) Realist novels. There is little doubt that the literary period discussed so far is characterised by discussions about Realism, what it is and what it might be, along with the part that the novel plays in this. The term 'Realism' is not therefore some abstract category imposed retrospectively, but a recognition of an aesthetic and cultural debate identified as such at the time. Our understanding of this debate is a mixture of placing it within its contemporary context – what it meant for these writers, artists and critics in the nineteenth century – and how we respond to that now, and trying to make sense of it. Realism was a dominant aesthetic with many facets which resound down to the present day. From the nineteenth century until now it has remained a contested idea, a way of coordinating thinking about representation and the world represented, at various levels of authorial and narratorial self-consciousness. Perhaps, rather than conceiving of Realism as a fixed category, it is more useful to think of it as an ongoing premise, one that we see differently argued and rendered in different ways.

The *typical* Realist novel

That just leaves me with having to suggest a typical Realist novel. The problem here is the obverse of *Middlemarch*'s status as 'the' Realist novel: no Realist novel is likely to have all of the features I have so far laid out. What I have tried to do is suggest a number of novels that, when taken together, give a good idea of the Realist novel. Trollope's *The Warden* and *Barchester Towers* are very typical – aware of discussions centred on Realism, and executing their art within this knowledge – yet not as philosophically intent as Eliot. The same can be said of the two Mrs Oliphant novels I have referred to, *Phoebe Junior* and *Hester*. They are firmly within the parameters of Realism, but it can also be pointed out that they have some reliance on other books, in particular, more than a passing reference to *The Warden*. But then *Middlemarch* owes something to Harriet Martineau's *Deerbrook* in its focus on a troubled doctor. *The Mill on the Floss* has greater typicality than *Middlemarch*, but on the other hand much of it is infused with elegiac and pastoral tones that are not typical of the Realist novel.

The lack of 'a hero' in *Vanity Fair* is part of the move to the commonplace, and the disposal of George part of that 'realistic' ordering of narrative that Realism depends upon, but its satirical frame often undercuts such Realism. The Gaskell novels I have drawn on – *Mary Barton* and *North and South* – are typical of the 'condition-of-England' Realist novel, therefore working within certain sub-generic constraints that a more general Realist novel such as *The Warden* does not do. The two Zola novels I have used, *L'Assommoir* and *Germinal* share many of the concerns of the English Realists, but also very sharply point up what the English Realists are doing and what Zola's brand of *Réalisme* provides. Taken together, however, along with *Middlemarch*, I think that here is enough to get a good idea of what the Realist novel might be.

Works cited and further reading

Acton, William (1857), *Prostitution, Considered in its Moral, Social and Sanitary Aspects, in London and Other Large Cities; with Proposals for the Mitigation and Prevention of Its Attendant Evils*.

Allott, Miriam (1959), *Novelists on the Novel*. London: Routledge.

Anderson, Amanda (1993), *Tainted Souls and Painted Faces: The Rhetoric of Fallenness in Victorian Culture*. Ithaca: Cornell University Press.

Austen, Jane (1965), Try *Persuasion*. London: Penguin.

de Balzac, Honoré (1951), *Old Goriot*. London: Penguin. Includes 'Author's Preface'.

Becker, G. J. (ed.) (1963), *Documents of Modern Literary Realism*. Princeton, New Jersey: Princeton University Press.

Beer, Gillian (1996), '"Authentic Tidings of Invisible Things": Vision and the Invisible in the Later Nineteenth Century', in Teresa Brennan and Martin Jay (eds), *Vision in Context: Reflections and Refractions*. New York: Routledge, 83–98.

Burney, Fanny (1994), *Evelina*. London: Penguin.

Carnall, Geoffrey (1964), 'Dickens, Mrs Gaskell, and the Preston Strike', *Victorian Studies*, 8.1 (September).

Correa, D. (2000), *The Nineteenth-Century Novel: Realisms*. London: Routledge.

Defoe, Daniel (1986), *Moll Flanders*. Oxford: Oxford University Press.

Defoe, Daniel (1987), *Roxana*. London: Penguin.

Dickens, Charles (1971), *Bleak House*. London: Penguin.

Doody, Margaret Ann (1996), *The True Story of the Novel*. New Brunswick, NJ: Rutgers University Press.

Eliot, George (1880), *The Impressions of Theophrastus Such*. Edinburgh: William Blackwood and Sons.

Eliot, George (1963), 'The Natural History of German Life', in Becker, *Documents of Modern Literary Realism*.

Eliot, George (1965), *Middlemarch. A Study of Provincial Life*. London: Penguin.

Eliot, George (2003 [1860]), *The Mill on the Floss*. London: Penguin.

Fielding, Henry (1985), *The History of Tom Jones*. London: Penguin.

Fielding, Henry (1985), *Joseph Andrews*. London: Penguin.

Flaubert, Gustave (2003), *Madame Bovary*. London: Penguin.

Frierson, William (1928), 'The English Controversy Over Realism in Fiction', *PMLA*, 43.2, 533–50.

Frierson, William and Edwards, Herbert (1948), 'Impact of French Naturalism on American Critical Opinion', *PMLA*, 1007–16.

Gaskell, Elizabeth (1997), *Ruth*. London: Penguin.

Gilbert, W. S. (1909), *Charity*, in *Original Plays by W. S Gilbert. First Series*. London: Chatto & Windus.

Gissing, George (1930), *The Unclassed*. London: Ernest Benn Ltd. Also available as e-text at Project Gutenberg.

Harsh, Constance (1992), 'Gissing's *The Unclassed* and the Perils of Naturalism', *ELH* 59: 911–38.

Levine, George (1993), 'By Knowledge Possessed: Darwin, Nature, and Victorian Narrative', *New Literary History*, vol. 24.

Levine, George (ed.) (1993), *Realism and Representation: Essays on the Problem of Realism in Relation to Science, Literature, and Culture*. Wisconsin: University Press.

Lewes, George (1865), *Principles of Success in Literature*. Available at Project Gutenberg.

Martineau, Harriet (1983), *Deerbrook* (1839). London: Virago.

Masson, David (1859), *British Novelists and Their Styles*.

McKeon, Michael (2002), *The Origins of the English Novel, 1600–1740*. Baltimore: Johns Hopkins University Press. Highly recommended.

O'Mealy, Joseph H. (1997), 'Rewriting Trollope and Yonge: Mrs. Oliphant's *Phoebe Junior* and the Realism Wars', *Texas Studies in Literature and Language*, 39.2 (Summer), 125–38.

Pinero, Arthur W. (1936), *The Second Mrs Tanqueray*. London: Samuel French Ltd.

Potolsky, Matthew (2006), *Mimesis*. London: Routledge.

Regan, Stephen (2001), *The Nineteenth-Century Novel: A Critical Reader*. London: Routledge.

Richardson, Samuel (1985), *Pamela*. London: Penguin.

Richardson, Samuel (1985), *Clarissa*. London: Penguin.

Shaw, Harry E. (1999), *Narrating Reality. Austen, Scott, Eliot*. Cornell University Press.

Spacks, Patricia Meyer (2006), *Novel Beginnings. Experiments in Eighteenth-Century English Fiction*. New Haven: Yale University Press.

Sterne, Laurence (2005), *A Sentimental Journey*. London: Penguin.

Sterne, Laurence (1984), *The Life and Opinions of Tristram Shandy*. Harmondsworth: Penguin.

Zola, Émile (1998), *Germinal*. Oxford: Oxford University Press.

4

The idea of poetry

It is to the poetical literature of an age that we must, in general, look for the most perfect, the most adequate interpretation of that age, – for the performance of a work which demands the most energetic and harmonious activity of all the powers of the human mind ...
(Matthew Arnold, 1857)

I hold you will not compass your poor ends
Of barley-feeding and material ease,
Without a poet's individualism
To work your universal. It takes a soul,
To move a body: it takes a high-souled man,
To move the masses, even to a cleaner sty:
It takes the ideal, to blow a hair's-breadth off
The dust of the actual.
(Elizabeth Barrett Browning, *Aurora Leigh*, II, 476–83)

The previous chapters have focused on the novel from the middle of the nineteenth century onwards as being at the forefront of literary Realism. Indeed, many critics and theorists regard discussion of literary realism as one related solely to the novel genre. However, Realism was such a dominant force in the nineteenth century that poetry and drama were obliged to respond to it. That this was the order of influence is repeatedly borne out by critical commentary and from within the literature itself, whether novel, poetry or drama. In Zola's essay 'The Experimental Novel' – that is, the novel as modelled after the manner of scientific experiment – he ends with: 'I have spoken only of the experimental novel, but I am firmly convinced that the method, after it has triumphed in history and criticism, will triumph everywhere, in the drama and even in poetry' (in Becker 1963: 155–6). It is that last part which gives a very good indication of the relationship between the novel, Realism and poetry, since Zola sees that poetry will be the most resistant form of writing to Realism. In this he was echoing a common sentiment, for the Realist novel was seen as the antithesis of poetry, and was felt to be in direct opposition to whatever it was (and perhaps is) that poetry stands for.

The sentiment that poetry was no longer required had begun early in the century. Bernard Richards cites Bentham's argument that the arts might have a utility value, similar to a game like 'pushpin', but could offer nothing more (1830); Thomas Love Peacock's *The Four Ages of Poetry* (1819) suggested that poetry belonged to the age of children; and Macaulay similarly noted that poetry could only operate its 'magic lantern' when the ages were dark (Bernard Richards, 'Introduction' to *English Verse 1830–1890*, pp. xviii–xix, for the above views). The nineteenth century was not such a period, and Peacock appears to foretell the century's subsequent prosaic character when he states: 'as the sciences of morals and of mind advance towards perfection, as they become more enlarged and comprehensive in their views, as reason gains the ascendancy in them over imagination and feeling, poetry can no longer accompany them in their progress, but drops into the background, and leaves them to advance alone' (Peacock 1972: 9). It is 'the idea of poetry' that is under siege.

The idea of poetry

Poetry has been broadly conceived of in two ways. First, it is formally distinct from prose writing in the way it is laid out on the page, and in its attention to rhyme, metre and line endings. It is also characterised by greater use of figurative and symbolic language, and sometimes by compression of ideas. Second, poetry has long been associated with what is 'ideal', noble and elevated, synonymous with the human spirit and thus, following on from discussion in previous chapters, what is more likely to exist in the realm of the invisible world rather than the empirical one. This is the contrast between what is 'poetic' and what is 'prosaic'. These two conceptions of poetry were dominant and intertwined in the nineteenth century, and have continued, if frequently contested, to the present day. Nor is it surprising that this should be the case because if you look for a definition of 'prose' in any dictionary you will see that it is defined as writing or speech that is not verse or poetry. You will also see that prose is often associated with a phrase such as 'common language', further boosting ideas that prose is inherently suited to the aims of Realism rather than poetry. Etymologically 'prose' is traced back to the Latin *prosa*, meaning 'straightforward', and this too would appear to inform what 'prose' stands for.

However, I would suggest a note of caution in the way I have characterised poetry versus prose. If 'prose' has retained a stable identity by its simply being opposed to 'poetry', the idea of poetry that the nineteenth century maintained until the end is very strongly shaped by the Romantics, and this tends to mask other ideas about poetry which, while not antagonistic to this idea, suggest that poetry could have other formal qualities and achieve things other than the imaginative and lyrical expression of the human spirit that the above offers. For instance, many Greek philosophers wrote their philosophy in verse; verse epistles are a major feature of the literature of the eighteenth century; Thomson's *Seasons* (1726–30) is a 'descriptive' work, focusing on landscape; and descriptive poetry in general is found in the sixteenth, seventeenth and eighteenth centuries. Nor should we forget that the Romantics were fond of verse narrative; and drama, again from the Greeks onwards, has often been in verse form. In other words, there appears nothing that is part of Realism which is necessarily outside of poetry. The idea of poetry as a literature of elevation and lyrical expression, while far from being exclusive to the Romantics, was nevertheless highly influential at the time the Victorians were writing. This passage from an 1829 essay by John Henry Newman perfectly encapsulates the idea and ideal of poetry that carried through the remainder of his century:

> It follows that the poetical mind is one full of the eternal forms of beauty and perfection; these are its material of thought, its instrument and medium of observation, – these colour each object to which it directs its view. It is called imaginative or creative, from the

originality and independence of its modes of thinking, conceptions
of ordinary minds, which are fettered down to the particular and
individual. At the same time it feels a natural sympathy with everything great and splendid in the physical and moral world; and
selecting such from the mass of common phenomena, incorporates
them, as it were, into the substance of its own creations. From living
thus in a world of its own, it speaks the language of dignity, emotion,
and refinement. Figure is its necessary medium of communication
with man; for in the feebleness of ordinary words to express its
ideas, and in the absence of terms of abstract perfection, the adoption of metaphorical language is the only poor means allowed it for
imparting to others its intense feelings. A metrical garb has, in all
languages, been appropriated to poetry – it is but the outward development of the music and harmony within. The verse, far from being
a restraint on the true poet, is the suitable index of his sense, and is
adopted by his free and deliberate choice. ('Poetry, with Reference
to Aristotle's Poetics', in Stasny 1986: 10)

Poetry's purpose is to represent the ideal rather than the actual,
and this is to be achieved by the minds of poets, which are minds
beyond those of common minds. The language poets will need to
use will chiefly be metaphorical, since ordinary language is too
feeble to achieve these ends. Further, this language is 'the
language of dignity, emotion, and refinement'. It is easy to see that
the Realist novel must fall down on one or more of these counts
when set alongside the idea and ideal of poetry, with poetry itself
still maintaining a superior position in the literary hierarchy. The
prose fiction of the Realist novel must use everyday language, with
metaphoric language by implication occupying a subordinate role
at best. And a further implication is that if poetry is the medium of
the imagination, (Realist) prose is the medium of all that is dull
and unimaginative. Again, these are sentiments which continue to
exert a force right down to the present.

There is a complimentary issue related to the opposition
between poetry and prose in the nineteenth century. Until well
into this period, poetry continued to be at the apex of the literary
hierarchy, partly because it was synonymous with a number of
things regarded as the domain and ambition of art: the ideal,
beauty, perfection. To be the best in literature was to succeed in
poetry. Poetry, in a broader sense, stood for the most complete

expression of what was noble in the world and in humanity, so any work of art, not just poetry as a literary genre, could be regarded as 'poetic' if it was able to realise the spirit of man, as the quotation from Arnold at the head of this chapter shows. It followed, therefore, that as prose in the form of the novel gained the ascendancy in popularity and significance, all those things associated with poetry were under threat. Just as the term 'poetic' had a wider application than just the literary association, so 'prosaic' meant something more than the medium of 'prose': it stood for everything we have discussed so far – the common, the everyday, the typical, all aspects of human life, including ugliness, the working classes, and 'less-than-human' behaviour. Poetry stood for beauty and an ideal of truth; prose stood for whatever was real, empirical, observable – a different kind of truth. So an idea of 'truth' still underpinned both of these genres, but ideas such as 'beauty' and 'spirit', so closely associated with poetry and so little associated with prose, created something of a problem for prose fiction writers.

Fernand Desnoyers, in his manifesto 'On Realism' (1855) addresses precisely the problem of poetry in light of the aims of Realism: 'Since the word truth puts everybody in agreement and since everybody approves of the word, even liars, we must admit that, without being an apologist for ugliness and evil, realism has the right to represent whatever exists and whatever we see' (in Becker 1963: 81). Desnoyers wants to make Realism 'poetic' by altering where poetry – in its wider sense – can be found:

> For my part, I believe that the poetry which everybody believes he has in his pocket is to be found in the ugly just as much as in the beautiful, in the fantastic just as much as in the real, provided that the poetry be naive and carry conviction and that its form be sincere. Ugliness or beauty is a matter for the painter or poet; it is for him to decide and choose; but one thing is sure, poetry, like Realism, can be found only in what exists, in what is to be seen, smelled, heard, and dreamed, provided you don't dream deliberately. (Becker 1963: 82)

It is important then for Desnoyers not to concede the ground to poetry, but rather to get people to understand that the subject matter of Realism is every bit as poetic as more traditional sources.

Flaubert, on the other hand, espoused both an absolute realism but also an idea that a work of art should be made beautiful out of nothing (and his argument for the self-sufficiency of art also suggests a removal from the edicts of realism; in Becker 1963: 89–90). Like Desnoyers, he too was urging that poetry could and should be found in anything: 'Let's extract [poetry] from no matter what, for it is latent in everything and everywhere; there's not an atom of matter that does not contain thought. So let's become accustomed to considering the world as a work of art, the ways of which we must reproduce in our works' (Letter To Louise Colet, 27 March 1853; in Becker). Again, this shows that although Realist tenets hold sway in the period under discussion, there is still a reluctance to let go of the idea of poetry since it continues to represent the highest of literary genres.

The clash between prose and poetry does not end there in the battle of associations. We have seen the importance of the scientific backdrop in the development of Realism and the Realist novel. For some, the inroads of science ensure that the world itself can no longer be considered 'poetic'. In *Sartor Resartus*, the fictional German Idealist philosopher Teufelsdröckh sees that 'God's world [is] all disembellished and prosaic' (Carlyle 1975: 52), thanks to science. It is further evidence of the notion that Realism is implicated in the materialism and capitalism of the age, that it is 'anti-spirit', anti-Ideal, and irreligious. I will give a couple of examples from our mini-canon of novels to show how the Realist novel is still in thrall to the idea of poetry, while at the same time by its very form continues to operate against the idea of it.

The first example is from Mrs Oliphant's *Phoebe Junior*. Northcote is a rich Dissenting minister, and here he reveals himself to be a connoisseur of pottery. But not so Phoebe or Reginald, who as the reader will realise by the end of the novel represent all that is financially and socially pragmatic in polite (and less-than-polite) English society. Phoebe tells Northcote: '[b]ringing poetry down to prose is not always an advantage, is it? Italy is such a dream – so long as one has never been there' (Oliphant 1989: 182). A little further on, Phoebe suggests that her grandmother present Northcote with a cup and saucer that he admires. Northcote says that it would not be right to break up the

set, and Phoebe confesses she was 'not prepared for such delicacy
of feeling – such – conscientiousness':

> 'Ah!' said Northcote, with a long-drawn breath, 'I don't think you
> can understand the feelings of an enthusiast. A set of fine China is
> like a poem – every individual bit is necessary to the perfection of
> the whole. I allow that this is not the usual way of looking at it; but
> my pleasure lies in seeing it entire, making the tea-table into a kind
> of lyric, elevating the family life by the application of the principles
> of abstract beauty to its homeliest details. Pardon, Miss Beecham,
> but Mrs. Tozer is right, and you are wrong. The idea of carrying off
> a few lines of a poem in one's pocket for one's collection – '
> (Oliphant 1989: 183)

This is the worth of poetry placed as the highest aesthetic value.
The unimaginative Reginald and the practically-minded Phoebe
are condemned by association at this point by not demonstrating a
poetic sensibility. However, by the end of the novel it is Reginald
and Phoebe's rather utilitarian view of the world that wins out,
and, by association, the Realist novel, which is precisely not
concerned with 'elevating the family life by the application of the
principles of abstract beauty to its homeliest details'. *Phoebe
Junior* is more interested in showing the very real difficulties
facing a young woman with a number of choices but within the
constraint of having to choose a husband. In passing, you might
note that poetry is associated with Italy, and this is something that
is a recurrent and organising motif in *Aurora Leigh*, as we will see
later.

The second example of the respective values of poetry and
prose as found in a Realist novel is from *Middlemarch*. Again, the
technique aligns the characters with prose and poetry. Dorothea
needs to tell Celia that she has accepted Casaubon's offer of
marriage, although she is wary of doing so:

> Dorothea was in fact thinking that it was desirable for Celia to know
> of the momentous change in Mr. Casaubon's position since he had
> last been in the house: it did not seem fair to leave her in ignorance
> of what would necessarily affect her attitude towards him; but it was
> impossible not to shrink from telling her. Dorothea accused herself
> of some meanness in this timidity: it was always odious to her to
> have any small fears or contrivances about her actions, but at this

> moment she was seeking the highest aid possible that she might not
> dread the corrosiveness of Celia's pretty carnally minded prose. Her
> reverie was broken, and the difficulty of decision banished, by
> Celia's small and rather guttural voice speaking in its usual tone, of
> a remark aside or a 'by the bye.' (Eliot 1965: 71)

Casaubon for Dorothea represents everything that is noble and
elevated in the world, and this is what attracts Dorothea to him.
He dwells in the world of the Ideal and the Abstract. By marrying
Casaubon, Dorothea is therefore wedding herself to a version of
the poetic. Nevertheless, she has to steal herself to the practicality
of telling her sister Celia about her engagement, who does not like
Casaubon and is typical of the general opinion of him as a dull,
unattractive academic. Where Dorothea sees 'beyond' the physical
to the (imagined) spiritual side of Casaubon, Celia sees only the
physical, material Casaubon. As ever, the writing here is quite
complex. Dorothea's belief in the spiritual, the ideal, the poetic
comes across as naive, and Celia's assessment of Casaubon comes
across as clear-sighted, 'realistic' and not tinged by any hint of the
aspirational. Nevertheless, there is a certain loading against Celia's
realism in Dorothea's horror of 'the corrosiveness of Celia's pretty
carnally minded prose', as if it is petty and mean to maintain
realism in the face of Dorothea's higher-mindedness. The
unwinnable contrast between the two is sealed in that final
sentence: 'Her reverie was broken, and the difficulty of decision
banished, by Celia's small and rather guttural voice speaking in its
usual tone, of a remark aside or a "by the bye".'

Such higher, poetic matters are in the realm of 'reverie', whereas
the 'prosaic' is confined to Celia's 'small and rather guttural voice'
and the common or vulgar interjection 'by the bye'. For Eliot, in
this novel and elsewhere, the conflict between poetry and prose is
unresolvable, as it represents the conflict between spirit and material, but the fact that we have this within the Realist novel genre is
once more indicative of the shift towards prose over poetry. It is also
interesting to note the following in relation to Eliot, as Pinney
observes in his gloss on her essay 'Notes on Form in Art' (1868):
'We know that she distinguished sharply between the limits of
prose and verse from her letter explaining her choice of prose for
the tale of *Silas Marner*: "I have felt all through", she wrote, "as if

the story would have lent itself best to metrical rather than prose fiction ... but, as my mind dwelt on the subject, I became inclined to a more realistic treatment'" (Pinney 1967). It is clear that a writer like Eliot would choose prose fiction as a particular tool to achieve particular ends with the material at hand, that the same material could be treated 'realistically' or poetically. But for poets who did not write fiction, the choice was much starker. Arthur Hugh Clough, for instance, partly in response to Arnold's defence of poetry as the higher truth, did accept the force of Realism and the novel, and argued for a change in poetic behaviour: 'For poetry "to be widely popular, to gain the ear of multitude", Clough thought it would have to deal "more than at present it usually does, with general wants, ordinary feelings, the obvious rather than the rare facts of human nature ... the actual, palpable things with which our every–day life is concerned" (Kerry McSweeney, 'Introduction' to *Aurora Leigh*, x).

STOP and THINK

Can poetry ever be Realist? Do the requirements of its form always undermine the possibility of realism, even where many of the elements of traditional poetry are dispensed with in favour of 'natural' language?

Elizabeth Barrett Browning: *Aurora Leigh*

It is Elizabeth Barrett Browning's 'novel in verse' which perhaps best represents the pressure in the nineteenth century for art to be 'realist', responding to concerns such as those articulated by Clough. Realism here means dealing with contemporary subject matter, rather than the princesses and fairies that those such as Tennyson, the chief poet of the Victorian period, had a reputation for. The dominant opinion is that the Realist novel is most suited and most successful in representing the age, one which is deemed at core to be 'materialist', in the sense of both capitalist and intent on the world in its physical appearance as 'material'. Like other poets of the time, Elizabeth Barrett Browning felt that poetry had fallen behind to the successes of the novel and should indeed look to the present time, as the novel did, rather than places that were historically or geographically far away. Why should not poetry tell a contemporary story, in the manner of a novel? As Aurora herself asserts:

> Nay, if there's room for poets in this world
> A little overgrown (I think there is),
> Their sole work is to represent the age,
> Their age, not Charlemagne's – this live, throbbing age,
> That brawls, cheats, maddens, calculates, aspires,
> And spends more passion, more heroic heat,
> Betwixt the mirrors of its drawing-rooms,
> Than Roland with his knights at Roncesvalles.

> (V.200–207)

And yet, what we find in *Aurora Leigh*, this 'novel in verse', is a defence of the idea of poetry at the very expense of Realism. Having accepted the Realist argument that art must deal with the contemporary and contemporary subject matter, the poem never-theless continues to uphold a poetic ideal, an idea that the poet sees beyond the visible, natural world to higher truths, God's truths. Just as it appropriates Realist conventions of characterisa-tion, description and narrative, it simultaneously undermines Realism by its prolonged emphasis on the invisible world, the value of poetry and its various associations.

The narrative of *Aurora Leigh* is centrally concerned with the value of poetry. Its eponymous heroine is cast adrift as a child after her English father and Italian mother die. Aurora is subsequently brought up by a strict religious aunt, and is given a traditional education for a woman, learning to play music, learning how to sew, and learning how to subordinate herself to men. But Aurora chafes under the regime, for she has a spirit that yearns for much greater things: 'I had relations in the Unseen, and drew / The elemental nutriment and heat / From nature' (I.474ff). Her restricted life with her aunt, and the entry of her cousin Romney Leigh, is described thus:

> I read her books,
> Was civil to her cousin, Romney Leigh,
> Gave ear to her vicar, tea to her visitors,
> And heard them whisper, when I changed a cup
> (I blushed for joy at that) – 'The Italian child,
> For all her blue eyes and her quiet ways,
> Thrives ill in England: she is paler yet
> Than when we came the last time; she will die.'
>
> (I.491–8)

The claustrophobia of polite English society is economically sketched here through the endless round of taking 'tea', visits from the vicar, and provincial gossip. Aurora's Italianness counts against her, partly because of English national prejudice against untrustworthy Mediterranean types.

Both still young, a friendship between Romney and Aurora develops, and the poem characterises Romney as mainly concerned with social injustice and struggling with the guilt of his privileged social position: 'agonising with a ghastly sense / Of universal hideous want and wrong / To incriminate possession' of Leigh Hall (I.519–20). His youthful reading concerns itself with statistics, and the poem continues to associate Aurora with what is elevated and Romney with what is earthly:

> Always Romney Leigh
> Was looking for the worms, I for the gods.
> A godlike nature his; the gods look down,
> Incurious of themselves; and certainly
> 'Tis well I should remember, how, those days,
> I was a worm too, and he looked on me.
>
> (I. 551–6)

Although there is some self-deprecation on Aurora's part when she looks back on her younger self, as the poem progresses the tendency is for Aurora's 'poetic' view to have the last word, for instance when Aurora claims that she read her books: 'Without considering whether they were fit / To do me good' (I.701–2), lost in a book's 'beauty and salt of truth' (1993: 708). Implicitly, she is guiding the poem's audience to read books 'poetically' rather than in the manner of her aunt's and cousin's utilitarian ways, 'calculating' how much good a book can offer. Also, of course, the poem continues to stand in contrast to all that Romney stands, and comes to stand, for. There is no doubt, even at this early stage in the verse-novel, that it is poetry that acts as a bulwark against all the material vulgarity of the age, against its capitalist endeavour, and against the empirical reality that Romney is immersed in. At one point she discovers her father's books, and this leads her to exalt poets. She answers the possible objections that could be raised against her praise of poets:

> What's this, Aurora Leigh,
> You write so of the poets, and not laugh?
> Those virtuous liars, dreamers after dark,
> Exaggerators of the sun and moon,
> And soothsayers in a teacup?
>   I write so
> Of the only truth-tellers now left to God,
> The only speakers of essential truth,
> Opposed to relative, comparative,
> And temporal truths; the only holders by
> His sun-skirts, through conventional grey glooms;
> The only teachers who instruct mankind
> From just a shadow on a charnel-wall
> To find man's veritable stature out
> Erect, sublime – the measure of a man,
> And that's the measure of an angel, says
> The apostle. Ay, and while your common men
> Lay telegraphs, gauge railroads, reign, reap, dine,
> And dust the flaunty carpets of the world
> For kings to walk on, or our president,
> The poet suddenly will catch them up
> With his voice like a thunder – 'This is soul,
> This is life, this word is being said in heaven,
> Here's God down on us! what are you about?'
> How all those workers start amid their work,
> Look round, look up, and feel, a moment's space,
> That carpet-dusting, though a pretty trade,
> Is not the imperative labour after all.
>   (I.854–880)

Romney, for his part, is damning of Aurora's view of things, that she can only understand very particular cases which she then generalises from, writing as if she were these very people:

> The human race
> To you means, such a child, or such a man,
> You saw one morning waiting in the cold,
> Beside that gate, perhaps. You gather up
> A few such cases, and when strong sometimes
> Will write of factories and of slaves, as if
> Your father were a negro, and your son
> A spinner in the mills.
>
> (II.189–96)

To write like this is to offer a sympathetic viewpoint without proper 'sociological' or statistical understanding. Despite their differences, Romney proposes marriage to Aurora, a proposal she stridently rejects, much to everybody's dismay. Her argument is that it is a wife he wants, not Aurora, as if once more it is the general idea which matters, rather than the individual. She chides him for wanting a 'helpmate' who can help him achieve his good works, whereas her understanding of love is something quite different. The associations continue to accumulate, therefore, with 'love' now enlisted on the side of the poet and poetry.

Aurora moves to London in the aftermath of rejection and makes a career for herself as a writer (Book III). The miserable position of the poet in mid-nineteenth-century England, as opposed to that of the prose writer, is bemoaned:

> I apprehended this –
> In England no one lives by verse that lives;
> And, apprehending, I resolved by prose
> To make a space to sphere my living verse.
> I wrote for cyclopaedias, magazines,
> And weekly papers, holding up my name
> To keep it from the mud. I learnt the use
> Of the editorial 'we' in a review
> As courtly ladies the fine trick of trains,
> And swept it grandly through the open doors
> As if one could not pass through doors at all
> Save so encumbered.
>
> (III.306–17)

The starving poet thus turns to prose, which she equates with hack-work, fit only for financial gain. To avoid her 'name' being sullied with prose, Aurora writes in this medium anonymously. Not only that, there is an implicit alignment of poetry with the individual and prose with a (fictional) mass when she notes that she must use 'the editorial "we"' in reviews. The implication is that the (lyrical) 'I' is the first choice for poets, and is more honest in being so. Although as we have already seen British novelists were no more able to let go of the 'noble' ideal than were poets, at least not until the 1880s perhaps, in the prosaicness of the novel it seems less compromising to Realist aims than it does here in *Aurora Leigh*, where the very genre is associated with 'elevation' and hence what is 'noble', or an idea of the noble, even when it is withering and satirical. It is the idea of poetry which here continues to be anti-Realism, wedded as Realism was to prose fiction and the utility of prose.

In this same Book III Aurora discovers from Lady Waldemar that Romney is to marry Marian Erle, a girl of 'doubtful life, undoubtful birth'. Lady Waldemar, in love with Romney herself, is dismissive of Romney's choice and automatically believes that Aurora will share her opinion. Aurora decides to visit Marian, and this section provides some very interesting material for a discussion of Realism.

Marian lives in a deprived part of London, and so the event of Aurora entering a world otherwise hidden from her, or known only through newspaper and Parliamentary reports, is the typical one of the middle-class descent into lower-class hell, such as we have already witnessed in *Mary Barton* and the passage that opens Gissing's *Workers in the Dawn*. Compare the latter with this:

> Two hours afterward,
> Within Saint Margaret's Court I stood alone,
> Close-veiled. A sick child, from an ague-fit,
> Whose wasted right hand gambled 'gainst his left
> With an old brass button, in a blot of sun,
> Jeered weakly at me as I passed across
> The uneven pavement; while a woman, rouged
> Upon the angular cheek-bones, kerchief torn,
> Thin dangling locks, and flat lascivious mouth,

Cursed at a window, both ways, in and out,
By turns some bed-rid creature and myself, –
'Lie still there, mother! liker the dead dog
You'll be to-morrow …'

(III.758–70)

The horror of it accumulates in detail, with threats of cholera and death hurled at Aurora, yet Aurora remains resolute enough to declare that 'I think I could have walked through hell that day' (1993: 779). It becomes gothic as she empties out her purse, 'when, as I had cast / The last charm in the cauldron, the whole court / Went boiling, bubbling up, from all its doors / And windows, with a hideous wail of laughs'. Amid this lower-class hell Aurora ascends some stairs to find Marian and her 'ineffable face', a 'soft flower' from 'such rough roots'. The whole nature of the episode is one that finds poetry within a stereotypical lower-class setting rendered as a pseudo-gothic event. Aurora, struck by Marian's angelic face, calls her 'cousin', an immediate declaration of social acceptance. Marian tells Aurora the story of her life, which Aurora then relays to us, the audience, 'with fuller utter-ance' (III.828).

I have talked so far very much at the level of the theme of poetry versus prose as it is manifest in the literature of the time and in some critical commentary. This section in the poem, along with other parts of *Aurora Leigh*, is indicative of the problems of Realist representation, both in general and specifically within poetry. The resort to the gothic imagery of hell's boiling, bubbling cauldron for a lower-class habitat suggests a disgusted middle-class response as filtered through other stereotypical representations of such scenes. In addition, although Marian's story is told at length, it is Aurora who gives it to us, therefore denying direct, self-representation from Marian's class. This problem with represen-tation is not confined to *Aurora Leigh*, as we have seen. However, Realist novels are not aiming to defend the form and spirit of poetry in the face of such scenes. *Aurora Leigh* thus operates at a complicated and contradictory intersection: it wants to show Romney's world, the world that Marian springs from, and yet show that poetry and all that it stands for is what we must cling to. The fact that Marian's face stands out against the faces Aurora has to pass by 'too quickly for distinguishing' (III.788) perpetuates the idea that we must strive to seek out what transcends these earthly horrors – we must cling to the poetic – and this is to be at the level of the individual rather than the social. The irredeemable social class from which Marian is the only one to escape reappears in the next book, Book IV, when Marian and Romney are to be married. Their marriage is intended to symbolically 'heal' the rift between their two classes. Cue more gothic imagery:

> Of course the people came in uncompelled,
> Lame, blind, and worse – sick, sorrowful, and worse,
> The humours of the peccant social wound
> All pressed out, poured down upon Pimlico,
> Exasperating the unaccustomed air
> With a hideous interfusion. You'd suppose
> A finished generation, dead of plague,
> Swept outward from their graves into the sun,
> The moil of death upon them.

(IV.542–50)

They inhabit a necropolis and emerge as the undead for the wedding feast. Again, the representation seems more reliant upon a stereotypical vision of the lowest classes, biblical in the scale of their misery, contaminating all that they touch and the air that they breathe.

If *Aurora Leigh* represents the lower classes en masse as the gothic 'Other', it must find a different way of representing Marian Erle, one of the same class, yet with a spotless soul. In terms of poetry versus prose, the question is how to maintain the spotless soul of poetry in the midst of sordid prose. It does this in a manner which we have seen some English Realist novels do when they wish to take into account the gentility of their audience. *Aurora Leigh* does it in a particularly telling way, indicative once more of the constraints upon English Realism, but also in a manner which continues to demonstrate the superiority of poetry over prose and Realism.

Marian does not turn up for the wedding, but finds herself by a rather convoluted route in Paris. She has been drugged and turned into a prostitute – just as Italy stands for the 'poetic', France stands for 'looser morals' where such things can happen. Marian recounts to Aurora the tale of how she was drugged and became 'lost', a euphemism for an unmarried woman becoming sexually active. However, in relating the tale to Aurora, Marian tailors and censors her own story according to the tasteful norms of the day. In this way, literary decorousness is awarded to Marian herself as she thoughtfully glosses over the details:

> Enough so! – it is plain enough so. True,
> We wretches cannot tell out all our wrong
> Without offence to decent happy folk.
> I know that we must scrupulously hint
> With half words, delicate reserves, the thing
> Which no one scrupled we should feel in full.
> Let pass the rest, then; only leave my oath
> Upon this sleeping child – man's violence,
> Not man's seduction, made me what I am.

(VI.1219–27)

It is Marian's narrative scrupulousness in the telling of her story which makes her, in Aurora's eyes and in the eyes of the reader, 'worthy' of being treated as Aurora's equal. Had she in fact given a 'fuller' description of her experience, this would have opened her (and the poem) up to charges of 'grossness' and 'vulgarity', qualities associated with the lower classes, and the kind of epithets to be hurled at Zola. Marian's ability to 'represent' her own story fully in accordance with what is and what is not allowed by polite society certainly puts her on a par with Aurora, and, by association, with the poem. It thus re-enforces the nobility of poetry at the expense of Realist detail. We have observed already that elsewhere in the poem, when it does attempt to represent the general horror it identifies as the lower classes, it resorts to non-Realist Gothicism.

Yet, even though in its execution *Aurora Leigh* may not match up to 'the faithful copy' of the Realist novel, and may wish only to be Realist in the sense of dealing with the contemporary age, it does recognise that there is a problem for representation, both as it is caught up in the poetry of the age and in this poem specifically. If the poem eschews representing certain details, it nevertheless understands that the science of its age sees that nothing is beyond representation, and that in this way science may be more honest than poetry. In the passage below, Aurora notes how the artist-poet is perhaps hindered by his or her dedication to beauty, and needs more courage to look at what may be unpleasant. Tellingly, it begins with a concern about the representation of 'crowds':

> These crowds are very good
> For meditation (when we are very strong)
> Though love of beauty makes us timorous,
> And draws us backward from the coarse town-sights
> To count the daisies upon dappled fields
> And hear the streams bleat on among the hills
> In innocent and indolent repose,
> While still with silken elegiac thoughts
> We wind out from us the distracting world
> And die into the chrysalis of man,
> And leave the best that may, to come of us,
> In some brown moth. I would be bold and bear
> To look into the swarthiest face of things,
> For God's sake who has made them.
>
> (VI. 136–49)

And yet it is precisely the crowds which Aurora has not looked into directly, feeling that it is to stare into the face of hell, and that the proper place to find the interest of the age is in drawing rooms (above). But the poem is then aware that 'men of science' adopt an attitude that might benefit poets when they view 'nought common or unclean' (VI.174). Yet this is not advocacy for French-style Realism – it is simply that poets might find beauty in 'nature's falling off' rather than being shocked by it (VI.178). So while there is recognition that there are parts of nature that poets deem beyond the pale, 'tethered' as they are to 'a lily or a rose' (VI.184), it is only that they fail to broaden their horizons in finding beauty elsewhere, as the scientists do, rather than a more materialist, prosaic approach to nature. The very fact, perhaps, that this is 'nature' rather than 'the world' or 'reality' suggests that 'nature', even when 'falling off', is inevitably the work of God, and for this reason deserves the poet's consideration. Once again, we can see that the idea of poetry provides resistance to the drive towards Realism that was common among nineteenth-century novelists. Rather than conceding to the arguments of Realism, other than its focus on the contemporary age, *Aurora Leigh* argues that poetry, and the ability to apprehend the world poetically, should be extended into all the realms that science fearlessly ventures into.

Other poetry

I have made *Aurora Leigh* bear the weight of poetry in this discussion of Realism. Partly it is because there is so little poetry in the Victorian period that takes up the battle cry of Realism, and partly because here is a poem that so comprehensively takes up the cause of poetry in the midst of Realism's dominance. The Realist novel itself was partly motivated by a reaction against Romanticism and, by extension therefore, a reaction against the tendency of poetry throughout much of the nineteenth century. Even if a certain 'modernity' can be located in some of the poetry of this period in that the central figures may be 'crippled' by self-conscious doubt and self-consciousness itself, and this in turn looks forward to the literature of modernism rather than backwards to Romanticism (other than Wordsworth's *The Prelude*, perhaps, which itself provides a model for *Aurora Leigh* and is regarded as a precursor of modern 'consciousness'), it is not a noted feature of the Realist novel. Any tortured artist-souls that may appear in a Realist novel must be seen in proportion to all the other different types of person who might plausibly be expected to populate society, rather than be the main focus of attention.

Robert Browning's monologue 'Fra Lippo Lippi' is a poem that enters into then current discussions of Realism, and is a poem which Eliot herself praised, saying that she 'would rather have *Fra Lippo Lippi* than an essay on Realism in Art' (cited in Bernard Richards, *English Verse 1830–1890*, 1980). Fra Lippo Lippi was an Italian painter in the fifteenth century and particularly significant in the move towards more realistic painting, part of what is characterised as the more general Renaissance movement towards humanism (or representing that period's embrace of humanism). Browning places Lippi as its originator, although the title should more accurately go to Tommaso di Giovanni

(1401–38), better known as 'Masaccio'. The realism of it is in its naturalistic rendering of dialogue as we are given the perspective of a monk speaking to an interlocutor. In one passage, one of Lippi's paintings stirs some debate amongst the monks. Initially it meets with approval, as its audience praises its verisimilitude:

> 'That's the very man!
> Look at the boy who stoops to pat the dog!
> That woman's like the Prior's niece who comes
> To care about his asthma: it's the life!'
>
> (Robert Browning, 'Fra Lippo Lippi', ll.168–71)

However, these monks are reproved by more senior ones who teach them 'what to see and not to see' (l.167). They also recognise the success of its verisimilitude, but condemn it for this very reason:

> 'How? what's here?
> Quite from the mark of painting, bless us all!
> Faces, arms, legs and bodies like the true
> As much as pea and pea! it's devil's-game!
> Your business is not to catch men with show,
> With homage to the perishable clay,
> But lift them over it, ignore it all,
> Make them forget there's such a thing as flesh.
> Your business is to paint the souls of men – '
>
> (ll.175–83)

and concludes with: 'Give us no more of body than shows soul!' (l.187) and 'Paint the soul, never mind the legs and arms!' (l.193). The arguments infused into the monologue are here obviously those we have observed throughout our discussion of Realism, about seen and unseen, and about the purposes of mimesis and verisimilitude. And although part of the same intellectual environment as *Aurora Leigh*, it produces a rather different take on the purpose of art. One of the claims that Lippi makes in the poem is that painting the everyday draws attention to what we have become habituated to, such that we delight in this. Unlike the argument in *Aurora Leigh*, Lippi asserts that it is not his job to 'instigate prayer' but it is the Prior's pulpit role to 'interpret God'. Instead,

by giving us the everyday afresh he is giving us God's works
afresh:

> For, don't you mark? we're made so that we love
> First when we see them painted, things we have passed
> Perhaps a hundred times nor cared to see;
> And so they are better, painted – better to us,
> Which is the same thing. Art was given for that …
>
>   (ll.300–5)

Whereas in *Aurora Leigh* it is the job of poetry to paint the soul as
well as the flesh, the argument here is that reproducing the faithful copy is to give us God without forcing an interpretation that
makes us 'see' in a specifically religious way.

George Meredith's *Modern Love* (1862) provides another aspect
of the relationship between Realism and poetry. The title is an
indication that Meredith is tackling a modern situation in respect
to age-old subject matter. While there is insufficient space here to
do any in-depth reading of the poem, there is one stanza in particular which relates directly to discussion in this book.

The poem details the breakdown of the narrator's marriage
when his wife has an affair. The story is told through fifty sixteen-
line sonnets, and so does not have the more prosaic Realist
approach to language that *Aurora Leigh* effects in its quasi-
naturalised iambic pentameter. However, exactly half-way through
the poem it does wonder about what can and should be represented, and about the related question of typicality.

> You like not that French novel? Tell me why.
> You think it quite unnatural. Let us see.
> The actors are, it seems, the usual three:
> Husband, and wife, and lover. She – but fie!
> In England we'll not hear of it. Edmond,
> The lover, her devout chagrin doth share;
> Blanc-mange and absinthe are his penitent fare,
> Till his pale aspect makes her over-fond:
> So, to preclude fresh sin, he tries rosbif.
> Meantime the husband is no more abused:
> Auguste forgives her ere the tear is used.
> Then hangeth all on one tremendous 'If': –
> *If* she will choose between them. She does choose;

> And takes her husband, like a proper wife.
> Unnatural? My dear, these things are life:
> And life, some think, is worthy of the Muse.

The stanza plays on the meaning of 'unnatural' as he attempts to comprehend the actuality of the *ménage à trois* he finds himself in, and to do this in the way that he and his wife represent the situation to themselves. She, reading a French novel, finds it 'unnatural' and questions which aspect of it is so. Is it the fact that it shows a *ménage à trois* – but, as he points out, that is precisely their own situation, so for him it is 'natural' in the sense that this is what happens in reality, and so it is only 'natural' for a French novel to represent this. The underpinning is essentially Realist: this is 'life', and it is the job of art – the Muse – to faithfully represent this. It can only therefore be 'unnatural' for the French novel to represent in terms of what is 'natural' for representation: the poem points up the national hypocrisy – 'In England we'll not hear of it' – showing that this is wilful ignorance and blind gentility rather than a refusal to give credence to what is presumed to be French abnormality. By implication, of course, Meredith's own representation of a *ménage à trois* in the poem cuts through this English prejudice against looking squarely at marital and sexual matters, and not surprisingly it came in for the kind of criticism we have seen levelled elsewhere at such 'frankness'.

Aurora Leigh, 'Fra Lippo Lippi' and *Modern Love* demonstrate that poetry did respond to the materialist pressures of the age, and other comments above show that some of this was in direct response to the success of the Realist novel and the dominance of prose as the medium of a rational, scientific age. Yet, just as in the last chapter it was shown that the Realist novel did not happen over night, that it was drawing on many techniques that had become established or experimented with in the modern novel's emergence, it would be wrong to paint a picture of poetry in the nineteenth century that predominantly wrestled with the legacy of Romanticism, or that Romanticism itself was concerned solely with the Ideal, or that this meant that it was always removed from everyday life. Just as at the start of the book I argued that 'the realist impulse' is found throughout history, elements of this same impulse can be found in the Romantic period and poets, in the

Preface to the *Lyrical Ballads* for instance, and in Wordsworth's
poem 'Michael'. It is also just as well to remember that Jane
Austen was writing at the same time as Keats, Shelley and Byron,
and her poetic equivalent could be found in the work of George
Crabbe. Just as Austen's novels share many of the characteristics of
what has been defined as the Realist novel, Crabbe's major works
The Village (1783) and *The Borough* (1810) offer much that might
otherwise fall within the domain of Realism. As well as a poet,
Crabbe was a coleopterist – a collector of beetles – and this
suggests that the natural historian's mind is at work in the cata-
loguing these poems take on. The interest in a scientific approach
might indeed take the work in a more solid Realist direction that
built upon empirical observation.

Once again, the answer is that here we have a work that predates
the self-conscious aggregation of features that constitute Realism,
but where the realist impulse is strong. *The Village* begins with the
aim of 'correcting' the typical view of the countryside as a place of
rustic harmony, and partly by the poem itself refusing the pastoral
mode. It wants to show 'the real picture of the poor' and in doing
so draws a broad brush over rural poverty that emphasises the
harsh nature of this type of life. Its aim is rather similar to that of
the natural historian viewing mankind in a particular habitat, as
we see Eliot doing later in *Middlemarch*. The differences are the
poetic form that Crabbe uses, and the manner in which he represents 'types'. Both of these features do tend to demonstrate how it
is that the novel perhaps came to be the preferred medium for
Realism, but also afford another means of putting Realism itself
into relief.

The Village is in heroic couplets, a metrical form associated with
the Augustans and a period of poetry largely preceding Crabbe's
own, which is coincident with that of the Romantics. By working
in such an obviously poetic mode any sense of the literary medium
approximating to the everyday in the way that the Realist novelists
(and a dominant strand of the novel genre) attempted cannot be
realised. It is a 'real picture', but within a poetic frame. Like
Aurora Leigh, it upholds the idea of poetry against the vulgar
ravages of the age – here symbolised by the 'harsh prose' of newspapers (the third and final part is devoted wholly to the deleterious

influence of the papers). In this way, it is the frame itself that militates against the Realist aesthetic. *Aurora Leigh* does not quite have
this problem since although it uses iambic pentameter, just as *The
Village* does, it is not in couplets and has a tendency to veer
towards a 'prosy' verse style. The second key way in which it
differs from Realism is the manner in which it draws its picture,
opting for a general commentary on the lives of the rural poor, and
using generic types which it has no interest in individuating in the
manner that the Realist novel does:

> 'A lonely, wretched man, in pain I go,
> None need my help, and none relieve my woe;
> Then let my bones beneath the turf be laid,
> And men forget the wretch they would not aid.'
> Thus groan the old, till by disease oppress'd,
> They taste a final woe, and then they rest.
>
> Theirs is yon House that holds the parish poor,
> Whose walls of mud scarce bear the broken door;
> There, where the putrid vapours, flagging, play,
> And the dull wheel hums doleful through the day; –
> There children dwell who know no parents' care;
> Parents, who know no children's love, dwell there!
> Heart–broken matrons on their joyless bed,
> Forsaken wives, and mothers never wed;
> Dejected widows with unheeded tears,
> And crippled age with more than childhood fears;
> The lame, the blind, and, far the happiest they!
> The moping idiot, and the madman gay.
>
> (Crabbe 2009: ll. 222–39)

It certainly portrays a 'real' world very different from that of
traditional pastoral verse, yet for the Realists this would tend to
be a general view which would need to have individuated such a
type and such a locale, and to offer accumulated psychological
detail and greater physical description. It is not the subject
matter, therefore, but the level of detail which is treated and the
manner in which it is represented. Again, I should stress that
this does not mean that *The Village* is a 'failure', it is just that
its aims and execution are not consistent with those of the later
Realist aesthetic.

The Borough is a more ambitious piece as it draws a comprehensive picture of an area. Its technique is similar to that of *The Village* as it identifies a large number of typical characters, places and events. Occasionally it tells the story of its inhabitants – Peter Grimes is the most famous – but the greater part of the poem is taken up with more generalised views of the borough. It certainly provides a model for Realism in its breadth of social detail, and its intention to cover all classes and places. Its delicacy in describing 'inns' suggests that it is mindful of literary decorum, and a reader familiar with the detailed physical and psychological descriptions characteristic of Realist novels may see little that is Realist in *The Borough*, but this and *The Village* bear analysis as related pieces of literature.

Summary

During the period of ascendancy for the Realist novel, poetry in Victorian England felt itself on the decline as the major literary form, and defended itself by defending the idea and the ideal of poetry. Elizabeth Barrett Browning's *Aurora Leigh* is the poem that most obviously and consciously represents this situation, making some concessions to the Realist novel by combining verse and novel forms, and by attending to the contemporary age, which, like Realist novels, it took to be mainly an issue about the lower classes, social problems and the general materialist tenor of the times. *Aurora Leigh* was atypical, nevertheless, in that most poetry of the period continued to operate with subject matter and form that was not within the Realist remit.

Works cited and further reading

Anderson, Amanda (1993), Chapter 5 on *Aurora Leigh* in *Tainted Souls and Painted Faces. The Rhetoric of Fallenness in Victorian Culture*. Ithaca: Cornell University Press, 1993.

Browning, Elizabeth Barrett (1993), *Aurora Leigh*. Oxford: Oxford University Press, including Kerry McSweeney's 'Introduction'.

Becker, G. J. (1963), *Documents of Modern Literary Realism*. Princeton: Princeton University Press.

Brett-Smith, H. F. B. (ed.) (1972), *Peacock's Four Ages of Poetry*. Oxford: Basil Blackwell.

Christ, Carol T. (1975), *The Finer Optic: The Aesthetic of Particularity in Victorian Poetry*. New Haven and London: Yale University Press.

Crabbe, George (2009), *The Village. Book I*. Representative Poetry Online, http://rpo.library.utoronto.ca/poem/574.html (last accessed 10 June 2009).

Davis, Philip (2002), 'Poetry' in *The Victorians*. Oxford: Oxford University Press.

Edwards, Gavin (1987), 'Crabbe's So-Called Realism', *Essays in Criticism*, 37.4: 303–20.

Flint, Kate (2000), *The Victorians and the Visual Imagination*. Cambridge: Cambridge University Press.

George, Meredith (1980), *Modern Love*, in *English Verse 1830–1890*, ed. Bernard Richards. London: Longman.

Pinney, Thomas (ed.) (1967), *Essays of George Eliot*, London: Routledge.

Richards, Bernard (ed.) (1980), *English Verse 1830–1890*. London: Longman.

Stasny, John F. (ed.) (1986), *Victorian Poetry. A Collection of Essays from the Period*. New York: Garland Publishing.

Whitehead, Frank (1989), 'Crabbe, "Realism", and Poetic Truth', *Essays in Criticism*, 39.1: 29–46.

For modern debates about poetry

Astley, Neil (2002), Introduction to *Staying Alive: Real Poems for Unreal Times*. Tarset: Bloodaxe.

Constantine David, (2004), 'Aspects of the Contemporary (i): What good does it do?' *Magma* 29 (Summer).

Forbes, Peter (1995), 'Why the New Popular Poetry Makes More Sense', *Poetry Review*, 85.3 (Autumn).

5

Realist drama

For the theatre must not be 'realistic'
(Guillaume Apollinaire)

drama is no mere setting up of the camera to nature . . .
(George Bernard Shaw)

'Cup-and-saucer' Realism versus melodrama

In turning to drama it is important to recognise that concentrating on the textual aspect alone would give us only a limited insight into its relationship with literary Realism. In this chapter, there-fore, as well as the texts themselves, I will look at other crucial elements such as stage design, and a technical feature often over-looked – the aside – something which seems inherently non-realistic, and which might therefore offer another view on Realism. If prose is by its very definition set in opposition to poetry, and hence to Realist fiction, when we examine drama's relationship to Realism we will find a different set of oppositions: to be dramatic is to be non-Realist, it is to order material in a manner which is other than what we find in the everyday, commonplace world from which Realism should take its stories. If we take the roots of drama to be in ritual, its existence as a genre would seem to be non-Realist at heart.

What is happening to drama in the period which we have desig-nated as Realist? Realism makes few inroads into the melodrama of the day that dominated the theatre, and literary history often has little regard for the period between 'Sheridan and Shaw', that is, a period from the end of the 1770s to the beginning of the 1890s. It is not the aim of this chapter to make any grand claim to counter this mainstream narrative, but on the other hand I would like to give a number of plays from this period their due, in their relation to Realism, hoping to show that they are not without their own merits, and once again to throw into relief the Realist novel.

Foremost in any discussion of Realist drama within what is characterised as Victorian theatre is the playwright Tom Robertson, whose plays *Society* (1865), *Ours* (1866) and *Caste* (1867), among others, were great successes in their time. He is sometimes portrayed as a playwright who single-handedly attempted to bring a greater realism to theatrical practice at a time when it was dominated by melodrama, pure entertainment and the spectacular. Indeed, his particular brand of drama was known as 'cup-and-saucer realism' because of its attention to domestic detail. From a modern viewpoint the realism of Robertson's plays can seem a very modest advance indeed, either in comparison with the Realist novels of the day or with the more evidently realist drama that was to come later in the century. Nevertheless, George Bernard Shaw regarded himself as a direct beneficiary of the work of Robertson and reminded people, in Robertson's defence, that the representation of everyday circumstances was hardly to be found before Robertson, and his comments, following a perform- ance of *Caste* in 1897 at the Court Theatre, give a good indication of what Robertson was up against:

After years of sham heroics and superhuman balderdash, Caste delighted everyone by its freshness, its nature, its humanity. You will shriek and snort, O scornful young men, at this monstrous asser- tion. 'Nature! Freshness!' you will exclaim. 'In Heaven's name (if you are not too modern to have heard of Heaven), where is there a touch of nature in Caste?' I reply, 'In the windows, in the doors, in the walls, in the carpet, in the ceiling, in the kettle, in the fireplace, in the ham, in the tea, in the bread and butter, in the bassinet, in the hats and sticks and clothes, in the familiar phrases, the quiet unpumped, everyday utterance: in short, the commonplaces that are now spurned because they are commonplaces, and were then inex- pressibly welcome because they were the most unexpected of novelties.' (Quoted in Tydeman 1982: 28–9)

Shaw's appreciation is of the realistic stage decor, the naturalistic dialogue and more commonplace characters. Although not alluded to here, Robertson is also credited with being a forerunner of the 'problem play', the type of play that Shaw and Pinero were to become known for, plays that deal with contemporary social issues. *Caste*, for instance, deals with the difficulties of a marriage between different social classes, and while this in itself is hardly new, it treats it seriously rather than simply as a vehicle for comedy, and the ending is nowhere near as pat as the term 'comedy' might lead an audience to expect. Tydeman's introduction to *Plays of Tom Robertson* asserts that:

> his plays do convey something of the quality of everyday existence where meals are eaten, watches consulted, pipes smoked, peas shelled, half-crowns borrowed, and galoshes fetched; behind the fiction some of the domestic and ethical pressures of the age can be dimly discerned, and in his far from facile characterisations intimations of psychological complexity filter through. (Tydeman: 1982: 15)

This assessment gives a good idea of what we can appreciate as Realist about the plays themselves and their productions, particularly that concerted effort to reproduce the texture of everyday life that the Realist novel excelled at. Reviews at the time certainly suggest that this was the effect that the productions achieved, but, as elsewhere with the reception of Realism, its value as 'art' was questioned in inverse proportion to its Realist achievements:

> In our day 'stagey' has become a word of reproach. An audience no longer enjoys the representation of what is beyond its reach. The present and the near now best satisfies it. In the drama, as in prose fiction, realism is wanted. Every man judges what is laid before him by his own experience. Truth to current existence is the criterion of merit he applies to a drama ... Mr. Robertson is a realist; the artificial and the ideal he eschews. Just as another dramatist introduces on the stage the real cab in which he has ridden to the theatre, so Mr. Robertson gives us the real conversation he has heard at the 'Owl's Roost', or in the West End Square where people come out at night to enjoy the evening breeze under a weeping ash in front of their houses. I cannot say we do not want the commonplace artistically represented on the stage, for it finds an appreciative public; I can

only express my surprise that people pay to hear other men say behind footlights what they hear in their own houses. (Thomas Purnell, 'Q', in the *Athaenaeum*, quoted in Tydeman 1982: 27)

Compare this with a recognition of the same qualities but with a positive reaction from an audience at the Theatre Royal in Glasgow, which was possibly experiencing the work of Robertson for the first time after an implied diet of melodrama. The London company's director Frederick Younge was asked to give an address to the audience following a successful performance of *Caste* that evening, and also took the opportunity to look back over two other of Robertson's comedies performed there in the same period by his company, *Play* (1868) and *School* (1869):

> It is very satisfactory, I think, that we have been able to obtain and retain your goodwill without having had recourse to outrageous sensations. I have never incited one member of my company to commit the crime of murder – (laughter) – even those amiable weaknesses forgery, perjury, and burglary have been omitted from our list of attractions ... Seriously, it is a hopeful sign for the future of dramatic art that large audiences can be deeply interested, and beguiled of smiles and tears, without the gathering of incidents from our police reports and prison records. (*Glasgow Herald*, Saturday 11 September 1869)

Nevertheless, Realism struggled in the theatre and Britain was not alone in having a theatre that was resistant to the wholesale uptake of the Realist aesthetic. Zola in his essay 'Naturalism in the Theatre' (1881) complains of something similar in France, and Strindberg, in his Preface to *Miss Julie* (1888) identifies a crisis in theatre across Europe as a whole. The resistance to treating social issues seriously and realistically was quite considerable in England. As we have mentioned, W. S. Gilbert's play *Charity* (1874), which attempted to offer a sympathetic understanding of 'a woman with a past', met with hostility and soon closed. Recognising perhaps that English drama had not achieved anything particularly notable in the nineteenth century, Gilbert wrote that the playwrights should not be criticised for producing the kind of plays that they did, because they were bound by what their audience would accept. The possibility of successfully importing the Realist aesthetic into drama was therefore quite remote.

The Ticket-of-Leave Man by Tom Taylor (1863) might be regarded as a play that exemplifies a certain Realist tenor which simultaneously concedes to the pressure of the theatrical status quo. Compared to the exemplary and extremely popular melodramatic offering *Black-Ey'd Susan* (Douglas Jerrold, 1829), Taylor's play has elements which are both Realist – the issue of a man released from prison on probation who tries to make a better life for himself – but also has enough features to be classed as a melodrama, since the good man escapes a downfall at the hands of out-and-out villains by the skin of his teeth. Indeed, *The Cambridge Guide to Literature in English* cites it as an example of 'melodrama'. However, the man who fulfils the role of what in melodrama would be 'the virtuous' protagonist – Bob Brierly – if initially shown to be naive (and hence possibly virtuous) is also shown to be capable of taking to drink and being violent. Such a figure might therefore be more accurately compared with Jem Wilson in *Mary Barton* rather than William, the wronged virtuous man in *Black-Ey'd Susan*. The difficulties Brierly faces are more plausible than thoroughgoing melodrama would normally call for, since the situation when he struggles to break free from his past reputation has some Realist merit. Nevertheless, the accommodation of the playwright to the demands of a nineteenth-century audience demanding the sensational are easily discernible as the play progresses.

If English drama of the Realist period was hampered specifically by the audience's desire for melodrama, it also faced a similar problem to that of the English Realist novel when it attempted to tackle subject matter that was deemed unsuitable for a genteel audience. When Charles Reade adapted the French dramatisation of Zola's *L'Assommoir* for the English stage (*Drink*, 1879), the play underwent significant changes in order to make it palatable. Reade's version was a great success and spawned many imitators, so much so that Reade had writs issued against a number of other playwrights for infringement of copyright. As Reade asserted, his version was based on a French dramatic adaptation by William Busnach and Octave Gastineau, and not based on the original novel. It was then easy for Reade to show that those who claimed they had adapted from Zola's novel had really pirated Reade's version, since this had incidents and characters not in the original novel. The disagreement tangentially throws up the differences between French and English audiences. The first reason Reade gives for taking from a prior adaptation rather than the source novel is that: 'Some four years ago Emile Zola wrote a novel full of genius, and fuller of filth, called "L'Assommoir"', from which 'Any Englishman had a legal and immoral right to dramatise and perform this novel' but none found it possible or advisable. The censorious English moral climate is clearly in evidence here, even if Reade at the same time acknowledges the brilliance of Zola's novel. Reade goes on to say that he 'adapted' more freely than the pirates have done, and in his adaptation he has altered the title to 'Drink', which is not a translation of 'l'assommoir', and has 'changed the moral character of the heroine' and transformed 'Gouget from muff to man' (Reade: 1882). It is noticeable that in changing all of these things, including the title, Reade is essentially offering his audience a stereotypical temperance narrative rather than following the 'unpredictable' trajectory that Zola's Realist novel ostensibly offers.

The idea of drama

Just as the idea of 'poetry' came to the Victorians loaded with certain expectations, 'drama' had its own history and dynamic. I have already suggested the Victorians mostly wanted melodrama, that is, drama characterised by comic-book villains and heroes, spectacular scenery and effects, and a highly wrought emotional tenor. To say that this is what the audience wanted, and got, is also to bring to the fore one of the features of drama – the economics of it make it much more dependent upon financial success than novels or poetry. Its collaborative nature involves theatre houses which need to make a profit, along with actors, producers, directors, stage hands, scene designers, and this makes the theatre of the time a labour- and capital-intensive business. For a play to close early is a financial disaster for many people, not just the playwright. It would not have been economically difficult for poets to embrace the Realist aesthetic, but they mainly chose not to. To turn around theatre, however, was a different matter. A dramatist who wanted to be Realist would need to convince the producer/-director and theatre company, and this in turn would necessitate convincing the stage designer(s) and actors that Realism was the way to go.

Another thing that should be pointed out is the way that the roots of a genre constrain the adoption of the Realist aesthetic. We saw this in Chapter 4 with poetry, and there is an analogous situation with drama. The roots of theatre are in ritual, with suggestions of 'magic' and transformation, and with older theatrical formats such as *commedia dell'arte*, and 'show'-style entertainments such as the circus, and while the past of the genre does not necessarily define its future or potential, they do somehow channel directions and possibilities. Realism, in its nineteenth-century version, does not really recommend itself to drama because 'real life' is by nature 'undramatic'. If one of the key characteristics of Realism is detailed description – physical, physiological and psychological – this cannot easily be rendered on stage. Action in drama is very often tied to time, place and a small number of characters and therefore is not suited to the wider social embrace of novels such as *Middlemarch* and *Germinal*. Inner thoughts are difficult to render naturalistically (see later discussions in the chapter of 'the aside', for instance). If the roots of the novel are in history writing, biography, autobiography, letter-writing, social observation and surveys, moral conduct books and journalism, there is a certain congeniality in these forms for the purposes of the Realist aesthetic, and discussion of the novel genre has focused on how central realism is to its essence. Analogous discussion about the idea of drama has often focused on precisely what 'drama' means, and just as 'poetry' is by definition opposed to 'prose', so 'drama' – the dramatic – appears inherently opposed to what is 'everyday', mundane and dull. To move into the twentieth century before returning to the specifics of the Realist period, two pieces separated by nearly 80 years argue for the essentially 'dramatic' nature of drama. Meyerhold's piece 'On the Theatre: The Fairground Booth' claims that the theatre had become dominated by realism, and argues instead that theatre is defined by what is anti-naturalistic:

> The public comes to the theatre to see the art of man, but what art is there in walking about the stage as oneself? The public expects invention, play-acting and skill. But what it gets is either life or a slavish imitation of life. Surely the art of man on the stage consists in shedding all traces of environment, carefully choosing a mask, donning a decorative costume, and showing off one's brilliant tricks to the public – now as a dancer, now as the intrigant in some masquerade, now as the fool of old Italian comedy, now as a juggler.
> (in Brandt 1998: 132–3)

Howard Barker's 'Theatre without a Conscience' in 1990 makes a similar point: theatre is precisely what is not in the world outside the auditorium. He argues that if it does draw from the real world in the manner of journalism and academic research then it is not theatre at all. At the heart of drama, then, runs a strong argument that in essence it is non-realist or anti-realist. And while the relative successes of Realist novels might be debated, there is little argument that the Realist novel has the means of being Realist within the theoretical tenets of that aesthetic.

However, there are suggestions that, not only is drama inherently anti-realist, but it intrinsically does not have the tools. For example, Eugene O'Neill's essay 'Memoranda on Masks' (1932) argues that there has been no convincing theatrical means to portray complex psychology. Those plays which are realistic can only offer something quite superficial. In arguing that masks can help achieve this for the modern dramatist, he is choosing a non-realistic tool to achieve one of the aims of nineteenth-century Realism. Nor is this just a twentieth-century view on drama. Not surprisingly, just as Realist prose fiction positioned itself in relation to its more elevated literary contender poetry, on occasion it also distinguished itself from drama and the dramatic. In *The Mill on the Floss* the narrator contrasts the way events are handled in drama and the way they happen in real life, and, by extension, the way they should therefore be handled 'non-dramatically' in Realist novels:

> Plotting covetousness and deliberate contrivance, in order to compass a selfish end, are nowhere abundant but in the world of the dramatist: they demand too intense a mental action for many of our fellow-parishioners to be guilty of them. It is easy enough to spoil

the lives of our neighbours without taking so much trouble; we can
do it by lazy acquiescence and lazy omission, by trivial falsities for
which we hardly know a reason, by small frauds neutralized by small
extravagances, by maladroit flatteries, and clumsily improvised
insinuations. We live from hand to mouth, most of us, with a small
family of immediate desires; we do little else than snatch a morsel to
satisfy the hungry brood, rarely thinking of seed-corn or the next
year's crop. (Eliot 2003: 28)

Just as elsewhere we have seen that poetry inherently has a tendency to idealise and elevate material, the dramatist is obliged to
distort the ways in which humans behave towards each other.
Eliot's argument is clear: only the Realist novel can produce the
faithful copy at this level. The idea of drama, unsurprisingly, is
that it is characterised by what is 'dramatic', and this is not the way
real life unfolds; put another way, when something is 'dramatic' it
is considered so because it is out of the ordinary. Nevertheless,
Tom Robertson does make some attempt to introduce the 'undramatic' into his plays. For instance, Philip Davis notes a tiny scene
(Act I Scene II) in Robertson's *Society* (1865):

which became famous for its understated delicacy, wherein an aris-
tocratic suitor, not having a key and unable to join his sweetheart in
the garden, looks up to see a nursemaid walking casually with her
guardsman-lover. The nursemaid simply lets the gentleman into the
square, the guardsman saying not a word and taking no further part
in the play. In this quiet new realism, the silent untold story of the
nursemaid and the guardsman is a piece of incidental life, which
creates *in* the play the sense of a world freely existing around it.
(Davis 2002: 264)

A detail like this is indeed equivalent to the accumulation of incidental detail in the Realist novel that aids the impression of 'the
faithful copy'. Something similar I think can be detected at the
start of *The Ticket-of-Leave Man*. It is set in the Bellevue Tea
Gardens, and the arrangement of the scene has waiters moving
between tables waiting on different groups in a way which
attempts to faithfully replicate the Tea Garden atmosphere. It is
not a piece of background business but the business around which
the scene is organised. Similarly, in a later scene, which could
equally be allowed a more fully-blown dramatic presentation, the

drama is submerged by the amount of time given to the inconsequential chattering of the landlady Mrs Willoughby after somebody has remarked how well she looks:

> Ah, my dear, you are very good to say so, which, if it wasn't for rheumatics and the rates, one a top of another, and them dustmen, which their carts is a mockery, unless you stand beer, and that boy, Sam, though which is the worst, I'm sure is hard to say, only a grandmother's feelings is not to be told, which opodolec can't be rubbed into the 'eart, as I said to Mrs. Molloy – her that has my first floor front – which she says to me, 'Mrs. Willoughby,' says she, 'nine oils is the thing,' she says, 'rubbed in warm,' says she. 'Which it's all very well, Mrs. Molly,' says I, 'but how is a lone woman to rub it in the nape of the neck and the small of the back; and Sam that giddy, and distressing me to that degree. No, Mrs. Molloy,' I says, 'what's sent us we must bear it, and parties that's reduced to let lodgings, can't afford easy chairs,' which well I know it, and the truth it is – and me with two beauties in chintz in the front parlour, which I got a bargain at the brokers when the parties was sold up at 24, and no more time to sit down in 'em than if I was a cherrybin. (Act II Scene 2)

It could be argued that this is nothing other than a comic turn from a lower class character, and as such has been a staple for centuries in drama, but again the amassing of such 'everydayness', rather than knowing its place as occasional light relief, is a consequence of the Realist aesthetic.

A review in *The Pall Mall Gazette* of a comedy titled *Humbug* by one Mr Burnand perhaps highlights the problems inherent when trying to accommodate drama to the Realist aesthetic along these lines, that is, by removing what is ostensibly dramatic from the drama. The reviewer regards Burnand's play as a piece of very poor theatre and suspects a failed attempt at 'cup-and-saucer' realism: 'The author had in view probably a play of the kind represented by Mr Robertson's "Caste" and "Ours," in which well defined characters and terse dialogue stand in the place of any great strength of plot or ingenuity in the contrivance of new situations' (*The Pall Mall Gazette*, 24 December 1867). The reviewer goes on to note that there are far too many characters uttering 'flat' and 'fatuous' dialogue. Again, part of the problem would seem to be the genre itself. Big, fat Realist novels abound with numerous characters who often have little bearing on the main narrative. The same novels can also have a wealth of inconsequential detail, observations, description and dialogue that are there perhaps for no other reason than that they reproduce 'reality' faithfully. To be sure, a criticism levelled at Realist novels is that they are 'dull', precisely for this reason, but somehow this is where this level of sustained 'everydayness' is most appropriate. A chapter in *The Mill on the Floss* entitled 'Enter the Aunts and Uncles' has much that is irrelevant to the story of Maggie and Tom, but which is a significant contribution to its Realism. Here, for instance, is one of the sisters talking in a way not dissimilar from the Mrs Willoughby excerpt above, as she gives her opinion of 'old Mrs Sutton o' the Twentylands':

> 'Ah,' sighed Mrs Pullet, 'she'd another complaint ever so many years before she had the dropsy, and the doctors couldn't make out what it was. And she said to me, when I went to see her last Christmas, she said, "Mrs Pullet, if iver you have the dropsy, you'll think o' me." She *did* say so,' added Mrs Pullet, beginning to cry bitterly again, 'those were her very words. And she's to be buried o' Saturday, and Pullet's bid to the funeral.' (Eliot 2003: 63)

Of course, while it does not move the narrative forward it does other things, such as establishing characters and, since this is one of Eliot's aims, it acts towards the representation of society as held together by these gossamer threads. The novel form easily accommodates this kind of extensive and comprehensive social detailing, whereas the dramatic form appears duty-bound to be sparing of such usage.

There is one final aspect I would like to discuss in the relationship between Realism and the idea of drama in the nineteenth century, and that is the role of the protagonist and the question of 'agency'. Ferdinand Brunetière, in his essay 'The Law of the Drama' (1894; reprinted in Brandt 1998) argues that in drama we witness (and expect to witness) 'the spectacle of a *will* striving towards a goal, and conscious of the means which it employs' (Brandt 1998: 21). He contrasts this with the novel, where the central character is acted upon: 'The proper aim of the novel as of the epic – of which it is only a secondary and derived form, what the naturalists call a sub-species or a variety – [...] is to give us a picture of the influence which is exercised upon us by all that is outside of ourselves' (22). No doubt Brunetière has in mind the Realist novel, particularly the French variety, where environment and heredity – factors outside of individual control and autonomy – significantly act upon characters. Here the 'law of the drama' is that drama can only work successfully when it has protagonists who have considerable agency. Brunetière is keen to separate out the novel from drama, and these genre traits are his key means of distinction. How far the distinction can be maintained is a moot theoretical point, but the way in which drama is traditionally structured around protagonists who are active agents suggests that it does not necessarily sit well with the way in which Realist novels often showed individuals whose lives were at the mercy of environment. We now return to some of the specifics of the nineteenth-century play as it comes to terms with Realism.

STOP and THINK

Is drama inherently unsuited to Realism? You might consider the following:

- Drama requires active protagonists, whereas Realism often shows inaction in the face of overwhelming, impersonal forces.
- Realism depends upon extensive psychological detailing which cannot be realistically rendered on stage.
- Realism is concerned with what is commonplace and undramatic.
- The idea of 'fourth-wall' drama, with the audience privy to the everyday, is mimetic without being realist.
- Strindberg's Preface to *Miss Julie* talks of the use of pantomine to produce what are essentially realistic effects. The fact that he underwrites such naturalism with a rather non-naturalist origin suggests that drama is destined to be non-realist. Does this interpretation seem reasonable?

Stage design and direction

> I did *so* want to see an office – a real one, you know, I've seen 'em set
> on the stage often but they ain't a bit like the real thing. (Tom Taylor,
> *The Ticket-of-Leave Man*, III.3)

William Tydeman's Introduction to *The Plays of Tom Robertson*
ranges across all the features which contributed to an appreciation
of Robertson as somebody involved in bringing greater 'intelli-
gence' and realism to Victorian theatre. The fact that he was able to
manage this is partly down to the theatre company that took on his
plays, the Prince of Wales at the Royal Olympic. The stage design-
er there, Madam Vestris, insisted on having rooms which could be
taken as copies of real ones. In this we can see that the realism
involved is visually mimetic, and visual mimesis has a long tradition in stage design. Innovations along the same lines in the
period include the introduction of 'real' physical objects and
actions. For instance, a 'pudding' is famously made on stage in
Robertson's play *Ours*. It does take place in the midst of the
Crimean War, but nevertheless it is of a piece with this more
general drive to introduce the Realist aesthetic into drama. Also
part of this visual mimesis were certain stage effects, for instance
the falling of rain on leaves and snow flurries when a door opened
(Tydeman 1982: 18). Such naturalistic directions are often written
into the plays. In *Ours* for instance we get: '(*Enter* PRINCE,
smoking a cigarette. CHALCOT *crosses*. PRINCE *seeing ladies raises
his hat, and throws cigarette on ground*.)' and the smoking continues
to be written in as part of the main stage business. At the beginning of the same play the scene is set thus:

> *An avenue of trees in Shendryn Park; the avenue leading off up right.
> Seat round tree in foreground right. Stumps of trees left. The termina-
> tion of the avenue out of sight. Throughout the act the autumn leaves fall
> from the trees.*

That direction at the end that the leaves should continue to fall
throughout the act is both realistic illusion and spectacle, and in
general these aspects of the move towards Realism are at the junc-
tion of the spectacular and the mimetic and highlight how what
seems appropriate in prose fiction produces results which may

seem to counter the Realist aims of the mid-century novelists and produce instead the 'spectacle' of the domestic. However, this scene-setting at the beginning of *Caste* can perhaps be regarded as an equivalent to Gaskell's descriptions of working-class habitats:

> *A plain set chamber, paper soiled. A window centre [back] with practicable blind; street backing and iron railings. Door practicable up right, when opening showing street door (practicable). Fireplace centre of left-hand piece; two-hinged gas-burners on each side of mantelpiece. Sideboard cupboard, cupboard in recess left, tea-things, teapot, tea-caddy, tea-tray, etc., on it. Long table before fire; old piece of carpet and rug down; plain chairs; bookshelf back left, a small table under it with ballet-shoe and skirt on it; bunch of benefit bills hanging under bookshelf. Theatrical printed portraits, framed, hanging about; chimney glass clock; box of lucifers and ornaments on mantelshelf; kettle on hob, and fire laid; doormats on the outside of door. Bureau centre of right-hand piece. [Door to bedroom?]*

This moves beyond the description of the avenue in *Ours* to something very akin to what we might expect from the Realist novel. Its level of detail puts it on the same plane as that of the Realist novel's mirror. Note that many of the items are to be 'practicable', that is, to work as they would in real life and to be available for use by characters on the stage. On the page it therefore reads as Realism, but with pointers towards a realisation in production of an equivalent visual mimesis.

Sybil Rosenfeld's *A Short History of Scene Design in Great Britain* claims:

> The trend towards realism was, in the early part of the century, irregular and sporadic. Tanks of water installed at Sadler's Wells from 1804 for aquadramas, and real horses and dogs in the huge patent theatres for hippo or canine dramas, represented an unhappy mixture of the actual with the simulated. Figures painted on canvas juxtaposed living actors. (Rosenfeld 1973: 111)

Although part of the more general drive towards 'realism' throughout the nineteenth century, this aspect is where mimesis equates with the spectacular end of dramatic production. Madam Vestris's reproduction of domestic interiors could be said to be similarly mimetic:

Vestris certainly gave verisimilitude to everyday rooms by abolish-
ing the unconvincing wings and by furnishing them with real, not
painted, furniture of taste and quality. She took pains to supply
good carpets, fine draperies, real blinds over practicable glass
windows and props such as clocks, fireplaces, mirrors and even
actual door knobs. Such realism was extended to the shop and the
garden. The shops in *Burlington Arcade* were built out with
transparent windows and had actual goods in them; the windows
opened, and showed people moving within, and a lamplighter lit
the lamps. In a forest scene a carpet was painted to look like soil
and grass and gardens were decorated with real statues and
potted plants. The stage was divided into six component parts up
which props could be sent, thus minimising waits. (Rosenfeld
1973: 113)

The whole effect towards which the stage design and management
is striving is 'verisimilitude'. In itself, of course, this is not
Realism, but it certainly assisted those playwrights who might
wish to endorse the Realist aesthetic. Again, there is the overlap
between a general 'realist' impulse and the mimetic: a horse on
stage might be both 'real' and 'spectacular'. However, these accurate domestic reproductions in themselves are not Realism, even if
they do aim for the 'faithful copy' at this visual level.

Again, *in itself*, therefore, this characteristic of Realism needs to
be treated with some caution, and only as an adjunct of other
Realist features. Here is a description of a scene from the popular
nineteenth-century melodrama *Black-Ey'd Susan* (1829) already
mentioned:

> *The Gun-Room of the Ship* – SENTRY *at the door – tiller working
> over head – seven canvas berths at the side – tomahawks crossed, and
> fire-buckets in a row* – WILLIAM *is seated, double-ironed, on a spare
> tiller* – LIEUTENANT, OFFICE OF MARINES, AND
> MASTER-AT-ARMS *in attendance* – WILLIAM's *chest is opened
> before him – the* LIEUTENANT *motions to* MASTER-AT-ARMS
> *to release the prisoner* – QUID, SEAWEED, *and others discovered.*
> (Act III, Scene 4)

There is certainly enough direction here to suggest that a realistic
setting is called for. The 'non-realism' lies everywhere else – in the
dialogue, characterisation, plot, recourse to song and the fact that

it is based on a well-known ballad. William is the too-pure hero and Susan the too-angelic heroine. This following is the scene direction for Act III, Scene II of Edward Bulwer-Lytton's *Money*, a typical mid-nineteenth-century play:

> SCENE III. *The interior of ****'s Club; night; lights, &c. Small sofa-tables, with books, papers, tea, coffee, &c. Several members grouped by the fire-place; one member with his legs over the back of his chair; another with his legs over his table; a third with his legs on the chimney-piece. To the left, and in front of the stage, an old member reading the newspaper, seated by a small round table; to the right a card table, before which CAPTAIN DUDLEY SMOOTH is seated and sipping lemonade; at the bottom of the stage another card table.*

Although once again the detail suggests Realism, and a Victorian audience certainly expects this visual verisimilitude, the framing of it has the aspect of a moral tableau, an impression partly supported by the opening dialogue:

> GLOSSMORE: You don't come often to the club, Stout?
> STOUT: No; time is money. An hour spent at a club is unproduct-
>   ive capital.

The play has no serious point to make about money or poverty, and its moral is the time-worn one of the necessity for true hearts over money. Mimesis, as we have seen before, can be used for different reasons, and in the theatre sometimes it creates the spec-tacular, and sometimes it reproduces the mundane. However, to return to Robertson, the following scene, carefully orchestrated around the taking of tea, is a perfect indication of how such repro-duction works at the level of 'the faithful copy' while it also successfully and quietly plays upon the main theme of social div-ision. To put you in the picture: the upper-class George D'Alroy has fallen in love with the lower-class actress Esther. His friend Captain Hawtree initially tells him that the law of 'caste' prevents him from marrying her. In Act III, Hawtree pays a visit to Esther. She is sleeping and he is entertained meanwhile by Esther's friend Polly and her fiancé Sam. The difference in class between Esther and Sam, and Hawtree, is confirmed when Polly says 'I won't ask you to take tea with us, Major – you're too grand.' He says, 'Not at all' and gives us the non-realistic, clunky aside: ''Pon my word, these are very good sort of people. I'd no idea –', which is followed by 'cup-and-saucer' realism:

> (SAM *cuts enormous slice of bread, and hands it on point of knife to* HAWTREE. *Cuts small lump of butter, and hands it on point of knife to* HAWTREE, *who looks at it through eye-glass, then takes it.* SAM *then helps himself.* POLLY *meantime has poured out tea in two cups, and one saucer for* SAM, *sugars them, and then hands cup and saucer to* HAWTREE, *who has both hands full. He takes it awkwardly, and places it on table.* POLLY, *having only one spoon, tastes* SAM's *tea, then stirs* HAWTREE's, *attracting his attention by so doing. He looks into his teacup.* POLLY *stirs her own tea, and drops spoon into* HAWTREE's *cup, causing it to spurt in his eye. He drops eye-glass and wipes his eyes.*)

Polly then points out that they have no milk, although it should be delivered any minute. The level of detail is not necessary for the comic element at the end of the stage direction, and here we can see once again how the Realist aesthetic shapes this aspect of the scene. The very fact that Hawtree takes tea within this level of detail provides a 'natural symbol' for the breaking of the rule of 'caste'.

But it certainly is a question of 'levels' with this and other plays. The milk does arrive the next minute: it is delivered by George, Esther's husband, who at this point is believed by Esther to have been killed in service overseas. The money he left for Esther has been squandered by her drunkard father, Eccles, thus leaving Esther and her baby in dire straits all this time. The very end of the play also provides the audience with a mix of the comic and the Realist, for rather than tying up all the loose ends in an unalloyed joyful fashion as might be expected for a comedy, Esther and George's happiness (and Tom and Polly's) is somehow compromised by the continued presence of Esther's father who turns up again, drunk. Quite clearly he is unreformable. Hawtree appears to neatly dispose of him in this comic interchange:

> HAWTREE: Mr Eccles, don't you think that, with your talent for liquor, if you had an allowance of about two pounds a week, and went to Jersey, where spirits are cheap, that you could drink yourself to death in a year?
> ECCLES: I think I could – I'm sure I'll try.

But the play actually ends with this interesting tableau:

> (ECCLES *falls off the chair in the last stage of drunkenness, bottle in*
> *hand.* HAWTREE, *leaning one foot on chair from which* ECCLES *has*
> *fallen, looks at him through eye-glass.* SAM *enters, and goes to* POLLY,
> *behind cradle, and, producing wedding-ring from several papers, holds it*
> *up before her eyes.* ESTHER *plays* [the piano] *until curtain drops.*)

There is no virtuous temperance narrative ending here, and the
audience is left with a semi-comic image of Hawtree espying
Eccles drunk on the floor. It would have been easy enough to have
Eccles absent from the scene, and it is not the case that Eccles is
presented as a comic drunk throughout. Rather, as well as
condemning his daughter to penury, he has previously been shown
as violent in a scene where Esther stands up for herself. She
discovers that her father is about to steal a piece of coral from the
child.

> ESTHER: (*confronting him*) If you dare! I am no longer your little
> drudge – your frightened servant. When mother died ... and I
> was so high, I tended you, and worked for you – and you beat me.
> That time is past. I am a woman – I am a wife – a widow – a
> *mother*! Do you think I will let you outrage *him*? (*pointing to*
> *cradle*) *Touch me if you dare!* (*advancing a step*)

With this characterisation of Eccles in the background, the ending
and play as a whole is not quite the comedy it is billed as, but, as
we have been suggesting throughout, does point to a penetration
into the dramatic genre of Realism at a time when circumstances
were not particularly conducive to it.

Acting style and the aside

It is always difficult to try to recover 'acting style' from before the
days of motion capture on film. When Hamlet instructs his players
not to overact it would seem that there has always been a tension
between the requirements for 'naturalistic' acting on the one side,
and 'expressionistic' acting on the other. How naturalistic the
acting can be for Shakespeare is always debatable since this can
only be achieved at a cost to the verse-form. In Fielding's *Tom*
Jones there is a scene at a performance of *Hamlet* where Partridge

appreciates a particular actor because it is easy to see that he is 'acting', whereas he gives no credit to those who do not appear to be acting since they are doing nothing other than what would actually happen at the sight of a ghost. Robertson's Realist success certainly appears to have been aided by a naturalistic acting style, which itself was helped by Robertson's own writing and by the small size of the Prince of Wales theatre:

> It may be noted that the limited size of the Prince of Wales Theatre is of real advantage to the class of plays Mr. Robertson is fond of producing; a story gains in strength and significance by being brought so closely to the view of the spectators; and the players are not constrained to unnatural shouting and grimacing in order that their speeches may be heard and the expression of their faces seen from distant portions of the house. Both author and actors are thus enabled to avoid the exaggeration of language and manner which has long been a prominent failing in dramatic writing and representation. (Dutton Cook review of Robertson's *School*, in Tydeman 1982: 16)

Again, we are dealing with perceptions of a rather relative nature, and acting that might seem 'naturalistic' to one generation can appear quite 'stagey' to a successive one. This brings me on to a rather minor matter in comparison, but one which shows how Realism and its assumed tenets can change things.

A staple feature of drama until the nineteenth century was the aside. This is a thought spoken out loud to the audience by a character in the presence of other characters. However, the other characters cannot 'hear' this dialogue since it is a direct address from the character to the audience. As a technical device it is nonrealistic: anything spoken in this way in reality would be heard by the other characters. It is (or was) therefore a dramatic convention accepted by theatre-goers. Presumably, it falls into disuse in serious drama precisely because of its non-naturalistic properties, and may have an association with Victorian melodrama, which writers would wish to distance themselves from. A pastiche of Victorian drama would do well to use this device as a marker of the form. But why should the convention of the aside be any worse than any other convention? What of the soliloquy? It is barely less realistic to have somebody speak their thoughts at such length –

most people are not given to speaking out loud in this manner, certainly not without having their sanity questioned. Yet a soliloquy might plausibly be incorporated into a realist play (see below).

Here is an example of an aside from *Black-Ey'd Susan*. The eponymous Susan is about to be evicted from her lodgings by her uncle landlord Doggrass. The character Hatchett plans to ingratiate himself with Susan by paying her overdue rent for her and telling her that her husband has died at sea. After Hatchett has paid the bill we get this aside: 'She's softened; a woman is like sealing wax, only melt her, and she will take what form you please. I've bought her heart with the chink, and tomorrow will secure it.' It is possible to imagine some moustache-twirling from the actor and hissing from the audience at this unsurprising revelation, with the convention now to be found only in pantomime and revivals of Victorian plays. This is no doubt most people's expectation of an aside.

However, as J. L. Styan shows in *The English Stage*, the use of asides had once been quite sophisticated, for instance Marlowe's use of it in *The Jew of Malta*, drawing the audience into a particular viewpoint and sympathy. Shakespeare likewise shows a sophisticated use. It allows (in theory at least) for a play to achieve certain effects and affects that illusionism does not. There is an equivalence here perhaps in the role of the narrator in the novel, where a direct, frame-breaking address to the reader is the equivalent of the theatrical aside. The difference is that in the play it is still the character who speaks, rather than a narrator-author voice. Nevertheless, as we have already attempted to establish, frame-breaking in itself should not be taken to identify a work as non-realist.

This brief digression into the nature of the aside suggests that the reliance on verisimilitude by the Realist aesthetic eliminates the aside from any drama that wants to appear 'realistic', but in itself shows that the Realism imported into the drama of the period relied on a particular interpretation of Realism that took it down the path of 'fourth-wall' productions: the equivalent of mimetic illusionism rather than the self-conscious Realism of Eliot.

Drama certainly lagged behind the novel in its ability to transform itself according to the tenets of Realism. I would suggest that towards the end of the century many of the ideas of Realism become incorporated into drama, but at the same time there is an emerging aesthetic which itself provides a challenge to Realism, and just as the theatre properly begins to take up the Realist aesthetic it is in conjunction with other ideas which are also a challenge to Realism. This new aesthetic comes to be termed 'modernism', and this is the subject of the next chapter.

Works cited and further reading

Apollinaire, Guillaume (1903), Preface and Prologue to *The Breasts of Tiresias*, in Brandt, 165–70.

Bargainnier, Earl F. (1977), '"Charity": W. S. Gilbert's "Problem Play"', *South Atlantic Bulletin*, Vol. 42, No. 4. (November), 130–8.

Bentley, Eric, (ed.) (1978), *The Theory of the Modern Stage*. Harmondsworth: Penguin.

Belsey, Catherine (1991), *Critical Practice*. London: Routledge. Belsey quite often uses drama to make her points about the classical realist text, particularly Chapter 4. (Belsey and the classic realist text is covered in Chapter 8, 'Theorists of Realism').

Brandt, George W. (1998), 'Introduction' to *Modern Theories of Drama. A Selection of Writings on Drama and Theatre, 1840-1990*. Oxford: Clarendon Press . The book includes a section devoted to 'Varieties of Realism'.

Davis, Philip (2002), *The Oxford English Literary History Volume 8. 1830–1880. The Victorians*. Oxford: Oxford University Press.

Lewes, George Henry (1850), 'The Old and Modern Dramatists', in *The Leader*, No. 19 (Saturday 3 August).

Reade, Charles (1882), Letter to the Editor, 'Mr Charles Reade and "Drink"', *The Era*, Saturday, 19 August; Issue 2291, and Saturday, 26 August; Issue 2292.

Reade, Charles (1991), *Drink*. London, Canada: Mestengo Press.

Rosenfeld, Sybil (1973), Chapter VII, 'Victorian Theatre: Realism and Spectacle', *A Short History of Scene Design in Great Britain*. Oxford: Blackwell.

Rowell, George (1972), *Nineteenth Century Plays*. London: Oxford University Press. Includes *The Ticket-of-Leave Man, Black-Ey'd Susan, Masks and Faces* (Tom Taylor and Charles Reade), *Money* and *Caste*.

Shaw, George Bernard (1952), 'Preface' to *Mrs Warren's Profession* in *Plays Pleasant and Unpleasant*, Volume 1. London: Constable.

Shaw, George Bernard (1978), 'A Dramatic Realist to his Critics', in
    Bentley, *The Theory of the Modern Stage*. Harmondsworth: Penguin,
    175–96.
Strindberg, August (1964), Author's Preface to *Miss Julie* (and the play
    itself), in *Selected Plays and Prose*, ed. Robert Brustein. New York:
    Holt, Rinehart and Winston.
Tydeman, William (1982), 'Introduction' to *Plays of Tom Robertson*.
    Cambridge: Cambridge University Press. *Caste*, *Ours* and *Society* are
    included in this selection.
Zola, Émile, 'Naturalism in the Theatre', in Becker, *Documents of Modern
    Literary Realism*.

I also suggest looking at the work of Chekhov and Ibsen, dramatists at the end of the century who appropriated many of the tenets
of the Realist aesthetic at the same time as developing their work
along modernist lines. For Ibsen: *A Doll's House*, *Ghosts* and *Hedda
Gabler*; for Chekhov: *Three Sisters*, *The Cherry Orchard*, *Uncle
Vanya*. In addition to Chekhov's plays, there is the related matter
of acting style. Stanislawski was part of the Moscow Art Theatre
Company, which helped Chekhov, but Chekhov found
Stanislawski's supposedly naturalist 'method' to produce just the
opposite of the type of realism Chekhov was aiming for. See
Ronald Hingley's 'Introduction' to *Five Plays*, Oxford: Oxford
University Press, 1991.

6

Modernism

Is it artistically strong? Is it good as a picture? There was a time when I might have written in this way with a declared social object. That is all gone by. I have no longer a spark of social enthusiasm. Art is all I now care for, and as art I wish my work to be judged. (Gissing, 1930, *The Unclassed*)

As a method, realism is a complete failure. (Oscar Wilde, 1891, 'The Decay of Lying')

From Realism to modernism

The group of writers that we have focused on in previous chapters regarded themselves as living in a new age which needed a new kind of art – one attuned to the science, materialism and social urgencies of the nineteenth century rather than the eternal verities and idealism that underpinned Romanticism. The succeeding generation of artists, from the 1880s and 1890s onwards, until the 1920s/1930s – a group subsequently referred to as modernists – also felt that the art that preceded it – namely, Realism – had outlived its usefulness. Some writers who straddled both periods gradually moved away from Realism to modernism: Henry James, for instance, whose writing overlapped with that of George Eliot at the beginning of his career, became increasingly 'modernist'. His works are attentive to their own construction through language in such a way as to draw attention to this aspect of the writing. Set this alongside a greater attention to the 'organic' form of the novel, narrative points of view restricted to the consciousnesses of the characters, and an interest in the workings of consciousness itself, and we are moving away from the aim of representing a consensual view of a plausibly constructed, contemporary social world.

The greater focus on the tools of the novelistic trade – language, narrative, characterisation, role of the narrator, the management of linear time – started to move novels and other art forms away from accessible, representational social art into one interested in art itself, and modes such as expressionism took elements of Realism to non-realist conclusions and realisations. I will look first at a novel which is predominantly in a Realist vein, as we have come to expect, yet which also shows signs of dissatisfaction with Realism and the aesthetic ideas which inform it, and then move on to an example of modernist fiction which dismantles virtually all of the tenets of Realism. Throughout both discussions we see the legacy of Realism trans-mute into ways which, even when ostensibly furthering the aims of Realism, amount to a quite strong refutation of it as an aesthetic.

George Gissing: *The Unclassed*

The Unclassed, published in 1884, was Gissing's second novel, and, rather like his first novel *Workers in the Dawn*, made little impact. However, I have chosen it as the opening to this chapter because it quite obviously struggles to emerge from Realist concerns and look to new ways of writing novels. The novel is set in London and has five main characters: Osmond Waymark, Julian Casti, Ida Starr, Maud Enderby and Harriet Smales. The novel begins with Casti, Starr and Smales as children, and after a few intervening chapters we are gradually reintroduced to them some years later as adults, although we are not given much of their life stories in between. Part of the theme, if not the main driving aesthetic concern, is to represent people who are 'unclassed'. This suggests that the novel wants to be more Realist than Realist novelists have hitherto achieved, aiming for a more comprehensive representation of reality, a better 'mirror'. Late in the novel we discover that Waymark has ambitions to become a writer and here

he talks about writing a piece on a socially deprived area he is
familiar with in his job as rent collector:

> 'I'm making an article out of Elm Court,' said Waymark. 'Semi-
> descriptive, semi-reflective, wholly cynical. Maybe it will pay for my
> summer holiday. And, apropos of the same subject, I've got great
> ideas. This introduction to such phases of life will prove endlessly
> advantageous to me, artistically speaking. Let me get a little more
> experience, and I will write a novel such as no one has yet ventured
> to write, at all events in England. I begin to see my way to magnifi-
> cent effects; ye gods, such light and shade! The fact is, the novel of
> every-day life is getting worn out. We must dig deeper, get to
> untouched social strata. Dickens felt this, but he had not the courage
> to face his subjects; his monthly numbers had to lie on the family
> tea-table. Not *virginibus puerisque* will be my book, I assure you, but
> for men and women who like to look beneath the surface, and who
> understand that only as artistic material has human life any signifi-
> cance. Yes, that is the conclusion I am working round to. The artist
> is the only sane man. Life for its own sake? – no; I would drink a pint
> of laudanum to-night. But life as the source of splendid pictures,
> inexhaustible material for effects – *that* can reconcile me to exist-
> ence, and that only. It is a delight followed by no bitter after-taste,
> and the only such delight I know.' (Gissing 1930: 112)

This functions as comment on *The Unclassed* itself, since it
describes the type of novel that *The Unclassed* seems to want to be.
The Realist project is there in the desire to 'get to untouched social
strata', to get at those classes which have thus far fallen outside the
Realist oeuvre. It also wants to be more Realist by moving beyond
the constraints of polite society on English Realism that we have
witnessed already, by dealing with subject matter that is fit for
adults, rather than producing material which has to be suitable for
children and family reading. The intended style also suggests
Realist writing of the type that informs a novel like *Middlemarch*,
that is: 'semi-descriptive' and 'semi-reflective', with 'cynical'
suggestive of a clear-sighted 'realism' in opposition to a Dickens-
style sentimentality. Yet at the same time as Waymark draws on the
Realist aesthetic, he talks of other things that do not belong to
Realism, but which belong instead to the 'art-for-art's-sake'
aestheticism, which was becoming increasingly significant as the
century came to an end, often referred to as *fin-de-siècle* writing.

This aspect is evident in the argument that Waymark puts forward about material being worthwhile only to the extent in which it is artistic, and in his argument that the artist is the only sane person around. The latter view is a return to a Romantic notion of the artist as a visionary. This return to Romanticism, with the artist as seer and as spiritual guide, is also part of a certain strand of modernism, where art becomes the only redemptive form available to modern man. And as to 'style', although he argues for description and reflection, he also looks for artistic 'effect', again, another feature of an aesthetic quite different from that of Realism, since Realism, while certainly attendant to elegant and emotional language, is more concerned with a prosaic communication of social realities.

Waymark thus argues for the type of novel which *The Unclassed* partly represents since it sees the blind-spots of the Realist novel while accepting its basic premises; it selects people who do not fit easily into class groupings and are not therefore classifiable in sociological terms. By digging into layers of social strata that are not normally covered in literature it gives a more accurate representation of all levels of society and the ways they are constituted. The potential here is for a greater Realism, in keeping with the type of Realist novel we have already seen. For instance, Osmond Waymark begins as a teacher, resigns, and then becomes a rent collector. His friend Julian Casti is a chemist who then becomes a dispenser at a hospital. These characters do not fit any ready social categories, at least not any that were too familiar to readers of Realist novels. In this way Gissing achieves a novel that is more Realist than is usual. This deeper digging is part of a desire to represent what is hidden beneath the observable – 'the spirit' – since both Julian and Osmond are interested in the arts and the spiritual side of life. Gissing's novel, therefore, continues the tradition of the Victorian Realist novel, with its focus on the representation of the commonplace, everyday world, but with one eye on the hidden. His social groups are the lower middle and the working classes, including, in Ida Starr, a prostitute.

In this way the novel consistently attempts to give 'realer' or more accurate representations. Waymark is less hampered by stereotyping than previously. Ida Starr, for instance, is not presented as a typical prostitute. In fact, she fits in with Amanda Anderson's observation that the reality for most 'fallen women' was that prostitution usually represented an episode in their lives, after which they would engage in other forms of work. There is an instance where Ida corrects Waymark when he falls into a stereotypical viewpoint, and thus simultaneously 'corrects' the reader's mis-representation of prostitutes, and by implication the misrepresentation by all preceding Realist novels of 'the fallen woman'. At their first meeting, after some interesting exchanges regarding Ida's wearing of a veil and whether her face is 'painted', she asks him to 'read her face' now that he has lifted the veil. Waymark says that he is sorry to have seen the face: 'I shall think of it often after tonight, and imagine it with all its freshness gone, and marks of suffering and degradation upon it' (1930: 83). This is a stereotypical prediction for a fallen woman, and she corrects him:

'Suffering, perhaps; degradation, no. Why should I be degraded?'

'You can't help yourself. The life you have chosen brings its inevitable consequences.'

'Chosen!' she repeated, with an indignant face. 'How do you know I had any choice in the matter? You have no right to speak contemptuously, like that.' (1930: 84)

In addition to these corrections and modifications of the standard picture of a prostitute, Gissing's novel distinguishes between different types of prostitute, and this is once more undoubtedly part of the novel's attempt at finer gradations of social strata. The conversation continues and then the tables are turned when Ida attempts to fix Waymark in a social class.

'But you are a gentleman,' she said, rising again, and rustling over the pages of the book she still held. 'Are you in the city?'

'The Lord deliver me!'

'What then?'

'I am nothing.'

'Then you must be rich.'

'It by no means follows. Yesterday I was a teacher in a school. To-day I am what is called out of work.'

'A teacher. But I suppose you'll get another place.'

'No. I've given it up because I couldn't endure it any longer.'

'And how are you going to live?'

'I have no idea.'

Waymark does not fit a social type – he is a gentleman, but that is rather vague in this context. He does not work in the city, nor is he not rich, and now he is an out-of-work teacher who no longer wants to be one. Ida's own surname, legally 'Woodstock', has been changed to 'Starr', a name taken from a character in a penny tale, again suggestive of a more constructed view of identity.

This questioning of social identity and the value of sociological labelling, and a certain amount of aestheticisation at the level of the characters' lives and the novel, are an indication that this puta-tively Realist novel is pushing at the limits of Realism. A further example is that the novel sets up a very obvious madonna/whore opposition with Maud Enderby and Ida Starr. Maud, a timid teacher whom Waymark meets at the school, has had a very strict religious upbringing, of the type that claims we are put on earth solely to suffer. Consequently Maud is racked by religious guilt. We have already seen that the novel attempts to undo the stereo-typing of the social group 'prostitute'; it now attempts to undo the stereotypical idea of woman as 'madonna', and charts how Maud moves beyond her religious straitjacket, thanks to her 'aesthetic temperament'. In doing so the novel overtly starts to separate out moral and aesthetic worlds. This separation of the moral from the aesthetic illustrates another change towards the modernist form.

Part of this 'aestheticising' tendency occurs in the novel from the fact that Waymark and Casti are themselves aspiring writers: Waymark wants to write a novel and Casti writes poetry on clas-sical models. In other words, art itself becomes central to the subject matter of the novel and begins to displace the social concerns prevalent in the Realist novel. Certainly there are artistic temperaments and narratorial digressions on art in Realist novels, in *Middlemarch* for example (Will Ladislaw; 'the pier glass'), but 'artists' in Realist novels are subsumed within a much broader social canvas, and discursive passages in Realist novels on art do not cast serious doubt on what can be achieved (and is being achieved) in the Realist novel we may be reading. *The Unclassed*, however, points to something different: it revives the status of the artist in a Romantic vein, in opposition to the materialism of the age, and begins to question the very achievements of Realism and the grounds upon which the Realist project stands.

Late on in the novel, Waymark and Ida are having a holiday together in Hastings, and Waymark wonders why they and people in general cannot always be happy. He answers his own question:

'We have not been content to live in the simple happiness of our senses. We must be learned and wise, forsooth. We were not content to enjoy the beauty of the greater and the lesser light. We must understand whence they come and whither they go – after that, what they are made of and how much they weigh. We thought for such a long time that our toil would end in something; that we might become as gods, knowing good and evil. Now we are at the end of our tether, we see clearly enough that it has all been worse than vain; how good if we could unlearn it all, scatter the building of phantasmal knowledge in which we dwell so uncomfortably! It is too late. The gods never take back their gifts; we wearied them with our prayers into granting us this one, and now they sit in the clouds and mock us.' (1930: 125)

This is a further blow to the Realism of the preceding decades, where the world was approached from a predominantly rational viewpoint in a belief that science would deliver up greater knowledge, which in itself would lead to greater happiness. Waymark now reflects on this and portrays it as man over-reaching himself instead of being content in relative ignorance. All that man has got for his troubles is a despair that can never be undone, there can be no going back to some pre-Fall Eden. Not only that, but Waymark takes his despair to its logical conclusion, and begins to talk of the possibility and necessity of suicide. This is a long way from the outlook shared by Gaskell, Eliot and those socially-concerned Realist novelists who precede Gissing.

While Gissing's novel may look to a greater Realism, it also starts to move away, as the realist impulse itself begins to give way to concerns about aesthetic effect and the role of the artist, amid a reflection on an age which perceives the hopes and achievements of rational endeavour to have been in vain: '"People kill themselves in despair," Waymark went on, "that is, when they have drunk to the very dregs the cup of life's bitterness. If they were wise, they would die at that moment – if it ever comes – when joy seems supreme and stable. Life can give nothing further, and it has no more hellish misery than disillusion following upon delight"'

(1930: 125–6). Both Ida and Waymark discuss the temptation of suicide, and Maud Enderby struggles against a severe religious upbringing. The narrator concludes that 'Maud's aesthetic sensibilities were in perpetual conflict with her moral convictions' (1930: 142), once again demonstrating how the aesthetic and the moral are being separated out. On more than one occasion issues which would normally be the focus of a social-issue Realist novel – poverty, prostitution, effect of environment on people – simply become 'material' for the artist. The techniques of Realism are no longer wedded to the subject matter of Realism.

In Maud's aesthetic transformation we have another feature of modernism, the idea that art itself can satisfy spiritual longings. The Realists' uncomfortable reconciliation of the observable world with a sensibility that there is something beyond the visible no longer appears to hold. Although Gissing's novel often talks of 'sympathy', this is the sympathy of like-minded souls, people drawn to literature, rather than a broader human sympathy. The novel evinces no sympathy from us for Casti's awful wife, Harriet, for instance. Once again, we can see that this later nineteenth-century period for literature signals a receding from the concerns with the social. It is noticeable that Maud shuns the possibility of society as she becomes more aesthetically aware, retreating into her own room and thoughts, and what impresses Waymark at this point is her spiritual otherworldliness allied to her aesthetic sensibility (1930: 148). There is a conventionality in seeing Maud as 'pure of spirit' and more noble than the man, but this is now directed towards art rather than moral and social improvement.

With respect to social improvement, Gissing's novel also registers the shift in the latter part of the nineteenth century towards a more despairing view of humanity. With the English novelists from Dickens through to Eliot there is always a sense that social amelioration is possible, even if, in Eliot's case (and indeed in Gaskell's) the solution is not necessarily to be found in governance, but rather in a notion of a motivated 'human sympathy'. Maud expresses her thoughts to Waymark, who in response tells her that she sounds just like Schopenhauer (1930: 210). Waymark declares that '"Art, nowadays, must be the mouthpiece of misery, for misery is the keynote of modern life"' (1930: 157). In this view,

social amelioration does not seem possible at all: despair is the
existential condition assigned to humanity, and his comment that
'We have a wonderful faculty for accommodating ourselves to
wretchedness' could have stepped out of Dostoevsky's *Crime and
Punishment*: 'Man gets used to everything – the beast' (Dostoevsky
1980: 44).

The move to a more significant concern with aesthetics and the
role of the artist, the misanthropic tone of despair and suicide in a
spiritless world, are all characteristic of nineteenth-century *fin-de-
siècle* art. Gissing's novel also starts to query and undermine
another feature of Realism and the Realist novel, and that is the
notion of 'character' as a stable identity. For instance, Waymark
struggles to understand Ida and his relationship with her. He sees
her as representative of a social group – 'He was well acquainted
with the characteristics of girls of this class' (135), but he also sees
her as 'unclassed', that is, she, like him, does not fit 'conventional'
social categories.

Gissing's 'unclassed' also stretches as far to the ways in which
we fix character and identity, and just as there is a dissatisfaction
with the representation of society through social groups, the novel
suggests that the way we understand 'character' itself is faulty.
Here is another facet which can be considered modernist, since
the identities of Waymark and Ida are not fixed, as they might be
in a more straightforwardly Realist novel. Again, the name
'Waymark' is a clue to this lack of fixity, along with the fact that
Ida's surname is a self-conscious fictional creation. 'Where was
the key of her character?' Waymark asks himself of Ida. It is not
that there is 'depth' necessarily, a peeling away of layers to get at
the 'real' Ida, it is simply that 'character' appears to escape normal
Realist representation. The novel alerts us to this early on when it
describes Ida as a child, able to occupy herself with her thoughts
without recourse to childish distractions, and yet the novel refuses
to offer a description of just what is going on in Ida's consciousness. As the novel progresses, Ida, Maud, Waymark and Julian
come to be regarded as 'unconventional'. Hence, Gissing's delineation of an 'unclassed', while ostensibly attempting to dig deep
into new social strata to achieve a greater social realism, in effect
points towards the focus on the untypical and highly individuated

characters prevalent in modernist fiction. Again, what is ostensibly a continuation of the Realist project – a more detailed picture of society and the particular individuals that constitute it – leads to something that is potentially anti-Realist, since when individuals are represented in too detailed a fashion they start to become 'unique' in their individuation to the extent that we lose sight of them as typical of a social group living out typical lives. Another consequence is that this greater individuation begins to undermine the whole notion of 'classification' which the Realist novel in part depends upon. If everybody is unique, by definition they cannot belong to a class or group.

Having prepared the ground for the modernist novel, let us look at an exemplary, more well-known production, Virginia Woolf's *Mrs Dalloway* (first published in 1925). Gissing's novel, for all its interest in 'the unclassed', remains, in many ways, within the Realist tradition. In contrast, *Mrs Dalloway* challenges virtually all of the tenets of the Realist novel and so will help us see the Realist novel from 'the outside'.

Virginia Woolf: *Mrs Dalloway*

Mrs Dalloway certainly has the potential to be a Realist novel. It concerns Clarissa Dalloway, a society hostess whose life revolves organising parties. This would allow for a reasonable cast of characters from the middle and upper classes. Parallel to Mrs Dalloway's life we are privy to the lower-class world of 'Mr and Mrs Septimus Warren Smith'. Clarissa's husband is an MP while Septimus suffers from shell-shock following his experiences in the First World War, and both these circumstances would give the opportunity to execute a novel with some degree of social concern and a wider social base than just middle and upper classes. These are all the ingredients for a Realist novel. This is how the novel starts:

> Mrs Dalloway said she would buy the flowers herself.
> For Lucy had her work cut out for her. The doors would be taken off their hinges; Rumpelmayer's men were coming. And then, thought Clarissa Dalloway, what a morning – fresh as if issued to children on a beach.

What a lark! What a plunge! For so it had always seemed to her when, with a little squeak of the hinges, which she could hear now, she had burst open the French windows and plunged at Bourton into the open air. How fresh, how calm, stiller than this of course, the air was in the early morning; like the flap of a wave; the kiss of a wave; chill and sharp and yet (for a girl of eighteen as she then was) solemn, feeling as she did, standing out there at the open window, that something awful was about to happen; looking at the flowers, at the trees with the smoke winding off them and the rooks rising, falling; standing and looking until Peter Walsh said, 'Musing among the vegetables?' – was that it? – 'I prefer men to cauliflowers' – was that it? He must have said it at breakfast one morning when she had gone out on to the terrace – Peter Walsh. He would be back from India one of these days, June or July, she forgot which, for his letters were awfully dull; it was his sayings one remembered; his eyes, his pocket-knife, his smile, his grumpiness and, when millions of things had utterly vanished – how strange it was! – a few sayings like this about cabbages.

She stiffened a little on the kerb, waiting for Durtnall's van to pass. A charming woman, Scrope Purvis thought her (knowing her as one does know people who live next door to one in Westminster); a touch of the bird about her, of the jay, blue-green, light, vivacious, though she was over fifty, and grown very white since her illness. There she perched, never seeing him, waiting to cross, very upright. (Woolf 1976: 7–8)

We have some remnants of the Realist novel, though these elements might reasonably apply to any novel: we are immediately given the name of the central character, Clarissa Dalloway, told that she lives in Westminster, given her age ('over fifty'), and that she has recently recovered from an illness. We are also given a sense of her character through the comparison of her to a jay. The narrative is third-person singular – 'There she perched' – and readers versed in the English class system will be able to place Clarissa in the middle- to upper-class bracket since we can infer that: she has a servant (called Lucy); her circle of friends, as represented by Peter Walsh (in India) is from this class; her childhood was privileged (French windows at Bourton); she lives in this class of neighbourhood since Scrope Purvis uses 'one' for the impersonal pronoun.

Yet in every other respect the 'method of realism' is nowhere evident: we have no sense of what the story is about; we are not even really sure where the story is set in either time or place, for it shifts in the opening between a putative here and now of London and a previous time-period when Clarissa was an 18-year-old ensconced in Bourton; there does not appear to be any rational causal logic to the sequence of thoughts; the narrative perspective is restricted to Clarissa's viewpoint, with a brief purview from Scrope Purvis. Even if the characterisation is unusual, and the thoughts chaotic, the narrator should at least put these in perspective for us, but he or she does not. And a related issue is that just as there appears to be no story, there is no clear theme either. The style of the writing is unhelpful – 'air ... like the flap of a wave; the kiss of a wave' – vaguely poetic, but certainly not informative. In sum, there is nothing here other than the random impressions of Mrs Clarissa Dalloway, and an impression of her by somebody else who has no obvious connection other than neighbourly proximity.

However, the above analysis of the opening is one carried out through the perspective of Realist expectations: the reader of a Realist novel expects to know who, what, where and why, whereas the opening to *Mrs Dalloway* confounds all of these means of orientating a Realist audience. Let us now look at it through modernist eyes and establish what this new aesthetic aims at as it supplants the 'outworn' Realist project.

Narrative perspective

The first thing to notice is that the narrative perspective is rendered predominantly through 'free indirect discourse', that is, although the narrative voice is in the third person it is not omniscient, and what it reveals is restricted to the point of view of a particular person. In this case, we are only told what Clarissa sees and knows and what Scrope Purvis sees and knows. A couple of lines suggest a more 'objective', or at least 'neutral' viewpoint, for example when the narrative puts into parenthesis '(for a girl of eighteen as she then was)' this would not seem to replicate Clarissa's thoughts but stand outside as narrative guidance to the reader. Similarly, 'She stiffened a little on the kerb waiting for Durtnall's van to pass' is a neutral viewpoint rather than free indirect discourse since, unless Clarissa Dalloway is prone to providing a running third-person commentary on her own actions, this is also an external viewpoint. It could arguably be that of Scrope Purvis who is introduced in the next sentence, but that seems unlikely since it is asserted/presented as narratorial commentary rather than the 'Scrope Purvis thought' which occurs later.

The whole novel is related in this manner, confining viewpoints through free indirect discourse to only what a particular character can know, see, feel and remember. In this way, apart from the occasional narratorial nudge highlighted above, there is no neutral, objective, or omniscient standpoint. Put another way, the world is revealed wholly through the subjectivities of characters, and in a manner which is complicit with these subjective viewpoints. As a consequence, the reader never gets a stable grip of the narrative, the characters, or the novel's themes. It would be possible to retain subjective viewpoints through free indirect discourse and still offer a stable viewpoint as to what is happening and what the general narrative thrust is – this is the narrative mode of *L'Assommoir* – but to have the subjective viewpoints rendered 'subjectively' in this manner, where thoughts and impressions and insights follow one another without any rational ordering or logical coherence, denies the reader any fixed, stable viewpoint from which to observe proceedings. It is a consistent feature of the Realist novel that there is a narrative perspective which oversees any and all individual perspectives of the characters, and this has the effect of making the world appear, to all intents and purposes, objectively describable and knowable. It is a world understood as a nineteenth-century scientist would or could conceive of it. To operate as *Mrs Dalloway* does is to imply that there is no one superior perspective, just perspectives, in the plural.

The consequences are quite profound. A (usually) unwritten assumption of Realist writing is that, as mentioned at the start of this book, there is a world that exists that in general upon which we can all agree. We might have different opinions about it or describe it in slightly different ways, but in essence we subscribe to the view that we are part of the same world and that collectively we can form a pretty accurate picture of that world.

Thus the belief that underpins Realism is that we share a common phenomenal world, a world replete with phenomena about which there is a general consensus. *Mrs Dalloway*, and perhaps enough other modernist works take the same stance for us to regard it as a dominant feature of modernist art and literature, assume a different philosophical baseline, coming at phenomena through wholly subjective viewpoints which may ultimately be incompatible and irreconcilable with each other.

There is an example of this incompatibility of viewpoints and its consequences in the novel, which suggests how we might 'read' *Mrs Dalloway* as modernists rather than realists. A crowd outside Buckingham Palace is drawn to an aeroplane that happens to be sky-writing, using its smoke to spell out letters: 'But what letters? A C was it? an E, then an L? Only for a moment did they lie still; then they moved and melted and were rubbed out up in the sky, and the aeroplane shot further away and again, in a fresh space of sky, began writing a K, and E, a Y perhaps?' (Woolf 1976: 24–5). The narrative perspective here is technically omniscient third person, but, rather like the other people watching, is unable to make head or tail of the letters, word or words in the sky. There is not a single viewpoint, therefore, which can tell us what the meaning of the skywriting is. All we have are multiple perspectives, each with a quite different view, since one person thinks it spells 'Kreemo', another 'Blaxo', and another 'toffee', and no possibility of agreement. The world exists, to be sure, just as nobody denies that the skywriting takes place, but other than that agreement there is no understanding of what is in front of us. Such a perception of the way we inhabit the world and the way the world is given to us is anti-Realist – we simply cannot agree what the world is and have no means of deciding between competing versions.

The novel also alerts the reader to the fact that it has no sympathy for the idea of 'proportion' in perspective, or at least any sense of objective or public 'proportion'. Parallel to Clarissa's day we follow some of the movements and life of Septimus Warren Smith, the shell-shock victim. The novel indirectly uses Septimus's madness to make many of the claims of Realism seem untenable. He is taken by his wife Rezia to see Dr Holmes and Sir

William Bradshaw to see if they can help. Septimus hallucinates, seeing his dead friend Evans everywhere. When Dr Holmes arrives, the narrative runs: '"You brute! You brute!" cried Septimus, seeing human nature, that is Dr Holmes, enter the room.'

This is an odd narrative aside, and the suggestion that human nature is represented by Dr Holmes seems a judgement independent of any of the character viewpoints, but one that has no faith in the idea of a human nature that is so necessary to humanism. At this point they are waiting for the arrival of Sir William Bradshaw, a Harley Street specialist. He is described as the 'ghostly helper', and, more significantly the 'priest of science', and on more than one occasion shown to be corrupt by making money out of other people's misery. Therefore, having dispensed with 'human nature' it also dispenses with the idea of science as a force for good and for progress. The name 'Bradshaw' would also have had a resonance for a contemporary audience since Bradshaws were synonymous with railway timetables – hence he not only represents science but 'public time', two elements antithetical to the subjective view. And then we get Bradshaw's philosophical and scientific view that everything depends upon 'proportion'. We saw in Chapter 2 how 'proportion' was key to the Realists and here *Mrs Dalloway* proceeds to ridicule the very idea of it by putting it into the mouth of Bradshaw, along with science, religion, medicine, public time, and meaning itself:

> To his patients he gave three-quarters of an hour; and if in this exacting science which has to do with what, after all we know nothing about – the nervous system, the human brain – a doctor loses his sense of proportion, as a doctor he fails. Health we must have; and health is proportion; so that when a man comes into your room and says he is Christ (a common delusion), and has a message, as they mostly have, and threatens, as they often do, to kill himself, you invoke proportion ... (Woolf 1976: 107)

Septimus is deemed mad because he lacks that sense of proportion. However, in the modernist view as represented by this novel, 'proportion' belongs to a rigid, Victorian, scientific, masculine view of the world which does not understand Septimus. Nor does it understand the world at all, for the paralleling of Septimus's and

Clarissa's lives suggests similar apprehensions of the world, one of degree rather than kind. Bradshaw also suggests to Septimus: 'Try to think as little about yourself as possible' (1976: 107), as if introspection itself is a symptom of an unhealthy attitude that can lead to madness. But the whole novel is taken up with 'introspection', with 'looking inside' the minds of people, and those minds also looking inwards at themselves. When Bradshaw also suggests to Septimus that 'Nobody lives for himself alone' (106), again this would seem to run counter to the novel's modernist, anti-Realist thrust, where it is exactly this care for oneself first and foremost that is the prerequisite for true existence.

Stream of consciousness

I have already noted that the first page of *Mrs Dalloway* gives us the thoughts and impressions of its protagonist, and that they are revealed without any apparent narrative or discursive logic. What we have here is an attempt to render the way the mind runs on, not in a linear, rational, ordered manner, but in a random jumble of ideas, images, memories and thoughts. This is termed 'stream of consciousness', a concept coined by the psychologist William James (Henry James's brother) who argued that our minds are always in the middle of things, rather like a stream. He asserted that to present the mind as one that operates in a strictly coherent, linear fashion, as if engaged in reasoned, consecutive contemplation, is to belie the way that it really operates.

The material on the first page of *Mrs Dalloway* does in fact hold together, but uses a binding altogether different from that of the expository prose we expect from Realism. Look again at the passage. Clarissa goes from the present to some thirty-plus years previously in the space of a few lines, thanks to a series of associations: this morning's freshness reminds her of the freshness of morning at Bourton, for 'fresh' occurs in relation to the present and the air in her memory. There may also be another association in that the novel begins with Mrs Dalloway about to buy 'flowers' herself while her memory of Bourton is standing at the window 'looking at flowers'. The associationism continues when she tries to remember what it was that Peter Walsh said, and this has to do with vegetables, and so there may be association by the category of gender, with women associated with flowers and men with vege-tables. Further, when Clarissa concedes to herself that she cannot remember specifically what he said she recasts him in terms of a general impression of sayings, and 'his pocketknife, his smile, his grumpiness'. The passage is also held together by other imagery, such as 'beach' and 'wave', which are purely metaphorical.

Whether this is how the mind actually works is beside the point, as is whether this technique of stream of consciousness adequately captures such workings. The importance for us is that by focusing in such a manner on what the mind is doing, by giving us the world as rendered solely by consciousness, we have moved from the social to the individual, from the objective to the subjective, from the external world to the interior one. It is not that the Realist novel omitted the inner lives of characters – far from it, for one of the achievements of the Realist novel is precisely its ability to represent the psychology of characters in a perceptive and plausible way. However, it is always done in a way which assumes and presumes that we can oversee and understand people in this way, that their psychology can be rationalised and put into social perspective, even where characters' thought processes are shown to be faulty, as they often are. But the point is that, with a Realist novel, they can be judged from the superior, rational, knowing perspective that the Realist narrative viewpoint offers.

At this point you may be thinking that what Woolf does through the stream-of-consciousness technique succeeds in being more realistic in its representation of the inner life than anything achieved by the Realist novel, no matter how good at psychological analysis the Realist novel might be. Where Eliot could show the myriad of influences on a single person's life, as we saw in *The Mill on the Floss* and *Middlemarch*, and certainly gave us access to the inner worlds of characters like Maggie Tulliver and Dorothea, she did not render these thoughts and impressions in 'real time' and wholly and consistently from the inside. This was the limit (or difference) of the Realist novel's psychological characterisations. Modernist novelists certainly advanced the idea and ambition that their psychological realism and representation of consciousness was 'realer' than anything produced by nineteenth-century Realists.

This is where we return to our definition of Realism, and the distinctions we have previously made between Realism, 'realistic' and 'mimetic'. The stream-of-consciousness technique certainly attempts to mimic mental processes rather than summarising, ordering and glossing them as the Realists did, and this in turn might lead us to describe it as 'psychological realism', but, as we have already seen, Realism has many other features, including a due sense of social and objective perspective which the modernist's concentration upon the life of the mind and consciousness, to the exclusion of external social perspective, intrinsically does not allow for. With modernist fiction (and poetry) we have moved inside people, and can only see the world looking out through such subjective eyes.

Time

Another profound consequence to this emphasis on incompatible subjective worlds is the way that time has significance for people, and this in turn affects the way that novels are ordered. If you remember the opening to *Middlemarch* it begins with the effect of Time on human character. The assumption here is that Time is a supreme external force acting on human lives – an identifiable force that exists in the world, or as part of the fabric of the universe, in a way which operates irrespective of human behaviour. Time in this sense is 'objective', that is, independent of individual human perception. The Realist novel 'copies' the way that objective time is deemed to work by unfolding narratives at a fairly steady, regular pace, and in a linear manner with one event following another chronologically. But if there is no 'objective' view of the world available, 'time' itself cannot exist independently in any meaningful way either. Although there may have been no agreement amongst modernist writers and artists about just how time did work, there was at least agreement that to proceed as if it were linear and objective was a misrepresentation.

For instance, *Mrs Dalloway* contrasts the idea of 'objective' (Realist) time with that of 'subjective' time. The opening of the novel shows Clarissa existing within two time-frames, the 'now' of London and the 'then' of Bourton. This is not the same as a character in a Realist novel remembering an event some time ago in their past, for, as the novel progresses, the memories of Bourton appear co-extensive with the contemporary to the extent that the idea that we experience our lives as a linear chronological sequence – events at Bourton followed by events now – is undermined. The constant foregrounding of events at Bourton puts them on the same ontological plane as the contemporary rather than represent-ing them as a distinct, distant time-period. 'Objective' time is represented by Big Ben booming out across London throughout the novel – it is a regular clock, public time, counting out hours in metrical fashion, regardless of individual lives. But *Mrs Dalloway* as a whole presents just one day in the life of its main character and gives her subjective experience of time. Again, it could be argued that this is much more realistic than the representation of time in the Realist novel, for indeed it is a common experience for time to 'fly by' or for time to 'drag', and a novel such as this renders that type of individual, subjective experience in a manner which gives the impression of happening in 'real time'. My copy of the novel has approximately 200 pages; reading at around 30 pages an hour it would take about a leisurely day to read, some kind of equivalent to the 'here-and-now' time-span of the novel. So both the representation of subjective time, and the slowing down of the time-span of the novel to a single day, suggest an increased fidel-ity to the individual experience of time, but, as already stated, such mimesis in itself does not give us Realism, as realistic as it might seem. The loss of a shared perception of a common phenomenal world, and the ousting of public time by private durations, consid-erably diminish the social consensus required for Realism to work.

Other modernist works attack received notions of time differ-ently, such as Conrad's *Under Western Eyes* (1911), which has significant, disjunctive time-shifts. His novel *The Secret Agent* (1907) not only has time shifts but in the central plot to blow up the Greenwich Observatory there is the suggestion that at differ-ent levels the world's 'standard' time (Greenwich Meantime) is under threat. James Joyce's *Ulysses*, to which *Mrs Dalloway* is a response in terms of its day-long time-frame, is probably the most extreme version of the representation of inner consciousness and the minutiae of mental processes – it takes far longer to read than the single day it covers. The Realist novel certainly wanted more 'detail' in order to produce its faithful copy, yet there was always a sense of what counted as due proportion in the relation between the narrative's timeline and the description of inner (psychological) and outer (social) worlds. Put another way, it did not want *that* much detail! *Under Western Eyes*, *The Secret Agent* and *Mrs Dalloway* all represent time in a disjointed, non-linear fashion, and Joyce's *Ulysses* magnifies it out of all Realist proportion.

Characterisation

In Gissing's *Unclassed* we saw that one of the features of the Realist novel under threat was a certain idea of 'character' as a relatively stable entity: we know what a character is because he or she is described in a way that 'fixes' them. Two things happen to 'character' in the modernist novel when compared to its place in the Realist novel: what constitutes 'character' changes, and simultaneously the way 'character' is represented changes.

In 'Mr Bennett and Mrs Brown', one of the seminal essays on what the new type of novel should be doing, Woolf focused on her approach to 'character' and how it differed from that of Arnold Bennett, a writer very much steeped in the tradition of the Realist novel: 'But now I must recall what Mr. Arnold Bennett says. He says that it is only if the characters are real that the novel has any chance of surviving. Otherwise, die it must. But, I ask myself, what is reality? And who are the judges of reality? A character may be real to Mr. Bennett and quite unreal to me' (Woolf 1966a: 325). At once we can see a breakdown in consensus of what constitutes reality, as outlined above. Woolf is wedded to the realist impulse of representing the world as it is, and claims that Bennett does not do it when it comes to character. I quote at length from Woolf's essay below because it also talks about the writing of character in a way that refers us back to stream of consciousness, our lives as mental experience, and the question of 'time'. Hilda Lessways is a character from Bennett's 'Clayhanger' series of novels:

> But we cannot hear her mother's voice, or Hilda's voice; we can only hear Mr. Bennett's voice, telling us facts about rents and freeholds and copyholds and fines. What can Mr. Bennett be about? I have formed my own opinion of what Mr. Bennett is about – he is trying to make us imagine for him; he is trying to hypnotize us into the belief

that, because he has made a house, there must be a person living there. With all his powers of observation, which are marvellous, with all his sympathy and humanity, which are great, Mr Bennett has never once looked at Mrs. Brown in her corner. There she sits in the corner of her carriage – that carriage which is travelling, not from Richmond to Waterloo, but from one age of English literature to the next, for Mrs. Brown is eternal, Mrs Brown is human nature, Mrs. Brown changes only on the surface, it is the novelists who get in and out – there she sits and not one of the Edwardian writers has so much as looked at her. They have looked very powerfully, searchingly, and sympathetically out of the window; at factories, at Utopias, even at the decoration and upholstery of the carriage; but never at her, never at life, never at human nature. And so they have developed a technique of novel-writing which suits their purpose; they have made tools and established conventions which do their business. But those tools are not our tools, and that business is not our business. For us those conventions are ruin, those tools are death. [...]

The problem before him was to make us believe in the reality of Hilda Lessways. So he began, being an Edwardian, by describing accurately and minutely the sort of house Hilda lived in, and the sort of house she saw from the window. House property was the common ground from which the Edwardians found it easy to proceed to intimacy. Indirect as it seems to us, the convention worked admirably, and thousands of Hilda Lessways were launched upon the world by this means. For that age and generation, the convention was a good one.

But now, if you will allow me to pull my own anecdote to pieces, you will see how keenly I felt the lack of a convention, and how serious a matter it is when the tools of one generation are useless for the next. The incident had made a great impression upon me. But how was I to transmit it to you? All I could do was to report as accurately as I could what was said, to describe in detail what was worn, to say, despairingly, that all sorts of scenes rushed into my mind, to proceed to tumble them out pell-mell, and to describe this vivid, this overmastering impression by likening it to a draught or a smell of burning. To tell you the truth, I was also strongly tempted to manufacture a three-volume novel about the old lady's son and his adventures crossing the Atlantic, and her daughter, and how she kept a milliner's shop in Westminster, the past life of Smith himself, and his house at Sheffield, though such stories seem to me the most dreary, irrelevant, and humbugging affairs in the world. [...]

Thus I have tried, at tedious length, I fear, to answer some of the questions which I began by asking. I have given an account of some of the difficulties which in my view beset the Georgian writer in all his forms. I have sought to excuse him. May I end by venturing to remind you of the duties and responsibilities that are yours as partners in this business of writing books, as companions in the railway carriage, as fellow travellers with Mrs. Brown? For she is just as visible to you who remain silent to us who tell stories about her. In the course of your daily life this past week you have had far stranger and more interesting experiences than the one I have tried to describe. You have overheard scraps of talk that filled you with amazement. You have gone to bed at night bewildered by the complexity of your feelings. In one day thousands of ideas have coursed through your brains; thousands of emotions have met, collided, and disappeared in astonishing disorder. Nevertheless, you allow the writers to palm off upon you a version of all this, an image of Mrs. Brown, which has no likeness to that surprising apparition whatsoever. (Woolf 1996a: 330–6)

Woolf's general dissatisfaction is with a style of writing – Edwardian – which is an ossified form of the Realist novel at the beginning of the twentieth century. It uses the technique of describing surroundings to indicate character, something we have seen was a feature of the Realist novel. By doing it this way, no matter how great the author's powers of observations might be as to physical detail, for Woolf the life of the character is 'inside' rather than tied to social environment: 'In one day thousands of ideas have coursed through your brains; thousands of emotions have met, collided, and disappeared in astonishing disorder.' This describes perfectly how Mrs Dalloway's life is portrayed, as consisting of this myriad of transient thoughts and emotions. It is still underpinned by the realist impulse – to reproduce the world accurately – but what that 'reality' is is also in dispute when it comes to people. Compare the opening of *Mrs Dalloway* with the opening to Bennett's novel *Hilda Lessways*:

The Lessways household, consisting of Hilda and her widowed mother, was temporarily without a servant. Hilda hated domestic work, and because she hated it she often did it passionately and thoroughly. That afternoon, as she emerged from the kitchen, her dark, defiant face was full of grim satisfaction in the fact that she had left a kitchen polished and irreproachable, a kitchen without the slightest indication that it ever had been or ever would be used for preparing human nature's daily food; a show kitchen. Even the apron which she had worn was hung in concealment behind the scullery door. The lobby clock, which stood over six feet high and had to be wound up every night by hauling on a rope, was noisily getting ready to strike two. But for Mrs. Lessways' disorderly and undesired assistance, Hilda's task might have been finished a quarter of an hour earlier. She passed quietly up the stairs. When she was near the top, her mother's voice, at once querulous and amiable, came from the sitting-room:

'Where are you going to?'

There was a pause, dramatic for both of them, and in that minute pause the very life of the house seemed for an instant to be suspended, and then the waves of the hostile love that united these two women resumed their beating, and Hilda's lips hardened. (Bennett 1968: 3–4)

STOP and THINK

How does this compare with the opening to *Mrs Dalloway*? In what ways is Woolf's representation more realistic than Bennett's? Does Bennett's writing technique seem old-fashioned ('Realist'!) in comparison to Woolf's? What are the advantages and disadvantages for the two styles of writing?

There are quite a number of common areas in this and the beginning of Woolf's novel: the establishment of character and the attention to domestic work for instance, down to the part about having to take on the servant's duty (and a bit further on in this chapter there is even talk of a door and hinges). The importance of time, both objective and subjective, is signalled here through the lobby clock (public time) and the suspension held in a minute's pause (subjective time), and we have seen how strongly that features in *Mrs Dalloway*. But the differences are quite obvious, for Bennett places everything in good Realist order – he arranges the scene for us, the relationship between mother and daughter (interestingly, 'waves' of hostile love), and the passage follows a logical sequence based on actions and thoughts that move in a linear fashion. The narrator tells us what Hilda is like – 'Hilda hated domestic work, and because she hated it she often did it passionately and thoroughly'. It is a psychological perception of an everyday 'type' that we have become familiar with as typical of Realist character presentation.

In the next chapter Bennett goes back to 1878 when Hilda was nearly 21 years old, and then back to when she was eight years old. There is a rapidity to this shift in time-periods not unlike that in Woolf. Unlike Woolf, however, the reader is always aware that the time periods are quite ontologically separate, another feature of the Realist novel.

This contrast between the Realist techniques of characterisation of Bennett and those of the modernist ones of Woolf may seem a little crude, but, among other things, Woolf clearly sets herself up in opposition to a style of writing that is basically Realist as it continued into the time of her writing. You may feel that, from our distance, she is wrong in her assessment of Bennett's achievement in portraying Hilda as a 'real' character, and you may even feel that his Realist method is preferable to Woolf's modernist stream-of-conscious impressionism. In fact, interestingly, *Hilda Lessways* is the second novel in the Clayhanger series and retells some events of the first novel from Hilda's perspective, a strategy a modernist novelist might have been proud of. Even Hilda's character suggests something of Clarissa's: 'Just as her attitude to her mother was self-contradictory, so was her attitude towards existence. Sometimes this profound infelicity of hers changed its hues for an instant, and lo! it was bliss that she was bathed in. A phenomenon which disconcerted her! She did not know that she had the most precious of all faculties, the power to feel intensely' (Bennett 1968: 8). Nevertheless, Woolf's dissatisfaction with Bennett and the type of Realist novel he stood for was shared by other writers with whom we are familiar as modernists – Lawrence, Joyce, James and Conrad. Lawrence, for instance, talks in a letter to Edward Garnett of how he is attempting to reconceive character in a new manner, against nineteenth-century novel conceptions. He is defending his work

The Wedding Ring, a working title for what became the novels *The Rainbow* and *Women in Love*:

> I don't agree with you about *The Wedding Ring*. You will find that
> in a while you will like the book as a whole. I don't think the
> psychology is wrong. It is only that I have a different attitude to my
> characters, and that necessitates a different attitude in you, which
> you are not prepared to give ... But when I read Marinetti – 'the
> profound intuitions of life added one to the other, word by word,
> according to their illogical conception, will give us the general lines
> of an intuitive physiology of matter' – I see something of what I am
> after. I translate him clumsily, and his Italian is obfuscated and I
> don't care about physiology of matter – but somehow – that which is
> physic – non-human, in humanity, is more interesting to me than
> the old-fashioned human element – which causes one to conceive a
> character in a certain moral scheme and make him consistent. The
> certain moral scheme is what I object to. In Turgenev, and in Tolstoi,
> and in Dostoievsky, the moral scheme into which nearly all the char-
> acters fit – and it is nearly the same scheme – is, whatever the
> extraordinariness of the characters themselves, dull, old, dead.
> (Lawrence 1956: 197–8)

The same underlying drive is there that we saw in Woolf, the perception that the Realist way of doing things is 'dead'. For Woolf, it was Bennett's method of description and the fact that he did not render the inner world of his characters and the way that the mind or consciousness works; for Lawrence, it is a different way of thinking about what a person is in the first place, and so he claims that there is an element of characters which has not been addressed. But this reconception of what a human is – partly 'inhuman' – has an effect on the way he executes a novel, just as it does for Woolf. For Lawrence there can be no standard moral scheme for characters, as there has been for the (Russian) Realists. Representation of character is strongly tied to represen-tation of a world that is moral, or has a moral necessity. Here, just as we saw in the projected future of the novel in *The Unclassed*, the 'moral' is severed from other concerns, and Lawrence appears to see it as irrelevant to characterisation. *Mrs Dalloway* ends with Peter Walsh filled with a feeling of ecstasy and asking himself:

> What is it that fills me with extraordinary excitement?
> It is Clarissa, he said.
> For there she was.

This feeling of standing on the brink of something about to happen, and being overwhelmed by the sense of 'now', of 'this-ness', of absolute presence, is what characterises Woolf's novel. There is no indication that these existential intimations are in any way of a moral nature.

Anti-humanism

Characteristic of novelists like Eliot, Gaskell and Dickens is what may be termed humanism, a belief in the value of the human spirit, respect for each other, a sense that things can be made better and that humans have it within their own hands to achieve this, whatever the forces of heredity and environment. Even Zola, focusing on what is miserable, perhaps vouchsafes for a humanism – otherwise why find it necessary to highlight this facet of human life? Woolf's novel ends on an apparent high note when Clarissa accepts the absolute present of her life, of this exact moment. However, it actually represents quite a retreat from a humanist perspective since this is nothing more than an individual's consciousness recognising and accommodating itself to nothing more than its own nature. It has no sense of going 'outwards' towards the social, and no sense of a world it shares with others. Despite her parties, Clarissa's victory demonstrates that subject-ive worlds must be anathema to an idea of society as a structural given.

There is a certain despair here which is easily identifiable in other works of art and writing characteristic of modernism. Edvard Munch's famous painting 'The Scream' might be taken as emblematic of this despair at the world: an androgynous figure stares out at us, terrified by something we cannot see but must imagine. The landscape itself is distorted into waves by the terror, as if the inner-world perception or consciousness distorts the outer world, again suggesting that there is no neutral, objective, fixed viewpoint. Simultaneous with the move to render the world subjectively is the move to show that this subjectivity cannot be escaped. Part of the despair would appear to be the consciousness of self-consciousness itself, that any view of the world is absolutely dependent upon consciousness and mind rather than external, social factors.

All of this feeds into a philosophical position that is anti-humanist. Just as modernism is characterised by writers and artists reacting against Realism, but often in quite diverse ways, they begin to adopt anti-humanist outlooks of various hues. Though this was not true of all of them – a writer like James would still seem to advance 'humane' values – as is evident above, Lawrence has little time for the stereotypical humanist ideology. In the novel *Women in Love*, the character Rupert Birkin asserts the new view, a view which often permeates Lawrence's work as a whole. Here he is talking to Ursula, who becomes a spokeswoman for humanity:

> 'And why is it,' she asked at length, 'that there is no flowering, no dignity of human life now?'
>
> 'The whole idea is dead. Humanity itself is dry-rotten, really. There are myriads of human beings hanging on the bush – and they look very nice and rosy, your healthy young men and women. But they are apples of Sodom, as a matter of fact, Dead Sea fruit, gall-apples. It isn't true that they have any significance – their insides are full of bitter, corrupt ash.'
>
> 'But there are good people,' protested Ursula.
>
> 'Good enough for the life of to-day. But mankind is a dead tree, covered with fine brilliant galls of people.' (Lawrence 1982: 186)

The sentiment here is partly a consequence of Darwinism – an idea that the development of the human race has come to an end, that it is no longer fit for purpose, or that it is fit only for low-level survival. Although Lawrence's particular vision of humanity may seem overly misanthropic and atypical, its anti-humanist bent is typical of modernist art and writing.

Anti-narrative

There is another anti-Realist consequence to the achievements of *Mrs Dalloway* as it renders consciousness in detail. It wants to give a sense of the thousands of ideas and emotions that flicker in us day after day, but it does not appear to want to tell a story. In itself the focus on character rather than narrative might seem simply a shift in emphasis, but once again it is a turning away from what informs the Realist aesthetic. Without an overt narrative, there is no 'shaping' of the material towards a shared understanding of the way the world is, or how we might order it among ourselves as part of the collective Realist endeavour. To reproduce the typical thoughts of an unremarkable person has something of the Realist ethos, but to do it to the exclusion of any other perspective is to deny the ability to comprehend the world external to any individual's apprehension. Hence, there is quite often a sense at the end of modernist novels that nothing is finished, there is no 'closure'. *Middlemarch* ties up all the loose ends, tells us the stories of all the people involved and how their lives continued after the main narrative. *The Mill on the Floss* ends with the deaths of Tom and Maggie Tulliver – that is their narrative. Even if we may not be sure what Gervaise's death at the end of *L'Assommoir* signifies, at least we do have an ending and the sense that we have had her story and those connected with her, a story that we are invited to make sense of, and upon which we can at least conclude that environment has powerful effects on character.

But where the novel *Mrs Dalloway* ends is to all intents and purposes arbitrary: there is no marriage, no death, no inheritance, no emigration, no sense that we have learnt anything of value, no moral, no anti-moral even. There is nothing, other than the sense of 'presence', of 'now' – and that is ever-present in the novel, such that the novel could quite easily end somewhere else. *The Mill on the Floss* has to end with the deaths of Maggie and Tom; *Germinal* has to end when the strike ends. Possibly *Mrs Dalloway* has to end after the party, or at the end of the day, but this is hardly 'the story' or a necessary 'end'. And without a proper narrative end it is hard to get at a 'meaning' or significance in the way that Realist novels offer and the Realist reader expects. The narrative does not give the meaning. There is certainly plenty of thematic material – issues of communication, gender, identity, age, the nature of consciousness and perception of reality, class – but the reader is not directed to these in the manner of a Realist novel. In the now-classic formulation, the novel 'shows' rather than 'tells', by which is meant that the reader is presented with the material to make of it what he or she will, whereas in the Realist novel the narrator acts as a friendly, omniscient, wise guide. Readers are on their own when faced with modernist writing and art, and this in itself represents a retreat from the idea of a shared world and a shared endeavour common to Realism and its humanist ethos.

Summary

The Realist aesthetic continued to be prominent until the end of the nineteenth century, and in some countries became important as a medium for asserting national identity and, in the case of America, for promoting a national literature and literary heritage. Nevertheless, in Europe, from the 1880s onwards there was a move away from Realism. Although the responses varied quite hugely across art and literature, there was a feeling that the Realist aesthetic as it had been perpetuated in the previous three or four decades had run its course, partly because the social and moral objectives of Realism no longer appeared to hold the attention of writers and artists who, for one thing, started to become at least as interested in the tools of their chosen medium as in any subject matter. Certainly there were many ideas in modernist art which can be traced back to Realism, especially with those novels that attempted to be more psychologically realistic than anything that had happened before, and this is partly because consciousness and the workings of the mind were becoming the subject of science through work in psychology and psychoanalysis, both of which are late nineteenth-century inventions.

In addition, the earlier confidence that science would deliver up the world to human knowledge, and that this would lead to an improvement in the human lot, dissipated. This was exacerbated partly by the acceptance of Darwin's idea of evolution, which helped to either remove God from the world, or place him at a very remote distance, and simultaneously diminished the status of the 'human' since it was now known to have descended from apes. This decline in the social nature of art and uncertainties about the way the world was constituted, and particularly how we perceived that world through a non-stable consciousness, meant that nineteenth-century realism – Realism – simply became an untenable aesthetic. The realist impulse perhaps lingered in the attempts to accurately mirror the mind, and produce what might be termed 'psychological realism', but this was certainly not Realism.

Works cited and further reading

Bennett, Arnold (1968), *Hilda Lessways*. London: Methuen.

Bradbury, Malcolm and James McFarlane (1991), *Modernism: A Guide to European Literature 1890–1930*. This remains one of the best books on modernism. London: Penguin.

Conrad, Joseph (1980), *The Secret Agent*. Harmondsworth: Penguin.

Conrad, Joseph (1980), *Under Western Eyes*. Harmondsworth: Penguin.

Conrad, Joseph (1997), 'Preface' to *The Nigger of the 'Narcissus'*. London: Dent.

Dostoevsky, Fyodor (1980), *Crime and Punishment*. Harmondsworth: Penguin.

Gissing, George (1930), *The Unclassed*. London: Ernest Benn Ltd. Available at Project Gutenberg.

James, Henry (1957), 'The Art of Fiction' in *The House of Fiction*. London: Rupert Hart-Davis.

Kolocotroni, Vassiliki, Jane Goldman and Olga Taxidou (2004), *Modernism: An Anthology of Sources and Documents*. Edinburgh: Edinburgh University Press. Includes much important modernist material, as well as critical statements from the Realist period.

Lawrence, D. H. (1956), Letter to Edward Garnett, 5 June 1914. *The Letters of D H Lawrence*. London: Heinemann.

Lawrence, D. H. (1982), *Women in Love*. Harmondsworth: Penguin.

Lewis, Pericles (2007), *The Cambridge Introduction to Modernism*. Cambridge: Cambridge University Press. Gives considerable attention to modernism's relationship with Realism.

Strindberg, August (1964), 'Author's Preface' to *Miss Julie*, in *Selected Plays and Prose*, ed. Robert Brustein. New York: Holt, Rinehart and Winston.

Wilde, Oscar (1985), 'Preface' to *The Picture of Dorian Gray*. London: Penguin.

Woolf, Virginia (1966a), 'Mr Bennett and Mrs Brown', in *Collected Essays. Volume 1*. London: Hogarth Press.

Woolf, Virginia (1966b), 'Modern Fiction', in *Collected Essays. Volume 2*. London: Hogarth Press.

Woolf, Virginia (1976), *Mrs Dalloway*. London: Grafton Books.

Woolf, Virginia (1992), *To the Lighthouse*. London: Penguin.

7
Before, during and after postmodernism

Attenuated modernism: realism in the 1930s and 1950s

The narrative thus far in relation to Realism and fiction goes something like this. Realism gains hold as a dominant aesthetic some time in the middle of the nineteenth century, partly as a reaction against Romanticism, partly as a response to the perceived issues of the age and the need for a socially-responsive and responsible medium, partly as a continuance of the development of the novel form, and partly as a response to scientific developments and thought. Realism has two distinct but related forms in England and France, and has different but related manifestations in other countries. Towards the latter half of the nineteenth century a new aesthetic, predominantly European in its earlier incarnations, reacts against Realism and produces what is now collectively termed 'modernism'. What next?

Inevitably, perhaps, modernism in turn becomes superseded. Again, it depends from which country you view these events, but in general it is thought that modernism is 'exhausted' by the 1930s, and that decade sees the 'high modernism' of works like *Finnegans Wake* (1939) as a logical dead-end, where the attention to 'language', for instance, predominates over other concerns, and leads to often impenetrable, inaccessible literature. In England there is an interesting reaction against modernism, which emerges at the end of the 1920s and continues beyond the Second World War. It is perhaps characterised by the perception that modernism has in part been a failed experiment in that its 'difficulty' means it has lost an audience, but also the perception that there are certain gains from the techniques of modernism which can enhance the novel in its Realist form. I would suggest that what happens round about this time is that the more broadly recognisable 'realist novel' takes shape as it assimilates modernist techniques to realist ends. Novels such as those by Elizabeth Bowen, Rosamond Lehmann and George Orwell are predominantly realist, but are not afraid to use free indirect discourse extensively, and to use disjunctive time-shifts, yet still maintain a commitment to an accessible, transparent language and a return to a belief in a common phenomenal world. In the wake of Freud and psychoanalysis, and in the midst of heated debates about the nature of capitalism and the merits of Marxism, writers in the 1930s are equally engaged by the workings of the mind and the workings of society, and an attenuated Realist form offers a means of handling both of these concerns. Again, I should emphasise that such broader social and cultural influences might be quite indirect, but they are arguably quite prevalent in this literature.

George Orwell's *Keep the Aspidistra Flying* (1936) is a good example of the return to realism by way of modernism. It follows the life of Gordon Comstock, a man with pretensions to be a poet but forced to make a living out of writing 'verse' for advertising. It shows a return to a realist outlook after the extremes of modernism: external and extensive descriptions of setting (London), solid temporal identification (1936), a central character with a full personal history, psychological consistency and behavioural plausibility, and a common phenomenal world. It renders detail at the level of minutiae, and moves between external description and a free indirect discourse which shades into stream of consciousness:

> His heart sickened to think that he had only fivepence halfpenny in the world, threepence of which couldn't even be spent. Because how can you buy anything with a threepenny-bit. It isn't a coin, it's the answer to a riddle. You look such a fool when you take it out of your pocket, unless it's in among a whole handful of other coins. 'How much?' you say. 'Threepence,' the shop-girl says. And then you feel all round your pocket and fish out that absurd little thing, all by itself, sticking on the end of your finger like a tiddley-wink. (Orwell 1983: 577)

This might not look out of place in *Mrs Dalloway*, whereas other parts are more overtly third-person omniscient, for example: 'The clock struck half past two. In the little office at the back of Mr McKechnie's bookshop, Gordon – Gordon Comstock, last member of the Comstock family...' (Orwell 1983: 577), although even here it catches the idiom of casual thought or speech.

The passage above focuses on Gordon's difficult monetary position. The theme of money is evident throughout the novel, and is given a material reality which is in accordance with Marxist precepts, but there is also a materiality of 'consciousness', thanks to modernism, and of social relations, thanks to Realism. Gordon himself has half-baked socialist ideals, which come up against the reality of having to get by and, eventually, having to support a family. Gordon's attempt to uphold literary value in the face of commercialisation and a perceived decline in civilisation echoes the cultural discontent seen in *Women in Love*, but also of course there is the looming threat of the Second World War.

Further evidence of the emergence of the realist impulse after modernism can be found in the poetry of the 1930s. In fact, the poetry that Gordon writes in *Keep the Aspidistra Flying* (1936) is typical of this return to 'traditional' verse forms, accompanied by a return to accessible language and a sense of shared social concern:

> Sharply the menacing wind sweeps over
> The bending poplars, newly bare,
> And the dark ribbons of the chimneys
> Veer downward; flicked by whips of air,
> Torn posters flutter; coldly sound
> The boom of trams and the rattle of hooves,
> And the clerks who hurry to the station
> Look, shuddering, over the eastern rooves,
> Thinking, each one, 'Here comes the winter!
> Please God I keep my job this year!'
> And bleakly, as the cold strikes through
> Their entrails like an icy spear,
> They think of rent, rates, season tickets,
> Insurance, coal, the skivvy's wages,
> Boots, school-bills, and the next instalment
> Upon the two twin beds from Drage's.

(Orwell 1983: 617)

Compare this with lines from the poem 'A Communist to Others' by W. H. Auden, published just three years earlier:

> Comrades who when the roar
> From office shop and factory pour
>   'Neath evening sky;
> By cops directed to the fug
> Of talkie-houses for a drug
> Or down canals to find a hug
>   Until you die:
>
> We know, remember, what it is
> That keeps you celebrating this
>   Sad ceremonial;
> We know the terrifying brink
> From which in dreams you nightly shrink
> 'I shall be sacked without,' you think,
>   'A testimonial.'
>
> We cannot put on airs with you
> The fears that hurt you hurt us too
>   Only we say
> That like all nightmares these are fake
> If you would help us we could make
> Our eyes to open, and awake
>   Shall find night day.
>   (in Skelton 1964: 54)

After the difficulties of reading modernist poetry such as that of Eliot and Pound, this is as clear as daylight. The language is 'accessible', in that the reader does not have to 'work' at the meaning of the poetry as the verse communicates directly to the reader. Both poems position themselves and their readers as sharing the same world and the same concerns – about employment and the possibility of redundancy, about money, and about an overwhelming sense of bleakness. We are back in the Realist world of typicality rather than heightened subjective individualism. Even though Gordon Comstock may not be the typical Realist protagonist – his artistic ambitions point more towards the artist-hero of modernism and its Romanticist strand – the fact that he fails in his artistic ambitions, ceding his life to the pressures of the 'real' world, moves him back onto the same plane of 'ordinary' life.

Such a predominantly realist mode continued in England into
the 1950s. There was 'The Movement' in England for poets, a loose
term that grouped together poets still concerned with the everyday
and a return to the traditional poetic mainstream. Even though
there was experimentation in the novel form in the 1950s, in itself a
continuation of modernist experimentation, it was often the 'first
novels' of authors that took the limelight, and these in turn were
often narratives that bore a close relation to the lives of their
authors, delivered through the accessible language and novelistic
form now established as the main form for the genre. Looking back
at that period, Malcolm Bradbury talks of this reaction against
modernism, as represented by the Bloomsbury set (Woolf and
others). This is from his introduction to William Cooper's *Scenes
from Provincial Life* (1950), a touchstone work for the 1950s
writers. Note that the title of Cooper's novel takes us back directly
to George Eliot, a conflation of the title *Scenes from Clerical Life*
and the subtitle of *Middlemarch*, 'A Study of Provincial Life':

> *Scenes from Provincial Life* is not of course an artless novel, but it is
> the novel in its empirical form. It could and did stand for an impor-
> tant swing away from the stylistic backlog of modernism, or what
> William Cooper calls the 'Art Novel': a swing towards an art of
> reason, an art of lived-out and recognisable values and predica-
> ments, an art, even, of the social places we associate with
> ordinariness – the provinces, the lower middle classes, the world of
> growing up and getting on. Virginia Woolf once suggested that
> modernism had set the writer free, led him from the kingdom of
> necessity to the kingdom of light, by allowing him to dispense with
> traditional plot and character, traditional detailing and chronology,
> the need to tell a story or report material reality. (Cooper 1969: iii)

There is no mistaking that this is the language of the Realist novel,
applied to the English novel a century or so later. This form of the
novel is about 'ordinariness' and reasonableness, about typical life
in the provinces, and the novel form itself returns to its 'traditional' elements of an identifiable plot, story, characters, detail, linear
chronology and a recognisable world. What is not there is the
specific claim to a scientific basis, but its mention of 'the novel in
its empirical form' points in that direction. There is also no doubt
that this approach to the novel remains viable up to the present

and retains a certain dominance. However, at the same time as realism was re-establishing itself after the turn to modernism, art and literature were taking another twist.

Postmodernism

Towards the end of the 1950s and beginning of the 1960s a new aesthetic came to dominate, called 'postmodernism'. The term itself gives an indication of its relationship to modernism as one which, in part, continues the project while going beyond it. However, if modernism and Realism had some common points of contact, the relationship between Realism and postmodernism is completely antithetical and antagonistic. When Woolf questioned Arnold Bennett's technique for rendering 'character' she wondered whose idea of reality was more correct. The premise, however, was still realist, for it assumes that there is a reality which can be described. The disagreement arose because Woolf believed her way of doing things more accurately reproduced this reality than Bennett's. For Woolf and other modernists, getting at the real world was certainly more problematic than the Realists had assumed, but they still believed it could be done if you looked hard enough and peeled away surface layers to get at the reality beneath.

Modernist works are often self-consciously 'difficult' to understand because they assume that reality itself is not self-evident: 'Our mistake lies in supposing that things present themselves as they really are' (Proust, in Stevenson 1992: 17). The Realists had a confidence in the observable world, even if they subscribed to ideas such as 'human spirit' and 'sympathy', forces which are not necessarily visible. The observable world for the Realists was informed by invisible forces. The modernists on the other hand sensed that there was a 'behind' or 'beneath' to the world which was more important than what was visible, so this created difficulties, and they believed that the tools to represent what was not observable might be faulty or not up to the job, hence the disposal of elements such as linear chronology, plot, stable identities, reasoned and proportionate narrative perspective. Nevertheless, the modernists retained a belief that the world was knowable and describable in some fashion, and that this, after all, could be communicated.

From the 1950s until the present this realist assumption has been radically questioned. What is 'real'? What is 'reality'? Does language describe a world that pre-exists the language, or does language in some way create the world, or worlds? This fore-grounding of language in the twentieth century is called 'the linguistic turn' and has dominated a considerable amount of thought about our relationship with the world and with each other. And specific to literature, if the world is made out of the language we use, it might follow that the way we engage with the world is not just linguistic but textual.

Simultaneous with this shift to the linguistic and the textual, is the question of how we tell ourselves about the world. From the 1960s onwards critical thought, accompanied by artistic produc-tions that concurred with these premises, began to see the world as constructed not just out of 'language' but out of narratives and discourse. The narratives and discourses that present the world to us do not describe the world but constitute the world we under-stand, and these narratives and discourses are deemed to be politically motivated by any, or all of such things as race, gender, class, nationality, religion and sexual orientation: there is no narra-tive or discourse which is independent of some vested interest, and this includes such disciplines as science and philosophy, two disciplines often regarded as not compromised by subjective considerations. The consequence of this, and the accompanying argument here, is that there is no objective ground and no objec-tive perspective from which we can talk about the world. The argument is that I cannot ultimately defend my view of the world as right and yours as wrong, or that one culture is right and another wrong, because from what grounds would I be starting?

The obvious response might be that science can give us hard facts about the world, but a certain strand of philosophy of science in the twentieth century (and again up to the present) has cast doubts on the certitudes that science might even offer this as a solid starting point. Newton was 'right' for a long time about the nature of the universe, then Einstein showed that this view of time and space was not the case. Is Einstein wrong? Could there be another view of the universe to supersede Einstein? And if this is how science operates, to what extent can it describe the real world to us at all? Who or what can tell us what the universe is like? And when scientists start talking about the make-up of the universe at its smallest and largest levels, and talk about things which are pure speculation and upon which there is no agreement, such as 'strings', this seems very far removed from the world we inhabit.

Just as there are questions over how we 'access' the world through language, discourse, representation and narrative – all elements which 'construct' the world rather than neutrally and objectively 'mapping' the world – what a human is, and what a human's identity might be, have been continually put into doubt, so much so that the competing versions of 'self', 'subject' and 'person', for instance, mean that there can be little prospect of a consensus on 'character', a feature that is central to realist representations. Part of postmodernism has been a concerted anti-humanism, one that does not see a human as an autonomous being able to have a say in his or her life, and does not see the possibility of progress through the advance of science and technology, or see the use of Enlightenment reason as the way forward. Instead, there has been a strong post-war sentiment which sees the self as 'constructed' by forces outside the individual self or beyond the control of the self. You can take your choice for what might be the most significant external force, from: economic systems (Marxist thought), the unconscious (Freudian and post-Freudian thought; psychoanalysis), cultural discourse and representation. The argument here is that we do not make our own lives but are born into language, culture, gender, race, class, discourses and representations which 'construct' the self and identity. Although many of these ideas can be discerned in modernist literature, their predominance over other elements makes for a fairly coherent and identifiable postmodern aesthetic, as exemplified in Margaret Atwood's novel *The Handmaid's Tale* (1995).

Margaret Atwood: *The Handmaid's Tale*
The story is set in a future dystopia where the ability to reproduce is at a premium. To further these ends the Republic of Gilead forces some women to become handmaids, with the sole purpose of giving offspring to childless couples. The protagonist is Offred. Although there is obviously nothing here which might form the

basis of the realist novel, part of the thrust of postmodernism is that realism simply is not possible, so in some ways it makes little sense in any case to rework typical realist materials in a postmodern manner, as the modernists often did. While it could be argued that the use of the science-fiction genre makes for a poor comparison with the realist genre, it is in accord with postmodern tenets, and will, nevertheless, allow us to see just how all the tenets of Realism are dismantled through the postmodern prism.

Narrative

Postmodernism is often seen as a 'return to narrative', by which is meant that modernist works had a tendency to reject narrative in favour of other means of ordering and unifying material – 'myth', poetic patterning, individual consciousness – and now postmodernism has returned to a concern with providing strong narrative interest. Atwood's novel certainly does this – we are intrigued by the world that Offred lives in, and want to know what fate awaits her and others.

However, there is a considerable difference between the way that *The Handmaid's Tale* treats narrative here, and the way a Realist text might, for it constantly questions how the narrative is being 'constructed'. Rather than just 'telling' the story, as Realists texts tend to, the narrator keeps suggesting that the story itself is put together in a particular way, and that it might indeed be reconstructed in other ways – with the consequence that the story would have other meanings – including a change in the sense of identity for the narrator. Realist narratives, by definition, are 'stable' – we 'trust' the story that we are told. In Realist narratives, even though we may get subjective viewpoints, there is always a perspective for the reader which allows us to put these things into 'objective' proportion. But in *The Handmaid's Tale*, and typical of postmodern narrative, the very nature of what constitutes narrative is questioned. So when Offred gives the reader a story about the past, about her past and how the present state of Gilead came about, and then says that this is a 'reconstruction' (Atwood 1995: 144), the 'contract' between the reader and the text is broken, or redrawn. If narrative is a 'construct' rather than a simple retelling of things as they are, then what is the truth of things?

In relating how the Commander gets Offred to play Scrabble with him illicitly, she tells the reader of how at the time she imagined planning to kill him: 'I think about how I could approach the Commander, to kiss him, here alone, and take off his jacket ... and slip the lever out from the sleeve and drive the sharp end into him suddenly', but then she says: 'In fact I don't think about anything of the kind. I put it in only afterwards. Maybe I should have thought about that, at the time, but I didn't. As I said, this is a reconstruction' (1995: 150). What is the reader to think? We seem to have a story, but not have a story. We have a narrator, but the narrator tells us that she is making it up. This chapter ends with: 'He was so sad. / That is a reconstruction too.' (1995: 150) The general point here about narrative is that all narrative is 'construct', but that we have no other option to get at the world except through narrative. Put another way, we cannot get at a world 'behind' narrative, a world that narrative might neutrally and objectively re-present (realism). It is narrative itself that creates the world we see. It is no coincidence that the forbidden game is Scrabble, drawing our attention to language at the same time as the chapter draws our attention to the constructive role of narrative.

While there is a constant undercutting of the belief that narrative can give us access to an unadorned truth, or any truth at all, the 'honesty' of the character in admitting to the constructed and reconstructed nature of her narrative suggests that at least there is something for the reader to get a grip on, as if we can at least hold on to the idea that Offred will own up to what is, and is not, reconstructed, and through this we can gain some semblance of what has really happened to her. It seems that there is always the possibility we will be able to work out the 'real story', despite the 'constructed' nature of the narrative, and narrative in general.

The constructed nature of narrative and how it affects what we can understand the truth to be takes an even more radical turn, however, in the last chapter, entitled 'Historical Notes on *The Handmaid's Tale*' – 'Being a partial transcript of the proceedings of the Twelfth Symposium on Gileadean Studies, held as part of the International Historical Association Convention, which took place at the University of Denay, Nunavit, on June

25, 2195'. Until this chapter we have followed Offred in her deal-
ings within Gilead, and although alert to possible failings in her
ability to give an accurate, trustworthy narrative, the reader is
still in the position of following a relatively chronological story
which makes sense. Now we are told that this story itself – 'The
Handmaid's Tale' – has been reconstructed in totality from voice
recordings on thirty cassette tapes. There is no guarantee that
the tapes are in the right order, or that they are not a forgery,
and the historians cannot identify the characters, and have no
way of knowing if there was such a character as Offred and, if
there was, whether she escaped Gilead or was killed. The novel
ends with: 'Are there any questions?' to which the reader cannot
help but feel there is nothing but.

While it may seem unbalanced to compare a novel so obviously
not realist with ideas of Realism, the issue here of narrative within
the context of postmodernism is quite germane. There are many
other postmodern novels that throw up similar or related issues
about the nature of narrative and how construction of the world
through narrative throws into doubt the possibility of arriving at
'truth' in the sense that those attached to Realist and modernist
aesthetics would accept, or those who believe in a more broader
realism would accept. Salman Rushdie's *Midnight's Children*
(1981) and *Shame* (1983), John Fowles's *The French Lieutenant's
Woman* (1969) are just a small example of postmodern novels that
do this. Robert Coover's *The Public Burning* (1977) imaginatively
reconstructs a key historical event in recent American history –
the execution of the Rosenbergs for giving away state secrets to the
Russians – and includes imagining the life of the then-living
Richard Nixon. It is as if the breakdown in the consensus as to
what constitutes reality entails that even something as recent and
'known' as this trial has to be rendered in ways which foregrounds
the question of the role of narrative in constructing our understanding of the world, and, by implication, meaning and truth.

Günter Grass's *The Tin Drum* (1959) and Thomas Pynchon's
Gravity's Rainbow (1973) both treat the Second World War in such
a radical way that alerts the reader to the issue of construction at
all levels. To conceptualise narrative in this manner is to radically
question how the world can be properly represented, or to accept

that what we have first and foremost is just 'representation', with no 'real' world beyond it. At one point Offred says, 'I am trying not to tell stories' (Atwood 1995: 60) and then 'We lived in the gaps between stories' (1995: 67) – the match between narrative representation and whatever it is that is supposedly represented remains intrinsically problematic. Narrative remains important within the novel and the Gileadean world – writing and language are under state control, suggestive of a continued power – but while it is central to the way we describe the world and our behaviour in it, what narrative is and what narrative can do is far removed from Realism.

Character

As well as reconceiving the nature of narrative, *The Handmaid's Tale* is also typical of postmodernism in the way it conceives of character. Again, 'self' and 'identity' may have different versions within works considered to be postmodern, but what underlies them is that characters do not have fixed identities as they do in Realism, and, to a certain extent, in modernism. Again, the underlying motif is 'construction', and just as the same narrative can be constructed in different ways (or the same narrative material can be ordered differently to create different narratives), there is a sense in postmodernism that what we understand to be our 'identity' or 'self' is a construction. The manner of construction varies considerably – in some postmodern manifestations we are able to reinvent ourselves continually. For instance, in Bharati Mukherjee's novel *Jasmine* (1989), the central character has a number of different identities throughout her life as she moves from an Indian village to America. Although her identity at each point is fairly well defined, the fact that her name and identity radically change suggests that character here has no ultimate stability.

In *The Handmaid's Tale*, identity is likewise far from a given, in the way that the reader is generally used to in Realist works: 'I wait. I compose myself. My self is a thing I must now compose, as one composes a speech. What I must present is a made thing, not something born' (Atwood 1995: 76). As already stated, one of the most impressive features of nineteenth-century

Realist fiction is the way it details 'character', the way it renders psychological nuances. But characters rarely behave 'out of character' – by definition, a 'character' consists of an identifiable group of characteristics. The interest, as Eliot states at the beginning of *Middlemarch*, is to see how 'character' responds in certain circumstances, to see how Lydgate's and Dorothea's characters fare under the microscope of provincial society over time. But for Offred to say 'My self is a thing I must now compose' suggests that there is nothing certain about the character at all, there are no definable characteristics. The self can be constructed, 'composed', virtually at will. This is not the Realist/realist understanding of self. Even Lawrence's notion of the 'allotropic' self retains a belief in a core element. In its various radical versions of what self and identity are, the postmodern aesthetic – underpinned by critical, philosophical, psychological and psychoanalytical understanding of self and identity – stands in opposition to the tenets of realism.

Metafiction

A common feature of postmodern works of art and literature is their self-referentiality. The final chapter of *The Handmaid's Tale*, mentioned above, is an example, since its discussion of the composition of 'The Handmaid's Tale' draws attention to the composition of the novel of the same name that we happen to be reading. In itself this may be regarded as an amusing or an annoying technique, but fiction that talks about fiction – 'metafiction' – has consequences for the way we might think about realism.

Although I deal with this in greater depth in the following chapters, a hostile view of Realism (and realism) is that Realist works represent the world as if the medium has no influence on what we apprehend – we 'see through' the language and narrative directly to the events and people depicted. With this view, we do not 'see' the tools by which this is achieved, we 'forget' that language and narrative are the means by which the worlds are constructed. This view of Realism therefore tends to regard metafictional technique as inherently anti-realist since it reminds readers that they are engaged with a piece of fiction, and thus by extension they are made aware that what is in front of them is purely a construct rather than an entry into a reasonably accurate reproduction of the real world. Any impression readers may get of experiencing the real world, or reality, is thus nothing more than an 'effect'. According to this view, Realist works in no way put the reader in touch with the real world, as a mirror or copy for instance, and do nothing other than create an illusion of reality, using illusion rather pejoratively in the sense of deception with sinister intent. However, we have already seen that in Realist novels, particularly in the work of George Eliot, for example, the narrator frequently draws attention to the fact that she is doing her best to give an accurate picture. Strictly speaking, such digressions are metafictional since within the novels the method of writing fictional narrative is brought to the attention of readers. But how can this be Realist, if it makes us aware of the constructed nature of narrative and representation?

Part of the answer is that it is clearly a mischaracterisation to see Realist texts as 'covering up' the fact that they are constructed. There is hardly a Realist novel that does not in some way draw attention to the writing or existence of novels, and certain novels such as those of Eliot offer extended metafictional consideration. The other part of the answer, therefore, must be that they are done with aims different from those of postmodern texts which also use metafictional techniques. For Eliot it is part of the contract with the Realist reader, an agreement that the author and the reader are engaged in working towards greater understanding and consensus as to the way the world is, with the attendant belief that language, narrative, characterisation, description and narratorial commentary can achieve this. This kind of metafiction is subordinated to the larger concerns and beliefs inherent in the Realist aesthetic. The metafictional elements, therefore, work towards greater stability. In postmodern works the metafictional elements are foregrounded to highlight the inherent instability of all these features, including the status of fiction itself. Metafiction in Realism works towards establishing clear boundaries between reality and fiction – fiction is not the real world, it is a representation of it, but one that we can agree on to a greater or lesser extent as true, accurate and faithful. Metafiction in postmodern works has a quite different rationale, since its assumption is that there is nothing to separate the world and the representation of the world – the world is a 'fiction' just as much as 'fiction' (novel) is fiction.

Authority

In addition to the increasing importance awarded to language, narrative and discourse, and changes in the conception of human identity and what 'human' itself means, a feature of postmodernism is what Jean-François Lyotard called 'the decline of metanarrative'. A metanarrative is a narrative which explains all other narratives; a metanarrative is therefore the 'master' narrative. For many cultures such master narratives are provided by religion and religious texts, such as the Bible. But a philosophy such as Marxism also functions as a metanarrative since it explains how societies came about, how they function, why humans are constituted as they are, and why they behave as they do. Lyotard's assertion, and one that has been accepted to differing degrees, is that we can no longer wholeheartedly subscribe to any metanarrative. There is no God-like position from which we can understand and judge. There are no authorities to which we can appeal.

Some of this is a consequence of what has been said about narrative, or, to broaden it out, representation in general. If there is no real world to be described, but instead competing narratives and representations, competing 'constructs', we are in a world which is shot through with relativism. Underpinning both the Realist and the modernist aesthetics is an idea that there are truths to be had. The manner of discovering these, and identifying those truths that are important, and how they can be then represented in art, differ. The postmodern ethos simply does not, and cannot, sign up to this. It would be different if we could all accept the same master narrative, or agree what truth was and what it should be truth about, or if science could guarantee that its version of the world was correct in all aspects; but none of this appears to be the case.

There are three epigrams at the start of *The Handmaid's Tale*, the first and third of which relate to this dismantling of the notion of authority. Taken within the context of the novel, they also lead on to the postmodern relativist view of the world, an idea that rather than fixity and stability and authority, it is not possible to judge between versions of the world.

The first quotation is from the Bible, and repeats the passage from Genesis where Rachel, unable to bare Jacob's children, suggests that he goes to her maid Bilhah where she can 'bear upon my knees, that I may also have children by her'. That this passage becomes the 'authority' for the authorities in Gilead to instigate the system of handmaids suggests that authority itself does not come to us as a clear communication but is itself subject to the forces of discourse, interpretation and representation. In other words the Bible cannot be taken as an authority, or rather it can be used to authorise one particular view of the world, with the novel's suggestion, therefore, that it could just as easily be interpreted and used in other ways and does not in itself represent any kind of ultimate authority.

The third quotation is a Sufi proverb: 'In the desert there is no stone that says, Thou shalt not eat stones.' What does this mean? One interpretation might be that we are in fact in a desert and so find ourselves without authoritative guidance. If such is our state, who is to tell us right from wrong? Again, where is the authority that can tell us what is right in the world, or how the world is? It might seem self-evident that we should not eat stones, but perhaps it also means that without authority we are free to do what we wish. There are certainly other possible ways of interpreting this, but this in itself indicates that we are caught up in interpretation and contested viewpoints, rather than in a position of being able to fix the world as it is.

Magical realism

A style of literature termed 'magical realism' coincided with postmodernism and postmodern fiction. It is sometimes regarded as part of the postmodern aesthetic, but also regarded as having a separate agenda, largely political and more in keeping with postcolonial art and literature. One history takes it back to 1920s Weimar Germany, with a second phase in 1940s Central America, and the more recognisable third phase beginning in Latin America in 1955 (Bowers 2004: 8). Gabriel García Márquez is its most famous exponent from Latin America, and Borges one of the notable influences. A European tradition is also often advanced,

with the work of Kafka significant (see, for example, the short
story 'Metamorphosis'), with later writers such as Günter Grass
(*The Tin Drum*, 1959), Salman Rushdie (*Midnight's Children*,
1981) and Angela Carter (*Nights at the Circus*, 1984) contributing.
Novels such as Toni Morrison's *Beloved* (1987) and Gloria
Naylor's *Mama Day* (1988) clearly might also bear a relation to
magic realist writing.

Gabriel García Márquez: *One Hundred Years of Solitude*

Much of what has been said about postmodern writing applies to
magical realism. At a base level it stands in opposition to all the
tenets of Realism that we have advanced, since it refuses to understand character, narrative, description, language and discourse in
the traditional manner. It is 'tradition' that is quite often the
contested term for magical realist literature, which is also quite
often postcolonial. Whose tradition is being referred to?
Postcolonial magical realist texts often usurp the 'Western' tradition of authority with other kinds of authority, usually emanating
from peoples and ways of life previously seen as marginal to the
white, male, European hegemony. Novels such as Márquez's *One
Hundred Years of Solitude* (first published in 1967) illustrate the
irreconcilable clash between Western modernity and indigenous
cultures. What distinguishes magical realist writing from other
related forms is its insistence on making no ontological distinction
between what is 'real' and what is 'magical'. One of the results of
this is that it inherently challenges a worldview which is that of the
Realist aesthetic, since it does not defer to Enlightenment reason
and rationality, and does not feel bound to separate fact from
fiction in order to arrive at Truth.

Magical realism revels in a carnival approach to the world,
embracing one or more of myth, folklore, the supernatural, the
inexplicable, the irrational and the surreal. The reason it is termed
magical realism is not just down to the placement of 'magic' and
'real' on the same ontological plane, but also because the techniques of realist writing are used to describe events, objects and
characters which are of a fantastic nature. Similarly, seemingly
normal items can seem quite magical when placed in a different
cultural context. Our exemplary text here is *One Hundred Years of*

Solitude.

The novel takes in the history of the village of Macondo in the South American jungle, and the history of a family living there. The book is prefaced with a family tree, and the reader immediately notices the similarity of the names, including Aureliano, of which there are nearly twenty. There are no birth dates, and no indication of time period, and the novel's opening line continues this disorientation: 'Many years later, as he faced the firing squad, Colonel Aureliano Buendía was to remember that distant afternoon when his father took him to discover ice' (Márquez 1978: 9). Where are we in time? At least with Woolf we know that Clarissa Dalloway is both 18 and 50 plus, even if there is a certain conflation of the time periods. Here, not only do we seem to be plunged into three time periods at once – the now, the later at the firing squad, the earlier in the distant afternoon – we have only just discovered ice, so that it seems like we might be ...? 'The world was so recent that many things lacked names, and in order to indicate them it was necessary to point' (1978: 9). We are at the start of the world, but surely we are not. Every March a family of gypsies comes to the village and bring new inventions, such as the magnet: '"Things have a life of their own," the gypsy proclaimed with a harsh accent. "It's simply a matter of waking up their souls"' (1978: 9). Thus, in addition to the Western nature of time and history being cast into doubt, the world itself is supernatural.

The novel continues in this fashion of casually creating a world that seems fantastical and real at the same time, in prose which is 'accessible' and down to earth in the face of what seems implausible and impossible. For instance, the village is stricken with a plague of insomnia, and in order that others are not infected with insomnia it goes into a state of quarantine (1978: 45). The people become used to it and so sleeplessness becomes the norm. In order to cope with the attendant memory loss Aureliano (the first one) decides to label every object, first in his laboratory and then in the whole village, marking things such as '*table, chair, clock, door, wall, bed, pan*' (1978: 46). However, he realises that people might be able to name things but not know what their use is, so objects are also given descriptions:

> The sign that he hung on the neck of the cow was an exemplary
> proof of the way in which the inhabitants of Macondo were
> prepared to fight against loss of memory: *This is the cow. She must be
> milked every morning so that she will produce milk, and the milk must be
> boiled in order to be mixed with coffee to make coffee and milk*. Thus
> they went on living in a reality that was slipping away, momentarily
> captured by words, but which would escape irremediably when they
> forgot the values of the written words. (Márquez 1978: 46)

The passage is intent on revealing the faulty mechanism of
language as our access to the world. The words initially seem to
map on to the world of objects – the physical world, the real world
– in an easy, one-to-one fashion. But this soon proves inadequate,
for the name of a thing does not give you the object in any way. The
attempt to circumvent this with added description only points up
how a word is nothing more than the symbol of a way of thinking
about something, which itself is wholly inadequate to represent
the object. Everything fails here: language, representation, understanding, classification. The ontology necessary for any kind of
realism is wholly missing: written using prose that indicates a
description of the real world, it is the fantastic which seems wholly
normal.

One other episode in the novel will serve to show the political
significance of blending what would seem to be two distinct
worlds. A massacre takes place, of 3,000 people involved in a strike
against a banana company. All the corpses are put on a train and
taken away. The only survivor is José Arcadio Segundo, but
nobody believes his story, and the government issues statements to
the effect that the strike has been resolved and the workers'
demands met. Any enquiry into lost relatives is simply met with
the official response: "'You must have been dreaming" ...
"Nothing has happened in Macondo, nothing has ever happened,
and nothing ever will happen. This is a happy town'" (1978: 252).
With no other witnesses to back up his story, the government's
version of events holds sway and their version of reality wins out.
What counts as real is therefore a consequence of who has the
authority over stories and, ultimately, history. The implication is
that what we take to be 'real' is here nothing other than the
discourse of those in charge. If the 'plague of insomnia' episode

signals a failure of language to give us reality, the massacre episode suggests that our access to reality is barred by the construction of authoritative narratives. In this, then, all possibility of asserting that there is a real world seems doomed, and with it (arguably) there is a considerable pessimism since reality is nothing other than a political construct. Just as the people who were massacred never existed, Macondo itself disappears at the end of the novel.

After postmodernism

The views and aesthetic designated 'postmodern' arguably held sway in the arts, science, humanities and other fields from the 1960s to the 1990s. As an identifiable aesthetic, rather like Realism and modernism before it, it has perhaps now run its course, although inevitably many of its characteristics and features continue into the present, even when commentators may not wish to use the term postmodernism. It is perhaps more accurate to say that the heat has gone out of many of the debates surrounding the more extreme, relativist versions of postmodernism. Whatever the case, the realist impulse, and realism, has remained throughout the twentieth and twenty-first centuries, and possibly remains popularly dominant, if still on the periphery of critical respectability. It is still the case that to work within realism is perceived by some critics to be the equivalent of using a mode which has long been superseded.

I end the chapter by looking at Joshua Ferris's *Then We Came to the End*, a novel published in 2007. It describes the minutiae of everyday life in the office of an advertising agency, with the unusual device of using the first-person plural for its narrative perspective. It is an example of a novel that is engaged with Realism/realism, and attempts to rework this aesthetic against a backdrop of the postmodern critique of realist representation.

Joshua Ferris: *Then We Came to the End*
Here is the opening paragraph of the novel, to give you a general flavour, and to show how the first-person plural works:

> We were fractious and overpaid. Our mornings lacked promise. At
> least those of us who smoked had something to look forward to at

ten-fifteen. Most of us liked most everyone, a few of us hated specific individuals, one or two people loved everyone and everything.
Those who loved everyone were unanimously reviled. We loved free
bagels in the morning. They happened all too infrequently. Our
benefits were astonishing in comprehensiveness and quality of care.
Sometimes we questioned whether they were worth it. We thought
moving to India might be better, or going back to nursing school.
Doing something with the handicapped or working with our hands.
No one ever acted on these impulses, despite their daily, sometimes
hourly contractions. Instead we met in conference rooms to discuss
the issues of the day. (Ferris 2007: 3)

Being unusual and overtly so, the narrative perspective immediately becomes foregrounded, and thus draws attention to the
narrative method itself in a way which we have seen is a feature
both of modernism and postmodernism. However, the focus on
mundane routine, detail, a group of white-collar workers, and as
we soon discover, the workings of post-industrial capitalism,
suggest that it is also very much concerned with the same areas as
the Realist novel. Indeed, as we discover, it is also concerned to see
how 'sympathy' plays out in the aftermath of a constant trickle of
redundancies, and the type of Realist novel typified by Gaskell is
here updated in the relations between the office workers and the
senior management responsible for hiring and firing.

What is new is Ferris's use of the first-person plural narrative
perspective in a way which I think addresses a problem for the
Realist novel. As previously stated, there is an argument that there
is a causal link between the novel's emergence as the dominant
literary form in the nineteenth century and the rise of the middle
classes. The argument is premised on the idea that the novel's
form reflects the interests of the middle classes, or the bourgeoisie, because the novel is the most appropriate medium for
portraying autonomous individuals who can succeed through their
own hard work. There is something about the form of the novel
which easily accommodates the progress of the individual or individuals, and obviously its ability to represent the life and
consciousness of an individual so well is largely down to its manipulation of narrative perspective. Conversely, the novel form has
had difficulty in dealing with groups *as groups*. In other words, the

novel genre can show groups from the outside as a collective, as a crowd, as the working classes often are thus represented in the nineteenth-century novel, or as a collection of representative individuals, so-called types or stereotypes, as, say, happens in novels such as *Middlemarch* and *Germinal*. What it has not seemed so able to do, or wanted to do, is show a group as a group from *inside* the group.

Ferris's novel itself is aware of the issue of realism and capitalism in relation to the novel, and although the book is predominantly realist, it appears to use a postmodern metafictional element towards the end of the novel when one of the people from the office gets a novel published, very much like the one we are reading, and talks about it with other people from the office:

> 'In the first book I tried to write,' he explained, 'the book I put down, I based a character on Lynn, and I made that character into a tyrant. I did it on principle, because anyone who was a boss in that book *had* to be a tyrant. Anyone who believed in the merits of capitalism, and soul-destroying corporations, and work work work – all that – naturally that person wasn't deserving of any sympathy. But when I decided to retire that book, thank god, and write something different, I knew she was sick, so I went to see her. Just on a lark. Because what did I know about her? Nothing, really. I didn't know her – not in any meaningful way. And it turned out she was very open to talking with me, not only about her sickness, but also her personal life, a lot of other things ...' (Ferris 2007: 377)

It is as if Joshua Ferris has read the Marxist critic Lukács on what the realist novel should do – that is, it should expose the workings of capitalism, and it should use a 'type' such as the tyrannical boss with which to do it – and has realised that this would not work because it would not be an accurate report from reality. So he finds out the real truth about the person and then writes the realist novel – which is very much in keeping with what literary realism is supposed to do. As argued above, it is sometimes claimed that such metafictional elements undermine claims to realism, but here is a case of it reinforcing a realist premise, for just as Eliot's narrators are constantly vigilant in maintaining a fidelity to reality, so here the putative novelist has adjusted his technique for precisely the same reason. As a whole, *Then We Came to the End* highlights the issues around the novel genre, realism, representation, capitalism and reality. It is an experimental realism that counteracts the post-modern version of the world, while accepting the fact that we cannot simply take reality on trust, nor represent it, in the manner of the nineteenth-century Realists. Nevertheless, it does return the reader to the idea that it is possible to get at a consensual view of the way the world is, and how it might be described.

Works cited and further reading

Atwood, Margaret (1995), *The Handmaid's Tale*. London: Virago.

Bowen, Elizabeth (1962), *The Death of the Heart*. Harmondsworth: Penguin.

Bowers, Maggie Ann (2004), *Magical Realism*. London: Routledge.

Carter, Angela (1985), *Nights at the Circus*. London: Pan Books.

Cooper, William (1969), *Scenes from Provincial Life*. London: Macmillan.

Drolet, Michael (ed.) (2004), *The Postmodernism Reader: Foundational Texts*. London: Routledge.

Ferris, Joshua (2007), *Then We Came to the End*. London: Viking.

Grass, Günter (1989), *The Tin Drum*. London: Pan.

Hutcheon, Linda (1988), *A Poetics of Postmodernism: History, Theory, Fiction*. London: Routledge.

Lee, Alison (1990), *Realism and Power. Postmodern British Fiction*. London: Routledge.

Lehmann, Rosamond (1991), *The Weather in the Streets*. London: Virago.

Márquez, Gabriel Gárcia (1978), *One Hundred Years of Solitude*. London: Picador.

McHale, Brian (1987), *Postmodernist Fiction*. London: Methuen.

Morrison, Toni (1988), *Beloved*. London: Picador.

Naylor, Gloria (1990), *Mama Day*. London: Vintage.

Orwell, George (1983), *Keep the Aspidistra Flying* in *The Penguin Complete Novels of George Orwell*. Harmondsworth: Penguin.

Pynchon, Thomas (1975), *Gravity's Rainbow*. London: Picador.

Sillitoe, Alan (1994), *Saturday Night Sunday Morning*. London: Flamingo.

Skelton, Robin (ed.) (1964), *Poetry of the Thirties*. London: Penguin.

Stevenson, Randall (1992), *Modernist Fiction*. Hertfordshire: Harvester Wheatsheaf.

Waugh, Patricia (1984), *Metafiction: The Theory and Practice of Self-Conscious Fiction*. London: Methuen.

Woods, Tim (1999), *Beginning Postmodernism*. Manchester: Manchester University Press.

Zamora, Lois Parkinson and Wendy B. Faris (eds) (1995), *Magical Realism*. Durham and London: Duke University Press.

Interlude

The previous chapters have discussed Realism in detail, along with modernism and postmodernism as they relate to this aesthetic. The assumption here is that art and literature can be organised into these categories, which themselves relate to broader cultural trends, and that these trends follow one another in a fairly orderly fashion. In adopting this approach I have also presented arguments and views in a rather general manner rather than tying them to particular theorists or theoretical views, other than those pertinent to arguments at the time. This approach is, therefore, Realism as it mainly appears in literary history. I hope that this has provided a very strong understanding of what Realism is, or at least shown solidly how it can be conceptualised within a broad literary historical view. Armed with this (you have finished 'beginning realism'!) the remaining chapters look at particular theories and theorists of realism. This will provide the opportunity to get more deeply involved with the issues surrounding Realism as they have developed throughout the twentieth century in relation to literature, and to cover certain issues which I have not dealt with at length for the sake of presenting a more readily comprehensible picture of Realism and realism. Chapter 9, on language, suggests again that there are other approaches to Realism/realism, one more obviously synchronic than historical. The chapters on philosophy and on realism in the age of new media again offer other perspectives on the concept of realism which are not dependent on literary history.

8

Theorists of Realism

Introduction

In this chapter I aim to give a sense of some of the most important critical work on literary realism from the mid-twentieth century to the present. The field is complex, contributing no doubt to the belief that realism is a 'slippery' term, and there can be no attempt here to be comprehensive. I begin by giving a sketch of the different channels of thought and arguments, and also place them in relation to the discussion on the preceding pages. One aspect that will emerge as significant, and which has not been quite so apparent as yet, is the political nature of discussions about realism. Although some of the earlier discussions listed below (1930s–1950s) might be viewed as past their sell-by date, particularly those which depend heavily on the viability of socialist structures, I think that there is more here than just historical interest in the fortunes of realist criticism over the last seventy years or so. It might be possible to argue for a 'poetics of realism' that aims to stand outside the political dimension, but that would be to miss the fact that as an aesthetic realism has always had a considerable political force, either as part of the status quo or as a challenge to existing political, cultural and social orders. Simultaneously, the 'poetics' strand of literary criticism that sees its task as the analysis and categorisation of technical features remains a persistent feature in literature on realism.

1930s–1950s

Auerbach's *Mimesis* (1946) is a seminal work in the field of literary realism, and close in time-period is Watt's equally seminal *The Rise of the Novel*, published in 1957, although drawing on work that he had begun twenty years earlier. Both of these books aim for a poetics of realism, that is, both books present realism as a particular 'form' comprised of specific techniques, developed and utilised by writers as the result of particular philosophical outlooks embedded within social practices and structures. Auerbach surveys European literature from Homer to the beginning of the twentieth century, whereas Watt focuses on Defoe, Richardson and Fielding as the main instigators of the novel form, a form that, he argues, is characterised by 'formal realism'. Implicit in Watt's book therefore is the idea that these novelists provide a blueprint for the novel genre, a genre which is defined by realism and understood to find its fullest expression in the nineteenth century. Similarly, although Auerbach takes us all the way back to Homer, he too finds literary realism's fullest realisation in the nineteenth century. As the reader will immediately see, that view of literary realism in this larger chronological context is one that has been followed by this book.

Neither of these books directly engages in a sustained manner with literary realism in a political context, although it can certainly be argued that they are the result of quite specific historical and political circumstances attendant upon the Second World War. It is interesting to compare Watt's and Auerbach's books in terms of their coverage. Watt's is resolutely Anglocentric while Auerbach's is firmly Eurocentric. This may simply be the result of the particular interests of the authors and their backgrounds, but it is worth suggesting that there is a political dimension to this, with both writers defending what is culturally valuable in the face of those totalitarian threats to the rich cultural heritage on which Auerbach and Watt draw. Auerbach's book becomes quite explicit about this defence of culture in its closing pages.

Outside of Auerbach and Watt in the period between the 1930s and 1950s there is an overt political discussion of the merits of realism, and just as Watt and Auerbach's work has had significant impact on the way we think about realism and the novel form, the ongoing debates between Lukács, Adorno, Brecht and others has had a lasting effect on the way realism is seen in political terms. This argument was largely concerned with which aesthetic was more conducive to a socialist agenda – modernism or realism. For Lukács modernism's inaccessibility to a popular audience meant that it could never be part of a project to empower the masses. For the opposing camp, still with the socialist agenda at the forefront, only by breaking through that artistic form which was capitalism's most powerful aesthetic tool – realism – could the establishment of socialism be effected in Europe.

1960s–

The end of the 1950s onwards saw the arrival of theories and theorists which come under the umbrella terms structuralism and poststructuralism. We have already seen, in Chapter 7 on post-modernism, what some of these ideas mean for literary realism, since these theories had a two-way relationship with the postmodern aesthetic and related philosophical and critical ideas. The notion of 'constructedness' remains central, but it is also usual for these discussions to emanate from a broadly left-wing, radical tradition. Hence the political-aesthetic arguments of Lukács and Adorno continue through into the work of the poststructuralists whose position is generally hostile to realism. For many poststructuralist critics, the realist aesthetic comes to be regarded as an intrinsically bourgeois aesthetic, and Barthes's essay 'The Reality Effect' is a well-known piece in the dissection of realist writing, part of the more general left-wing critical attack on all things bourgeois. Lukács's earlier left-wing position therefore loses out to later arguments, but it might also be argued that the earlier left-wing assertion that modernist avant-gardism is an inherently anti-realist/anti-bourgeois aesthetic is overtaken by the postmodern and poststructural arguments of writers like Barthes, where modernism becomes less of an issue.

Influential in its popularisation of this anti-realist critique is Catherine Belsey's *Critical Practice* (1980). Belsey offers lucid accounts of the structuralist and post-structuralist positions and, drawing on the work of Colin MacCabe and Stephen Heath, she provided a solid attack on realist literature and its proponents. Besley's book is also important because it suggests that readers themselves need to break out of 'realism' in their own reading practices.

The work of Riffaterre and Kearns is less familiar, offering a different kind of challenge to critical perceptions of realism outside the mainstream or what is critically fashionable. While I am not really persuaded into seeing realism as they do, their deliberate provocations open up realism in ways that more straightforward accounts cannot always achieve.

The general drift throughout the twentieth century, and into the current one, is a certain hostility towards what realism is believed to stand for, most forcefully put in the work of Belsey and others. However, the strong defenders of realism, and its particular manifestation in the novel, are Auerbach, Lukács, Bakhtin and Watt. 'Defenders' may be too strong a word, other than in relation to Lukács, since these writers are often presenting realism in an analytical fashion, both historically and as a poetics. Hopefully there is enough here to point the reader in the direction of the large field of interesting critical work on literary realism.

Eric Auerbach: *Mimesis* (1946)

Auerbach's immense work surveys the whole European tradition of literature, from the Greeks, through the Romans and into Christian writing, and covers the great works and writers of European literature: Homer, the Bible, Dante, Boccaccio, Shakespeare, Cervantes, Proust. It is not possible in the space here to do justice to all the subtleties of argument, but I will outline the main threads, and in doing so hopefully reinforce and enhance the picture of literary realism that we have already built up.

The first thing to consider is Auerbach's use of the term 'mimesis' rather than realism. The book tends to regard the terms as interchangeable and when looking at Auerbach it is perhaps wise to bear in mind the distinctions I made earlier between realism and mimesis. For instance, he is very keen to argue that Dante is a realist, even if the setting is in the world beyond the empirical one and the characters are not involved in earthly matters. In the way that Realism has been defined in this book, we would say that Auerbach is interested in mimetic effects, which are part of a realist impulse, but it is not what we would say amounts to 'realism'. What Auerbach's book does do is trace 'the realist impulse' in literature over this large tradition. As he works his way towards the eighteenth and nineteenth centuries, he picks out those major trends in philosophical thought, changes in social structures and political ideology, which help make a fully-blown realism possible. What are these forces?

As part of our picture of realism I have suggested that a fundamental concern is its serious interest in the everyday lives of ordinary people. For Auerbach, a prime reason for this is the 'Christianisation' of Western civilisation, and Auerbach's book and argument has a religious subtext of Christian progression. The fact that the Bible, in particular the story of Christ's Passion, has the most dignified material mixed in with the lowliest (Christ's life is lived among the humbler elements in society), dissolves a traditional 'separation of styles', that is, the 'elevated' style is no longer reserved for upper social strata but can be used as the style to treat 'lowly' characters and subject matter. The realist novel example he gives is Stendhal's *Le Rouge et Le Noir*, published in 1830 and set in that year. Its protagonist is Julien Sorel, the son of a carpenter: 'So logically and systematically to situate the tragically conceived life of a man of low social position (as here that of Julien Sorel) within the most concrete kind of contemporary history and to develop it therefrom – this is an entirely new and highly signifi-cant phenomenon' (Auerbach 1991: 457–8).

This is a constant theme throughout Auerbach's book – the argument for realism that the life of somebody not of an elevated social class is worthy of substantial literary treatment. Significant for Auerbach is that the life of a lowly person can be 'tragically conceived'. Previously, such realism was only suited to low comedy, that is, in the interests of literary decorum it was only possible to have representations of society's lower orders if they were not treated as seriously as the more noble elements. For Auerbach, progress of Christianity in Western civilisation means that art and literature increasingly becomes more predisposed towards a realism which has no 'separation of styles', and therefore towards an art and literature which is able to accommodate all that needs to be accommodated of reality (although even here it is complicated, see p. 120).

The notion that realism is part-characterised by its serious regard for the lives of the majority, and not just the privileged, is thus here given a particular motivation, that of Christian democratic levelling – we are all equal in God's eyes. Although the general point about democratisation is one usually accepted in conceptualising realism, the strength of Christian belief as an influence is a moot point. Later appreciations of Auerbach often put him firmly into his time of writing, as I have done above. In this aspect of the book, as well as the book as a whole, there is seen to be an attempt to make Western literature a bastion of civilisation against National Socialism, a plea that the book itself makes towards the end (1991: 551).

This place for realism as a counter to Nazi ideology is bolstered by a humanism that Auerbach assumes his audience has and desires, and which is also part of a fully-exercised realism. He assumes that his humanist audience will appreciate a particular kind of sentiment: an elevated style, which at the same time embraces the humblest (the argument again for the Bible's representation of Christ's life) and to which a particular kind of reader is sympathetic. Here is a good example of Auerbach discovering the humanism that underlies realism in Dante's *Inferno*:

> When we hear Cavalcante's outburst ... or read the beautiful, gentle, and enchantingly feminine line which Pia de' Tolomei utters before she asks Dante to remember her on earth ... we experience an emotion which is concerned with human beings and not directly with the divine order in which they have found their fulfillment. Their eternal position in the divine order is something of which we are only conscious as a setting whose irrevocability can but serve to heighten the effect of their humanity, preserved for us in all its force. The result is a direct experience of life which overwhelms everything else, a comprehension of human realities which spreads as widely and variously as it goes profoundly to the very roots of our emotions, an illumination of man's impulses and passions which leads us to share in them without restraint and indeed to admire their variety and their greatness. (1991: 201–2)

The argument for realism here is that although set in hell, Dante's work is able to render the 'reality' of human emotion within the context of 'humanity'. Auerbach downplays the religious context in favour of humanism when he states that such an emotion as displayed here does not belong to the 'divine order'. He thus identifies in Dante elements which we see as also crucial to our definition of Realism: the emphasis on the world as experienced on earth by a human nature common to all. And in general for Auerbach, it is humanism in the sixteenth century which introduces a wider perspective for artistic representation, one that includes historical depth and an inclusion of different peoples.

With different emphases, all of the above accords with our picture of those features which act as a prelude to nineteenth-century Realism. However, there are parts to Auerbach's argument which have not been part of our picture of Realism, but which are also worthy of attention.

Auerbach finds different realisms in different historical periods, with the underlying impression that modern realism represents the most thoroughgoing. Although I have argued that we might reconceive Auerbach's version as one that traces the ever-present realist impulse through until we get the dominance of the Realist aesthetic in the nineteenth century, there is rather more to his argument than this allows. For Auerbach, the kinds of realism to be found prior to modern realism are not complete. Each period in history has its own particular forms which permeate all of society, not just the upper strata, and which are not to be understood just through major political events (1991: 444). This kind of understanding of the past, 'Historism', also comes to be applied to the present. It then seems for Auerbach that realist works must appreciate and represent these deep structures. Realism, in other words, has to be able to fully appreciate how a society is structured in order to be able to function properly as realism. But this is complicated because not all societies have been definable in this way, and it is only those that can be identified as homogenous at a structural level which can be understood and appreciated. For realist writing to be able to flourish, then, the writer has to be living in a society which is organised in a homogenous way.

In Goethe's time, for instance, 'the social picture was

heterogenous', so it was not possible to provide a coherent, 'realist' picture. 'Organic' then becomes a key concept for Auerbach and his argument for realism. It has to be possible for a realist writer to firmly place a character in his or her social milieu, and that can only be attempted and achieved if there is a unity to the milieu. The use of the organic metaphor for character and society also reads as a continuation of the idea that Realist writers are obliged to see characters as absolutely tied to their environment. Accompanying this organic view there also needs to be an understanding of the reality of a country as a whole. For instance, Auerbach argues that France could be understood as a unity at the time of Balzac, whereas Germany could not (1991: 473), hence we get Balzac's realism.

Although I have not advanced such a line of argument about the importance of coherent pictures of societies and nations, it is one that in different manifestations has appeared intermittently. By definition, the condition-of-England novels of authors such as Gaskell and Disraeli are premised on the idea that they have a sense that what they describe is the state of England at that time – 'the way we live now', to quote the title of one of Trollope's novels. Simultaneously, there is the assumption on the part of the usually omniscient narrators that they are speaking to a relatively homogenous audience about a society which was either instantly recognisable (middle-class) or seen as completing the social picture (the revelation of working-class conditions, for instance). Implicitly, and in keeping with the Realist idea of empirical reality and a concomitant social specificity, it may be seen that this part of Auerbach's argument bears some relation to an understanding of Realism.

But how specific to realism (and Realism) this is must be debatable, since art of many types may lay claim to taking the temperature of the society depicted. Nevertheless, the nation-state is a relatively new formation and the perception of it as a means of social and political management and unification might have some bearing on the way that Realism is conceptualised. The influential American critic William Dean Howells argued that America's national literature should be Realist, and that it was a national duty to be Realist in order to represent American society to the American people. There were similar arguments in other European countries – that a Realist literature was required in order to help build a sense of national identity.

There is an added political dimension to this which remains part of the argument about realism up to the present. On reading *Mimesis* it becomes clear that Auerbach sees that one of the main features of realism is its treatment of the underlying social and economic forces and conditions of any given society and epoch. In this way, realism – in societies where to reveal such conditions might run counter to the prevailing ideology of the governing body and class(es) – has the potential to be read as revolutionary or dangerous. This view of Auerbach's is worth holding on to, for it suggests that realism always has a potential as a political force. It is one that was held by Lukács (in a different way), as we shall see, but one that has since been consistently opposed, for reasons already mentioned (mainly, a perceived intrinsic conservatism). For Auerbach, however, it was another feature of realism's ability to stand up to immoral political regimes, regimes that ran counter to his humanist outlook and humanity in general.

STOP and THINK

Is realism the best means of uncovering and representing abuse in society? Does it provide the most powerful tool for artists who wish to challenge social and political convention? Or do the aesthetic tenets of postmodernism, postcolonialism and magic realism offer more credible artistic challenges? Or are they evasions of, and escapes from, reality?

If the political context for Auerbach was the rise of National Socialism, the aesthetic context was modernism, which offered the most recent major achievements in literature, such as the work of Woolf and Proust, and Auerbach spends some time on Woolf's *To the Lighthouse*, published in 1926, little more than ten to fifteen years prior to Auerbach's research. What he says about these works and modernism provides an interesting additional perspective on our discussion of realism, modernism, and will return us once again to the political nature of these debates.

To the Lighthouse focuses on the thoughts and impressions of

the Ramsay family, and is similar to *Mrs Dalloway* in its rendering
of consciousness as the means to represent our apprehension of
the world. Auerbach talks about Woolf's use of free indirect
discourse in relation to this (1991: 536–8). He sees the novel's use
of multiple consciousnesses as an attempt to approach an objective
view of Mrs Ramsay, the central character, rather than seeing such
a technique as a withdrawal from an objective worldview. The
modernist use of multiple subjective perspectives therefore adds
up to a kind of triangulation for Auerbach that he sees as continu-
ous with the precepts of Realism. He sees the technique of free
indirect discourse everywhere in modernism, but claims that the
abandonment of external realities for these multiple perspectives
makes for a 'richer and more essential interpretation of them'
(1991: 545).

However, just a few pages further on, this view of modernism as
a continuation of Realism has quite a dark political aspect, and this
relates again to notions of organicism and national unity (1991:
551ff), and taps into despair at a world that has witnessed two
global wars in the space of thirty years. He describes the technique
of the modernists as one of 'dissolving reality' into multiple
perspectives, and sees in this a hopelessness that is part of that
decline of civilisation which has led to two world wars and the rise
of fascism. That Joyce's *Ulysses* (1922) itself is unfathomable is
symptomatic of the bigger picture – the world itself is unfathomable. Auerbach concludes by arguing that the focus on 'the
random moment' viewed without prejudice – something typical of
modernists like Woolf, Joyce and Proust – means that what is
common to all people (elemental) comes more to the fore and is a
possible means of finding a 'common life of mankind on earth'.
Hence, at the same time that modernist writing appears to be the
result of Western civilisation's descent into barbarity, the fact that
it can mirror modern chaos by detecting those moments which
represent a common humanity means that there is as yet (humanist) hope. However, this is perhaps where we need to return to a
distinction between Realism and mimesis, and our discussion of
modernism. As mentioned, 'mirroring' in itself might be mimetic,
but it is not necessarily Realism. The dissolution of a consensual
view of what the world looks like or what it is, and the dissolution

of a common moral framework, suggest that the tenets of Realism are indeed strained to breaking in modernist works and thought.

Ian Watt: *The Rise of the Novel* (1957)

I should point out immediately that Watt and Auerbach have two quite different aims. Auerbach wants to observe how mimesis – our realist impulse – culminates in the achievements of literary realism, and to do this he ranges across European literary history. Watt's is a narrower focus, for his aim is to identify works by Daniel Defoe, Samuel Richardson and Henry Fielding that are central to the development of the novel form. For Watt it is these three novelists in the eighteenth century who lay down the blue-print for the novel, significantly aided by a new reading public and a change in the social and moral climate. However, to illustrate how these authors created the novel form, Watt has first to iden-tify the characteristics of the novel, and it is in doing this that he outlines what realism is. His argument observes the transform-ation from the worldview of the Middle Ages, its belief in the world beyond and ideal forms, to the modern worldview (sixteenth century onwards) and its increasing interest in the earthly human. I quote the following passage at length since it gives a good account of Watt's argument.

> The narrative method whereby the novel embodies this circumstan-tial view of life may be called its formal realism; formal, because the term realism does not here refer to any special literary doctrine or purpose, but only to a set of narrative procedures which are so commonly found together in the novel, and so rarely in other liter-ary genres, that they may be regarded as typical of the form itself. Formal realism, in fact, is the narrative embodiment of a premise that Defoe and Richardson accepted very literally, but which is implicit in the novel form in general: the premise, or primary convention, that the novel is a full and authentic report of human experience, and is therefore under an obligation to satisfy its reader with such details of the story as to the individuality of the actors concerned, the particulars of the times and places of their actions, details which are presented through a more largely referential use of language than is common in other literary forms.

Formal realism is, of course, like the rules of evidence, only a
convention; and there is no reason why the report on human life
which is presented by it should be in fact any truer than those
presented through the very different conventions of other literary
genres. The novel's air of total authenticity, indeed, does tend to
authorise confusion on this point: and the tendency of some Realists
and Naturalists to forget that the accurate transcription of actuality
does not necessarily produce a work of any real truth or enduring
literary value is no doubt partly responsible for the rather widespread distaste for Realism and all its works which is current today.
(Watt 1957: 32)

Some of this readily accords with the picture we have built of
Realism and realism, especially the emphasis on particularity of
time and place, and the plausibility of actions. We should note that
Watt is keen to point out that although the novel may have appropriated to itself the appearance of greater authority in its 'report
on human life' in comparison to other art forms, this is an illusion
partly fostered by the Realists and Naturalists themselves.
Compared with other art forms, Realism is not intrinsically superior in its ability to represent human experience.

Leading up to the passage above Watt argues that one of the
major shifts of worldview from that of the Middle Ages to that of
the modern world is that instead of timeless truths there is an
insistence on the authentic report from experience of the individual, and this is the result of philosophical work such as that of
Locke and Descartes. Instead, in the modern world, what is true is
not to be given to us by tradition and received wisdom handed
down by religious and other established authorities, but only what
can be verified by our sense impressions and the mind's scepticism
as it is applied to empirical reality. This empirical reality is also
one characterised by an interest in earthly time, and the idea that a
person's 'character' is under the influence of this kind of time
(rather than subject to eternal time), means that experience has to
be rendered more 'slowly' than other art forms are able to deal
with. This, in turn, leads to the works of Defoe and Richardson,
whose novels such as *Moll Flanders* and *Pamela* are interested in
the very particular experiences of individuals, rendered in such a
way as to seem to be authentic accounts and where we observe the

influence of time on character. Such kind of biographical narrative organisation – Watt's formal realism – then becomes central to
his understanding of the novel form.

While much of the above contributes to the way *Beginning
Realism* has described the Realist novel, Watt's emphasis on the
'individual authentic account' as the central interest, along with
his assertion that 'the term realism does not here refer to any
special literary doctrine or purpose', does mark a difference from
our picture of the Realist novel. Remember that Watt's intention is
to identify the characteristics of a new literary form, 'the novel', in
order that he can then delineate the social and moral environment
that allowed such a form to flourish. I have argued that the realist
novel is just one manifestation of the novel genre, and that the
Realist novel has quite particular characteristics, some of which
are direct descendants of the eighteenth-century novels that Watt
describes, but which has other characteristics specific to the nineteenth century. Although Watt includes Fielding in his discussion,
he admits that the majority of features he identifies as formal
realism have already been established by Defoe and Richardson.
However, again this is a result of Watt's focus on the individual's
authentic experience, which is at the expense of a broader social
perspective.

Later on in the book Watt does highlight that one of Fielding's
contributions is that he offers a broader social canvas than
Richardson, and that human reality is more than consciousness,
but the main thrust of Watt is certainly the idea of the uniqueness
of individual experience (Watt 1957: 288–9). The reader might
remember an earlier point I made about the difficulty Realist
novelists face – if their central characters are too individuated,
they become atypical and unrepresentative and thus unable to be
related back to an agreed-upon world.

Although I have said that Watt does not make a particular political case for realism, he does see the rise of the novel as being
linked to the rise of the economic and political class of the bourgeoisie, making a direct correlation between the rise of the two.
For Watt, 'Moll Flanders, like Rastignac and Julien Sorel, is a
characteristic product of modern individualism in assuming that
she owes it to herself to achieve the highest economic and social

rewards, and in using every available method to carry out her resolve' (Watt 1957: 94). The focus on 'economic individualism' as the heart of the change in the economic order sees Watt align the capitalist individualist, therefore, with the protagonist of the novel genre. However, it could be argued contra Watt that the novel emerges because it is able to provide an analysis of capitalism, that is, it does not inherently favour the autonomous individual striving for material gain, nor does it reflect a world in which the Protestant work ethic is desirable and prevails. This leads us neatly into the work of Lukács.

Georg Lukács

Lukács enters the debate about realism in the 1920s, and defends it against the works of modernism through to the 1950s. As he sees it, the problem with modernism is that it refuses the possibility of understanding society as a totality, focusing as it does on consciousness and 'moments'. Modernists argue that the world is fractured, and some left-wing critics argue that capitalism is likewise fracturing. Again, Lukács says that this is superficial: capitalism is a unity, a coherent totality, independent of consciousness (Adorno et al.1977: 31, 'Realism in the Balance', in *Aesthetics and Politics*). The focus by works of modernism on superficial or transient aspects of reality denies a proper recognition of the functioning of capitalism and its totality of relations. This view might also be contrasted with Auerbach's view of modernism, as he, too, argued that there was a breakdown in the coherence of society, but for Auerbach the concentration on 'moments' by modernism accurately reflected the breakdown rather than conspired with it.

Auerbach's view may seem a relatively neutral, stylistic analysis, but when set alongside Lukács we can see that the way realism is defined depends upon how 'reality' is characterised in the first instance, that is, the conception of 'reality' which precedes stylistic analysis of realism has to be a political perception. For Lukács, for someone to say that society is fractured is in itself a misrepresentation of the state of social (and economic) affairs and is thus politically suspicious. Further, for Lukács, modernism's concentration on the content of consciousness, and the apprehension of the world through subjective consciousness alone, itself represents a refusal of that objective point of view which is intrinsic to realism and essential for socialist critique, for the denial of the objective point of view within a work of art or literature means that there can be no objective critique. The distortions and psychopathologies of modernism lead to a position whereby when these elements are dominant and universal, as they are in modernist literature, there is nothing to judge them against, that is, there is no longer any 'normal' against which to judge these things. Modernism also therefore deprives literature of a sense of perspective (Adorno et al. 1977: 32–3). We have seen throughout this book that 'a sense of perspective' is essential to the aims of Realism. For Lukács, then, those left-wing critics who advance the claims of modernism at the expense of realism fail to grasp the nature of reality and the manner in which modernism is complicit with capitalist ideology.

But Lukács also makes a point about the very method of criticism and analysis which proponents of modernism use. Their focus is on 'form' or style, and this in itself hinders a true understanding of realism in comparison to modernism. In 'The Ideology of Modernism' (Lukács 1963) he claims that the emphasis on form is not only part of the modernist aesthetic but also part of the bourgeois-modernist critic's approach – that is, the bourgeois-modernist critic is firstly concerned with making distinctions on the basis of formal criteria (1963: 17–19). For Lukács this hides the fact that the same formal techniques, for example interior monologue and stream of consciousness, can derive from quite different purposes and authorial worldviews. One use might be a concern to show all of human activity, as the works of Thomas Mann do, where the workings of an individual consciousness are just one part of the totality, and the other use might derive from a belief that the world is constituted by the 'perpetually oscillating patterns of sense- and memory-data' (Lukacs 1963: 18). For Lukács, the opposition is false, and we should be looking at the underlying content and *Weltanschauung* (worldview) since this is what determines the formal aspect of any given work of art. Style is therefore 'rooted in content' (1963: 19). For Lukács this is also because man is always in context – man's

'ontological being' cannot be separated from his 'social and historical environment' (1963: 19). For Lukács, therefore, the
promotion of modernist literature at the expense of realist literature also denies the way in which realism understands the
relationship between individuals and the totality of society.

Lukács argued that the best kind of critique available from
literature was that presented by what he called bourgeois critical
realism. Although the ultimate aim for literature should be socialist realism, it was not in a fit state or could not match the
achievements of the great bourgeois realists, who, according to
Lukács, were successful in critiquing their societies because even
though ostensibly compromised by their bourgeois class positions,
they were able, nevertheless, to go beyond this position (part of
the argument for their greatness).

Lukács goes further when he argues how realist novels best
work, for which he has a theory of 'types', and this provides an
interesting contrast with Watt's argument that the novel's realism
is dependent on the rendering of authentic individual accounts,
whereby 'individual' is understood as 'unique' rather than representing a 'type' of any kind. He suggested that there were three
kinds of novel. The first was the novel that was interested purely
in society as an entity and not in the life of the individuals within
it. A second kind tended to be interested in the inner person alone,
without paying much attention to their external circumstances,
such as the society they lived in. Lukács does not support either
type of novel, for neither of them fulfils the role of true realism,
which is to present the whole picture, of how individuals and
society are interwoven. This is how he puts it:

> Realism is the recognition of the fact that a work of literature can
> rest neither on a lifeless average, as the naturalists suppose, nor on
> an individual principle which dissolves its own self into nothing-
> ness. The central category and criterion of realist literature is the
> type, a peculiar synthesis which organically binds together the
> general and the particular both in characters and situations. What
> makes a type a type is not its average quality, not its mere individual
> being, however profoundly conceived; what makes it a type is that in
> it all the humanly socially essential determinants are present on
> their highest level of development, in the ultimate unfolding of the

possibilities latent in them, in extreme presentation of their extremes, rendering concrete the peaks and limits of men and epochs.

True great realism thus depicts man and society as complete entities, instead of showing merely one or the other of their aspects. Measured by this criterion, artistic trends determined by either exclusive introspection or exclusive extraversions equally impoverish and distort reality. Thus realism means a three-dimensionality, and all-roundedness, that endows with independent life characters and human relationships. (From the Preface to *Studies in European Realism*, Lukács 1972: 6)

Lukács's commitment to a realist aesthetic is a commitment to an organic society, and his notion of the type is one of a character who reveals any particular given epoch. Works which are overly subjective or sociological fail to properly render societal structures. There is underlying this view a sense of history as defined by specific epochs, and history itself as an unfolding of potentiality, typical of Marxist thought. Of course, it would be possible to advance an idea of realism that did ask for a type that 'lived' and was neither average nor excessively introverted and still not be dependent on a Marxist historical view, but it is clear that for Lukács true realism can only come through a perfect understanding of historical circumstance and an individuated exemplary character type.

STOP and THINK

Is it necessary to understand a society in totality in order to understand character? This may seem rather a tall order, but much literary criticism is concerned with placing literature and its characters within social and historical contexts, such that even for those kinds of works dealing with intensely subjective viewpoints – the Brontës, modernism – the tendency is to make the characters understandable according to the social and cultural forces impinging upon them.

Catherine Belsey: *Critical Practice* (1980)

Belsey's book was first published in 1980, and is fully immersed in, and approving of, poststructural criticisms of realism. The poststructural attack is on realism's intrinsic belief that it can give us an objective view of 'reality', and on realism's belief that language is largely unproblematic in its ability to give us an agreed-upon reality. Belsey's book appeared in the *New Accents* series, which was a popular route into literary theory for many undergraduate and postgraduate students. Although not 'seminal' in the way that the above theorists are, its encapsulation of post-structural arguments, the way in which it dismantles realism's reliance upon 'common sense', and the way it critiques the 'classic realist text', make it an excellent way into this area of discussion. We will see how the poststructural viewpoint undoes all the basic tenets of realism/Realism: accessible (transparent) language; belief in a common phenomenal world; belief in an existing empirical world which can both be described and known; belief in a pre-existing human nature; autonomous individuals; a broadly liberal humanist worldview.

Belsey's central argument is that the dominant mode of literature since the Renaissance has been one of 'expressive realism', by which she means a combination of mimesis and Romanticism. She claims that 'the Aristotelian concept of art as mimesis, the imitation of reality, was widely current throughout the Renaissance' (Belsey 1991: 7–8), and when this becomes fused with 'the spontaneous overflow of powerful feelings' by the heightened sensitivity of the artist, we get 'expressive realism'. She goes on to link this to the way we read:

> the commonsense view of literature [proposes] a practice of reading in quest of expressive realism ... Common sense assumes that valuable literary texts, those which are in a special way worth reading, tell truths – about the period which produced them, about the world in general or about human nature – and that in doing so they express the particular perceptions, the individual insights of their authors.
>
> Common sense also offers this way of approaching literature not as a self-conscious and deliberate practice, a method based on a reasoned theoretical position, but as the 'obvious' mode of reading, the 'natural' way of approaching literary works. (Belsey 1991: 2)

In addition, Belsey claims that expressive realism is a product of industrial capitalism, and belongs to that particular historical period of the 'last century and a half' (1800–1950). Therefore, expressive realism is in itself a political ideology. Because it represents the 'common sense view' the ideology is not overt, but buried in common-sense assumptions about the way the world is and the way people relate to it and live within it. In other words, this view seems to be 'common sense', but this should certainly not be taken to mean that it does, in fact, represent the way things are. For Belsey and others, this 'common sense' is in reality bourgeois ideology, which is made to seem as if it is the natural order of things.

While expressive realism has been widely challenged in the twentieth century, these challenges have themselves 'failed finally to break with the empiricist-idealist problematic'. They have provided 'new ways of approaching literary texts but [failed] to construct a genuinely radical critical practice'. Hence, Belsey's book is not just an overview of the attack on 'common sense' and 'expressive realism' by much of twentieth-century literary theory, but does itself propose a new 'critical practice', that is, a new way of understanding literature which draws on literary theory but avoids its contradictory effects.

The following quotation from Belsey, discussing the work of the critic Stanley Fish, shows the nature of her political direction in an attack on expressive realism, both as a reading practice and as certain species of literary production:

> It is worth noting that Fish still connects literature directly with truth, even though the truth in question is 'discovered' by the reader. His model of the text is not precisely expressive, though it is implicit throughout that the author as dialectician is in control of the discourse which constitutes the text. Nonetheless, Fish's position is radical to the extent that it sees readers as participant in the construction of meaning, and it therefore provides a possible basis for a genuinely radical and productive critical practice. (Belsey 1991: 33)

The valued terms here for Belsey are 'genuinely radical' and 'productive', which is the language of the political left at this time and the language of a more general liberatory politics which continues into contemporary criticism. The political angle has already been established by Belsey when she identifies expressive realism with industrial capitalism. Her left-wing viewpoint is clearly not that of Lukács but is a vaguer gesture towards 'radicalism' and 'plurality', which perhaps has its roots in Anglo-American 1960s anti-authoritarianism rather than that kind of socialist commitment more common to the French poststructuralist critical tradition. It also falls in with a modernist and postmodernist/poststructuralist critical orthodoxy that realism cannot 'challenge' the reader, since it ultimately satisfies its audience rather than disturbing it. Whereas Watt and Auerbach could look at realism from a putatively politically-neutral point of view by focusing on the formal elements that contribute to realism, in the critical work of the 1960s (and arguably to the present) there is no such viewpoint possible and, as we can see here, whatever we say about realism has a political aspect to it.

I will deal with two major planks of Belsey's attack on realism – the role of language, and her conceptualisation of the classic realist text.

Language

I have previously mentioned that 'the linguistic turn' has been one of the most significant factors in critical and philosophical discussions in the twentieth and twenty-first centuries. Belsey signals this importance for her argument early on: 'The transparency of language is an illusion' (Belsey 1991: 4) and it is a point to which she constantly returns. According to Belsey, the reason why the theories which attack the expressive realist ideology fail is because they subscribe to the same view of language as does expressive realism: that language is a tool which is adequate to represent the author's and the reader's experience of the world, and can communicate this in a relatively trouble-free way. Belsey's view, following post-Saussurean Linguistics ('the linguistic turn') is that language itself is the key player in the way the world works, the way we represent the world in art and literature, and how we understand the world. Language is the medium through which we understand the world, and, so Belsey argues, we cannot move outside of our linguistic constructions; all that it is ever possible for literature to do is reflect these constructions. It is not possible for literature to reflect the real world itself because language (so conceived) is responsible for its very creation (1991: 46–7).

In order to produce a critical practice which recognises the role of language in constructing our view of the world, Belsey turns to Althusserian Marxism and Lacanian psychoanalysis, even as she recognises that they may have certain incompatibilities. Following on from Althusser's reading of Marx:

> ideology is both a real and an imaginary relation to the world – real in that it is the way in which people really live their relationship to the social relations which govern their conditions of existence, but imaginary in that it discourages a full understanding of these conditions of existence and the ways in which people are socially constituted within them. (Belsey 1991: 57)

As readers, we consume literature according to the prevailing ideology, which is essentially bourgeois. Hence, to put it bluntly, we only tend to see in works of literature what bourgeois ideology wants us to see. Ideology is here 'real' in that this is how we actually relate to the world and literature (following Althusser's version of Marxist thought), and 'imaginary' in that the way we believe ourselves to be relating to and understanding the world is the 'common sense' view that the ruling bourgeois ideology has conned us into accepting. Only by realising the constructed nature of our world, our relations within it, and the role of language and ideology in constructing both our world and our relations, can we break out of this.

Classic realist text

The idea of the 'classic realist text' is drawn by Belsey from the work of Stephen Heath and Colin MacCabe, which appeared in the magazine *Screen* in the 1970s (and MacCabe's *James Joyce and the Revolution of the Word*, first published in 1978). It is a particular formulation of 'classic realism', which Belsey mainly aimed at the realist novel, but is indicative of a wider poststructural conceptualisation of realism: 'Classic realism is characterized by *illusionism*, narrative which leads to *closure*, and a *hierarchy of discourses* which establishes the "truth" of the story' (Belsey 1991:

70). I will look at each of these three elements in turn, occasionally looking at MacCabe (1985 and 2003) as well as Belsey.

Illusionism

Illusionism means that the reader is not made aware of the writing as writing. The narrative discourse is 'unmarked', it does not reveal itself as writing, but appears to be an objective and transparent window on reality (in 'The end of a meta-language, from George Eliot to *Dubliners*' in MacCabe 2003:.13ff). In the context of the preceding comments (by Belsey), it should be clear that 'illusionism' does not simply identify a key stylistic trait of realist writing, but is a technique (or group of techniques) which hide the fact that there is a particular medium here which gives the illusion of representing reality or the world directly. 'Illusionism' is thus also intended in the sense of 'deception'. Not only does this illusionism hide the role of language in constructing the world, in doing so it makes invisible the bourgeois ideology that classic realism serves.

Closure

The idea of closure is relatively straightforward: 'the movement of classic realist narrative towards closure ensures the reinstatement of order, sometimes a new order, sometimes the old restored, but always intelligible because familiar' (Belsey 1991: 75). We saw earlier on that according to Realism's own tenets, endings should be problematic since there are no natural endings, other than the death of an individual. *Middlemarch*, nevertheless, ties up all the stories of the characters for us, as do any number of Realist novels. The reader expects a proper ending. The wider import of this for Belsey and the position she represents is that this is inherently conservative, not necessarily because there is no change in the order of things, but because where there is change it is offered up in a way that is intelligible according to the status quo that the reader is familiar with. Once again, the argument is that this particular feature of classic realism is in the service of bourgeois ideology.

Hierarchy of discourses

Discourses within the classic realist text are organised hierarch-
ically, and it is the surrounding narrative discourse which acts as
the meta-language. For example, although characters will express
themselves quite coherently in dialogue, it is the accompanying
narrative, delivered as the authoritative view, which will put such
discourse into the proper perspective. The reader is placed in the
same position as the narrator and consequently the reader and
critic are in a position of dominance; they do not have to agree
with the contents of the meta-language, for the position of authority that the meta-language offers to the reader is sufficient.

Conjoining the hierarchy of discourses and the narrative movement towards closure the basic delineation of the classic realist
text is that its endpoint is always a convergence of the views of the
author, narrative and reader towards agreement of what they
already knew about the world (Belsey 1991: 75 ff). This, in turn,
reinforces the bourgeois humanist view that individuals (subjects
in this terminology) are autonomous, generators of their own
actions and meanings – again a view that is 'naturalised', made
'common sense' by the operations of the classic realist text here
described:

> Initially (and continuously) constructed in discourse, the subject
> finds in the discourse of the classic realist text a confirmation of the
> position of autonomous subjectivity represented in ideology as
> "obvious". It is possible to refuse that position, but to do so, at least
> at present, is to make a deliberate and ideological choice. (Belsey
> 1991: 83–4)

Although, as I have,suggested, the heat has gone out of some of
this debate, particularly since the collapse of the Berlin Wall, the
suspicion that realism is complicit with a suspect bourgeois (right-
wing) ideology lingers. However, this is an observation which is
more an acknowledgement that much of the above informs current
discussions of realism, and within which theorists and critics
orientate themselves.

Other readings

My intention above has been to present a reasonable cross-section
of theoretical work on realism so that the reader is relatively well
placed in taking his or her own research further. Inevitably, there
are other works which might be regarded as central, and there are
certainly other writers and publications I would want to point to. I
sketch some of these below, but again, even here, there can be no
attempt at comprehensiveness.

Of recent work there is Pam Morris's *Realism* (2003, in the *New
Critical Idiom* series). This gives more attention to the history of
realism in France than I have done, and more clearly identifies
particular critical groupings, such as the Frankfurt School
(through which Morris looks at the modernism versus realism
debate). It offers sections on specific critics as well in relation to
Realism which I have not covered, particularly in relation to the
role of the reader: Stanley Fish, Wolfgang Iser and Hans Robert
Jauss. It ends by paying attention to Habermas's idea of 'communicative reason', and how this and like-minded approaches might
be enlisted in the cause of realism today. Another book that offers
an overview of realism, and includes selected essays, is Dennis
Walder's *The Realist Novel* (1995). Other books of this kind are D.
Correa (ed.) *The Nineteenth-Century Novel: Realisms* (2000),
Elizabeth Deeds Ermarth, *Realism and Consensus in the English
Novel* (1983), Lillian Furst (ed.) *Realism* (1992), and J. P. Stern,
On Realism (1973). Then there is George Levine (ed.) *Realism and
Representation: Essays on the Problem of Realism in Relation to
Science, Literature, and Culture* (1993) and *The Realistic
Imagination. English Fiction from Frankenstein to Lady Chatterley*
(1981). Kearns's book (below) quite often has Levine in the back-
ground.

Raymond Tallis's *In Defence of Realism* (1988) directly
confronts postmodernists and poststructuralists. It is rather thin
on the Realists themselves, preferring instead to demolish all the
claims of contemporary critical theory, and it makes no attempt to
offer a theory of realism of its own, often falling back on common-
sense claims about the nature of language, life and reality, and
using 'realism' and mimesis interchangeably with discussion of

'the realistic novel'. Its approach to a definition of realism is thus to proceed 'negatively', saying what it is not rather than what it is, and thus (for Tallis) avoiding the political, philosophical and social morass that awaits anybody who attempts to define it. One of the problems with dealing with realism 'negatively' in this way is that it means that Tallis spends more time on arguments that are against realism (more precisely in his book, against 'realistic fiction'), focusing on mainly postmodern texts and post-Saussurean literary and critical theory, and that there is hardly any attention paid to realist literature, realist criticism or realist theory.

Katherine Kearns's *Nineteenth-Century Literary Realism. Through the Looking Glass* (1996) is both sympathetic and provocative. It has an impressive command of those critical and philosophical positions which impinge upon discussion of realism, and places its own methodology within the philosophical claims and methodological practices of realism. She argues that the nineteenth-century Realist novelists are aware of those pressures which are antithetical to realist endeavour, of the difficulties of language, literary self-consciousness, the gaps between theory/philosophy and practice, the paradox that concentration on the familiar and everyday can lead to surreality, the gap between representation and experience, relativism of truth claims, and instability of 'character'. Rather than being the naive purveyors of illusionist, realist fiction, these novelists believe that in the interests of communication and a shared humane endeavour, these features are to be sacrificed for the greater good.

For Kearns, this superficially often appears to be an acceptance of a rather reductive Benthamite view of the world, where reality is that which is agreed upon by the majority, and that 'the good' is to be counted as what is good for the majority. Part of the Realist's balancing act, however, is to always acknowledge that this is what they are doing. In portraying the nineteenth-century Realists in such a way it can sometimes seem as if they themselves are writing within the context of twentieth-century poststructural criticism, and refuting such criticism through their pragmatic engagement with the world and precepts antagonistic to it. Kearns is alive to the historical narratives of realism, and to her own seeming ahistorical approach, but it does still have a tendency to distort the work of the nineteenth-century writers. Kearns's approach also offers detailed readings and reference to works which are not usually regarded as central to the Realist canon – *Wuthering Heights*, *Frankenstein*, *The Blithedale Romance* and *Dracula* – and there is the tendency to conflate mimesis with Realism. Nevertheless, this is one of the most engaged works on realism that there is.

For those interested in the more technical and stylistic aspects of realist writing there is Phillipe Hamon's work (see the essay in Lillian Furst's *Realism* 1992). An interesting book in this field is Michael Riffaterre's *Fictional Truth* (1990) which argues that realism is a particular rhetorical effect dependent upon diegesis rather than mimesis. For Riffaterre, realism works by expanding upon semes – basic units of meaning – in self-validating processes which explain, and therefore 'verify', their own assumptions. Such rhetoric is therefore 'intratextual', that is, a function of operations within the text itself, and not dependent upon reference to any external reality. As such, this is one (extreme) version of the linguistic turn as applied to realism. The issue here is how words and symbols refer to the world, and is part of the more general scepticism of the ability of words to refer to things in a way which is amenable to realist literature.

Although I have denominated this chapter 'Theorists', there is often no easy separation between some of this and the next two chapters on language and philosophy, so the above should be treated as complementary with the following. These chapters will also return to some of the issues and theorists mentioned here.

Works cited and further reading

Adorno, T. et al. (1977), *Aesthetics and Politics*, London: New Left Books. Includes essays by Bloch, Lukács, Brecht, Benjamin and Adorno.

Auerbach, Erich (1991 [1953]), *Mimesis*, trans. Willard R. Trask. Princeton, New Jersey: Princeton University Press.

Belsey, Catherine (1991), *Critical Practice*. London: Routledge.

Correa, D. (ed.) (2000), *The Nineteenth-Century Novel: Realisms*. London: Routledge.

Ermarth, Elizabeth Deeds (1983), *Realism and Consensus in the English*

Novel. Princeton, NJ: Princeton University Press.

Furst, Lilian R. (ed.) (1992), *Realism*. Harlow, Essex: Longman.

Kearns, Katherine (1996), *Nineteenth-Century Realism. Through the Looking-Glass*. Cambridge: Cambridge University Press.

Levine, George (1981), *The Realistic Imagination. English Fiction from Frankenstein to Lady Chatterley*. Chicago and London: University of Chicago Press.

Levine, George (ed.) (1993), *Realism and Representation: Essays on the Problem of Realism in Relation to Science, Literature, and Culture*. Wisconsin: University Press.

Lukács, George (1972), *Studies in European Realism*. Original writings 1935–39. London: Merlin Press.

Lukács, George (1963), *The Meaning of Contemporary Realism*. London: Merlin Press.

MacCabe, Colin (1985), *Theoretical Essays: Film, Linguistics, Literature*. Manchester: Manchester University Press.

MacCabe, Colin (2003), *James Joyce and the Revolution of the Word*, second edition. Basingstoke: Palgrave Macmillan. The additional essays include 'Joyce and Benjamin' (1983) and 'Realism: Balzac and Barthes' (1985).

Morris, Pam (2003), *Realism*. London: Routledge.

Riffaterre, Michael (1990), *Fictional Truth*. Baltimore: Johns Hopkins University Press.

Tallis, Raymond (1988), *In Defence of Realism*. London: Edward Arnold.

Trollope, Anthony (1994), *The Way We Live Now*. London: Penguin.

Walder, Dennis (ed.) (1995), *The Realist Novel*. London: Routledge.

Watt, Ian (1957), *The Rise of the Novel*. Berkeley and London, University of California Press.

9

The language of Realism

> The reader of realism naturally focuses on content, not style.
> (Spector in Bloom 1987: 231)

I have made repeated reference to the importance of language in discussions of realism, and in this chapter we look at the different ways in which language is conceptualised in relation to discussion of realism. As I pointed out at the end of Chapter 8, such a discussion cuts across both literary critical concerns and philosophy. The title 'The language of Realism' is not intended to suggest that there is a single aspect to the use of language in realism, but to cover these different uses, some of them falling directly within stylistics, some of them a mix of stylistics and politics, and stylistics and philosophy. It also means we can return to some of those features discussed earlier, such as the use of 'detail'.

Prose

> 'In the prosaic neighbourhood of Middlemarch' (*Middlemarch*, Ch. 34)

The chapter on poetry made some observations on the nature of prose as virtually unfit for the literary arts in comparison to poetry. Conversely, we can now take the opportunity to see just how it is that prose as a medium has been seen as eminently suitable for the work of realist literature.

Auerbach makes a general point about language as a tool in aid of realism. He firstly makes connections between the kinds of society there have been and the types of literature they have produced, and concomitantly he views language itself as a medium which is mastered differently, or employed differently, at different times. Only when it has a particular kind of capacity – for example, handling and conveying 'complex factual data' (Auerbach 1991: 219) – can it move towards realism, or be said to be realist. Watt sees the issue somewhat differently, and in its aim to reproduce authentic(-seeming) accounts of experience argues that perhaps the most important feature in the development of realism was 'the adaptation of prose style to give an air of complete authenticity' (Watt 1957: 27). More specifically, Watt argues that prior to the work of Defoe and Richardson, even where attention in literature might have been given towards the humbler elements of everyday life, there was an expectation that literary art should always heed the expectations of 'beauty', such that attention was always given to 'writing' (a similar historical perception about writing is held by Barthes in his article below). Thus, up to and including the eighteenth century there

> remained a strong literary expectation that they would use language as a source of interest in its own right, rather than as a purely referential medium.
>
>   In any case, of course, the classical critical tradition in general had no use for the unadorned realistic description which such a use of language would imply. (Watt 1957: 28)

Conversely, there is little prior interest in the denotative and referential functions of language (1957: 29) – features which are now habitually associated with realist writing. We might add to this that if realism depends upon the refusal of ornate or highly stylised writing, it has often turned to opposite models where the use of unadorned prose is prevalent, such as writing concerned with the presentation of facts – science, journalism, Parliamentary reports and history, for instance.

Metonymy

Following on from this, and perhaps the major concern in the discussion of the language of realism, is the distinction between metaphor and metonymy, and the association of the figure of metonymy with realism. The distinction derives from the article 'Two Aspects of Language and Two Types of Aphasic Disturbances' by Roman Jakobson (published in 1956 in *Fundamentals of Language*). Jakobson was researching aphasia, a speech disorder in which people have difficulty in comprehending language or in expressing themselves verbally. In order to understand this speech disorder, Jakobson argued that it was first necessary to understand the way language works, and he proposed that speech – and, in fact, all sign systems – operate according to two principles, that of 'similarity' (metaphor) and that of 'contiguity' (metonymy).

To use a familiar example, although not Jakobson's, 'The ship ploughed the ocean' is a metaphor based on a perceived similarity between the action of a ship moving through the sea and the action of a plough on land. The link between the two is 'imaginative' since there is no connection between them in the physical world. Metonymy, at the other linguistic pole, is characterised by the substitution of one item for another on the basis of some form of 'contiguity' (adjacency) between the two items. In 'all hands on deck', 'hands' is the metonymic substitute for 'sailors', wherein hands are deemed to be 'contiguous' with the sailors by virtue of the fact that they 'belong' to the sailors; they then 'stand in' for the sailors by virtue of the fact that they are that part of the person most required by the command to get on deck and help out. Although 'all hands on deck' would appear to require little analysis as an example, 'contiguity' is actually rather a complicated matter, as we shall see. In essence, contiguity tends to mean things which are physically adjacent or connected. Therefore, intrinsic to the metonymic pole of language is the idea that items connected metonymically belong to the same spatio-temporal world and are linked ontologically, which is not the case for metaphor, as already noted. This is how Jakobson characterises metonymy in realism in opposition to the metaphoric in poetry:

> The primacy of the metaphoric process in the literary schools of romanticism and symbolism has been repeatedly acknowledged but it is still insufficiently realized that it is the predominance of metonymy which underlies and actually predetermines the so-called

'realistic' trend, which belongs to an intermediary stage between the decline of romanticism and the rise of symbolism and is opposed to both. Following the path of contiguous relationships, the realist author metonymically digresses from the plot to the atmosphere and from the characters to the setting in space and time. He is fond of synecdochic details. (Jakobson and Halle 1971: 91–2)

In the context of literary history, Jakobson places realism between romanticism (at the end of the eighteenth century/beginning of the nineteenth century) and what he calls symbolism, which is a characteristic mode of modernist writing (end of the nineteenth century/beginning of the twentieth century). In the context of linguistic analysis he says here that study has favoured the processes of metaphor over metonymy, where 'nothing comparable to the rich literature on metaphor can be cited for the theory of metonymy' (1971: 95). This prejudice has arguably continued until the present time, with linguistic research into metaphor far outweighing discussion of metonymy. I mention this as indicative of a further critical prejudice against realism, since it is another version of the alignment of metaphor-poetry with what is interesting, and metonymy-realism with what is dull. Since metonymy relies on contiguity, there is little required in terms of imagination, unlike the brilliancies of metaphoric apprehension and insight where a writer must make connective leaps that do not present themselves within the same spatio-temporal world (so the argument goes).

To describe a room by listing its contents, and from there to read the character, requires less imagination than describing a character by his or her similarity to an animal or bird, or any other number of images not connected in a way other than through similar, though not contiguous, attributes. The other thing to take from this quotation, and the most germane for our discussion of realism, is what Jakobson calls 'the path of contiguous relationships' where 'the realist author metonymically digresses from the plot to the atmosphere and from the characters to the setting in space and time'. The metonymic pole of language binds characters to environments, and appears to offer a cohesive totality to the fictional worlds of realism, which can replicate our understanding of the actual world of objects and the totality of relations that obtains between them. And one final comment before we launch into examples of metonymy at work in realism is to mention the figure 'synecdoche'. This is a notable metonymic trope, in which the part is substituted for the whole. The example of metonymy used above, 'hands', is synecdochic, since a body part is taken to represent the person.

Let us begin with some mid-nineteenth century non-fiction prose, not too dissimilar from descriptive passages we might come across in novels from the period. This description of Manchester and its inhabitants is taken from Friedrich Engels's *Condition of the Working Class in England in 1844*, and we can see that the main figure for organisation is metonymy:

But the most horrible spot (if I should describe all the separate spots in detail I should never come to the end) lies on the Manchester side, immediately south-west of Oxford Road, and is known as Little Ireland. In a rather deep hole, in a curve of the Medlock and surrounded on all four sides by tall factories and high embankments, covered with buildings, stand two groups of about two hundred cottages, built chiefly back to back, in which live about four thousand human beings, most of them Irish. The cottages are old, dirty, and of the smallest sort, the streets uneven, fallen into ruts and in part without drains or pavement; masses of refuse, offal and sickening filth lie among standing pools in all directions; the atmosphere is poisoned by the effluvia from these, and laden and darkened by the smoke of a dozen tall factory chimneys. A horde of ragged women and children swarm about here, as filthy as the swine that thrive upon the garbage heaps and in the puddles. In short, the whole rookery furnishes such a hateful and repulsive spectacle as can hardly be equalled in the worst court on the Irk. The race that lives in these ruinous cottages, behind broken windows, mended with oilskin, sprung doors, and rotten doorposts, or in dark, wet cellars, in measureless filth and stench, in this atmosphere penned in as if with a purpose, this race must really have reached the lowest stage of humanity. This is the impression and the line of thought which the exterior of this district forces upon the beholder. But what must one think when he hears that in each of these pens, containing at most two rooms, a garret and perhaps a cellar, on the average twenty human beings live; that in the whole region, for each one hundred and twenty persons, one usually inaccessible privy is provided; and that in spite of all the preachings of the physicians, in

> spite of the excitement into which the cholera epidemic plunged the
> sanitary police by reason of the condition of Little Ireland, in spite
> of everything, in this year of grace 1844, it is in almost the same state
> as in 1831! Dr. Kay asserts that not only the cellars but the first
> floors of all the houses in this district are damp; that a number of
> cellars once filled up with earth have now been emptied and are
> occupied once more by Irish people; that in one cellar the water
> constantly wells up through a hole stopped with clay, the cellar lying
> below the river level, so that its occupant, a hand-loom weaver, had
> to bale out the water from his dwelling every morning and pour it
> into the street!

The movement of the passage is metonymic, shifting as it does
between objects that are geographically adjacent (contiguity in
space). Location, atmosphere and environment are all wedded
together, forging causal links between the various features, and as
such, therefore, potentially providing an explanation for the
conditions. The movement of the passage is also metonymic at the
discursive level, as Engels states that he will use this particular
spot as representative of all the horrible spots in this part of
Manchester, that is, he will substitute this part for the whole.
Metonymy is also at work when he assumes what the inhabitants
must be like by observing the condition of the houses, that they
must have reached the lowest form of humanity. He then says:
'This is the impression and the line of thought which the exterior
of this district forces upon the beholder.' Engels here explicitly
informs the reader that he apprehends the characteristics of the
inhabitants metonymically, that is, he extrapolates along the
metonymic chain from the environment to the inhabitants.
Nevertheless, he backs up the supposition with evidence from
another source, Dr Kay, as if metonymy is not in itself sufficient.

This factual support for the metonymic supposition, however,
serves to reinforce the validity of reading metonymically – we are
assured that we can indeed read the lives of the working classes
from the conditions they inhabit because the evidence about the
workers is underwritten by an appropriate, independent authority.
And note that it is an unnamed hand-loom weaver who synec-
dochally stands in for the working classes, defined by occupation
rather than individuality. To anticipate later discussion in the

chapter, we might notice that the lives are described in their external circumstances and that there is no attempt to read 'character'
from this, that is, there is no attempt to render the inner, subjective lives of the workers. Over the whole passage there is the
interpenetration of all the elements, of sights and smells, and the
element of 'contagion' which makes the general tenor of contiguity to be one of disease. None of this is to ignore the metaphoric
usage evident in the passage, but the dominant trope is clearly
metonymy. Interestingly, the metaphoric association of the inhabitants with the lives of pigs ('as filthy as the swine') perhaps
obviates the necessity to deal with the inner lives, since to cast
them as living lives little better than pigs removes any notion of
human consciousness. Without reasonable metonymic access to
the consciousness of the individuals, Engels switches to metaphor.
But even here, a few lines on, Engels blurs the metaphorical nature
of the observation by calling the houses 'pens'.

The way that Engels manages his material metonymically, and
the cognitive assumptions associated with this trope, transfer
intriguingly into Realism. This way of describing conditions is
typical of Realist writing that deals with the industrial working
classes, as we saw when we looked at Gaskell and in *Aurora Leigh*.
Another example is in Disraeli's *Sybil* (1845):

> Here during the days of business, the sound of the hammer and the
> file never ceased, amid gutters of abomination and piles of foulness
> and stagnant pools of filth; reservoirs of leprosy and the plague,
> whose exhalations were sufficient to taint the atmosphere of the
> whole kingdom and fill the country with fever and pestilence.
> (Disraeli 1980: 205)

It is partly that such fiction adopts the method and language of
this kind of sociological reporting, but it is also that Realist works
are using the material as the basis of research which is then
adapted to the literature. The replication of the style of a report
thus lends the air of authenticity to the writing, and so the
metonymic method is reproduced. Nevertheless, there is a difference between the metonymic process of the type used in the
Engels passage and its use within Realist novels. This is certainly
not to argue that such reports as Engels's are neutral and objective

writing, but this is very much the manner of producing 'authenticity' that the Realist novels adopt. Having dealt with the basics of metonymy, we now turn our attention to a more nuanced view of its use in Realism.

J. Hillis Miller's 'The Fiction of Realism: *Sketches by Boz*, *Oliver Twist*, and Cruikshank's Illustrations' (1971) and Stephen J. Spector's 'Monsters of Metonymy: *Hard Times* and Knowing the Working Class' (1987) make good use of Jakobson's theory of the two linguistic poles. Miller argues that the pieces in *Sketches* – Dickens's journalistic records of London life – use the metonymic process for apprehension, in the way we have seen laid down by Jakobson. Miller quotes one passage where Dickens says that there is no need to describe a character at all since we can read all that there is to know about him from the way he dresses:

> We needn't tell you all this, however, for if you have an atom of observation, one glance at his sleek, knowing-looking head and face – his prim white neckerchief, with the wooden tie into which it has been regularly folded for twenty years past, merging by imperceptible degrees into a small-plaited shirt-frill – and his comfortable-looking form encased in a well-brushed suit of black – would give you a better idea of his real character than a column of our poor description could convey. (Quoted in Miller 1971: 99)

As Miller says, Dickens's assumption is that 'An objective description of what he looked like and how he dressed will convey immediately his inner spiritual nature' (Miller 1971: 98–9). Yet, as we have seen in previous chapters, the relationship between Dickens and Realism is a complicated one, and this apparently straightforward use of metonymy as a cognitive process masks the way that Dickens rarely stays within metonymy. Miller argues that it is typical of Dickens to use metonymy as the basis for metaphoric substitution. For instance, in 'Meditations in Monmouth Street', Dickens moves from the clothes of the dead to the lives of those who wore them: 'The clothes are metonymically equivalent to their absent wearers and give Dickens access to them. The life which properly belonged to the wearers is transferred to the clothes', but then the 'waistcoats have almost burst with anxiety to put themselves on' and so this personification of an inanimate object becomes metaphorical rather than metonymic: 'The metonymic reciprocity between a person and his surroundings, his clothes, furniture, house, and so on, is the basis for the metaphorical substitutions so frequent in Dickens's fiction. For Dickens, metonymy is the foundation and support of metaphor' (Miller 1971: 97). This partly explains, perhaps, the 'correction' of Dickens by other Realist writers who stay more firmly within metonymic arrangements of discourse.

Spector's article on *Hard Times* argues that Dickens relies on metonymy as his method for rendering character, at the same time as he finds metonymy unequal to the task (and Katherine Kearns, mentioned in Chapter 8, discusses how Dickens struggled with the constraints of the Realist aesthetic in this novel). He argues that Dickens, like Engels, used metonymical association as the method to understand the lives of workers. That Dickens fails to give us the inner lives of his working-class characters was a contemporary criticism of the author, and Spector quotes George Eliot's review of *Hard Times*: 'We have one great novelist who is gifted with the utmost power of rendering the external traits of our town population; and if he could give us their psychological character – their conception of life, and their emotions – with the same truth as their idiom and manners, his books would be the greatest contributions' (Spector 1987, 229–30). Spector notes that when Dickens made the trip to Preston to observe the strike, his middle-class expectation that the workers would constitute an angry mob was not realised when he found them to be well-organised and peaceable (1987: 235).

According to Spector, although the novel begins confidently enough in its belief that it can indeed portray the lives of the workers, it gives up half-way through where Louisa Gradgrind realises that she has no idea whatsoever what their lives are like, and their lives remain a 'mystery' to her. The assumption that external features are an index of the subjective life is thus abandoned, and the metonymic chain that goes from environment to dress to character is no longer causal, that is, the elements in the chain remain contiguous but no one element can be used to predict the nature of the next. Thus, although metonymy is a stylistic feature here, it does not allow us to comprehend the nature of causal relations.

The above has dealt with contiguity as it relates to the links between character and environment. But you may have also noticed that in the descriptions in Disraeli, Engels (and previously in Gaskell) there is always the fear of contamination, that is, a person may become tainted, corrupted or infected by that which is adjacent. This essentially metonymic apprehension of the order of the social world (if overlain with sometimes metaphoric flights) is consistently represented as such in Realist texts in relation particularly to class. A recurrent theme, therefore, is 'proximity' – distance rather than nearness needs to be maintained between social classes, otherwise the one class will become infected by the other. In Gilbert's *Charity*, Mr Smailey objects to being in the same room as Ruth Tredgett, the 'tramp', whom Mrs Van Brugh takes under her wing. When Mrs Van Brugh is out of the room, Smailey openly objects to Ruth that they have now been put on the same social level.

> MR S: Don't – don't approach me – we have nothing in common. Listen at a distance. Mrs. Van Brugh has thought proper to place you on a pedestal that levels you, socially, with respectable Christians. In so doing that she has insulted respectable Christians. She thinks proper to suffer you to enter my presence. In so doing I consider that she has insulted me. I desire you to understand that when a woman of your stamp enters the presence of a Christian gentleman, she – (Gilbert 1909: 105–6)

Ruth recognises him from her past and so, in one way, the metonymic assumption is correct – his physical proximity reveals a one-time moral proximity. However, as the drama proceeds and both Mrs Van Brugh and Ruth are vindicated as good people, there is some undercutting of metonymy as the means to understanding the nature of behaviour. In effect, the attempt to redeem 'fallen women' by Gilbert is also an attack on the metonymical cognitive process.

Mrs Oliphant's novel *Phoebe Junior* is partly premised on the idea of what happens when the distance between unequal social types is forcibly collapsed, for Phoebe leaves London to visit her grandfather, a grocer, and therefore a class beneath her. He is read metonymically by Phoebe on her first meeting with him, unable to recognise him because his clothes belong to a class she does not deal with other than on commercial terms. She is shocked to discover that he is indeed her relation – and thus the narrative sees Phoebe having to overcome her repulsion at this blood contiguity: 'He looked neither more nor less than what he was, an old shop-keeper, very decent and respectable, but a little shabby and greasy, like the men whose weekly bills she had been accustomed to pay for her mother' (1989: 83), and the novel sets this mainstay of Victorian mores against another Victorian ethical anchor: 'The first glimpse of old Tozer, indeed, made it quite evident to Phoebe that nothing but duty could be within her reach' (1989: 85). However, again there is some validation of Phoebe's metonymic apprehension of her grandfather because he does in fact turn out to be something of a brute, but, of course, that cannot gainsay her proximity to him through heredity. I should also point out that Tozer is just as shocked at Phoebe's appearance.

All of the above examples serve to show that while metonymy is indeed characteristic of Realist writing in various ways, it is rarely treated unproblematically. I would suggest that while metonymy is clearly a major feature and rhetorical marker of the Realist novel, its execution is open to some further refinements. Eliot's criticism of Dickens shows that her argument for Realism was that it had to show the inner as well as the outer, again confirming the picture of Realism as one which has to find the correct perspective and ratio for the subjective response to social environment. The fact that, in *Middlemarch*, nobody can read Bulstrode's character from his actions or anything else about him shows the failure of metonymy, whereas the opening of the novel, which reads the contrasting characters of the sisters Dorothea and Celia through their attire, suggests that it might still be a reasonable first port of call for the way we engage with the world. *Middlemarch* in fact quite explicitly warns us off metaphors, since they are the enemy of reason:

> Poor Mr. Casaubon had imagined that his long studious bachelor-hood had stored up for him a compound interest of enjoyment, and that large drafts on his affections would not fail to be honoured; for we all of us, grave or light, get our thoughts entangled in metaphors, and act fatally on the strength of them. (Eliot 1965: 111)

Dickens's problematic relationship with Realism is partly down to his use of metonymy as a way into metaphor rather than as the prime cognitive process and mechanism for ordering material. I hope also to have shown that metonymy can be every bit as fascinating as metaphor.

Roland Barthes: 'The reality effect'

Although formal rhetorical analysis beyond metaphor and metonymy is no longer popular, 'description' is a long-standing rhetorical characteristic associated with realist writing, and the look at metonymy above can be seen as part of this exploration of description. Riffaterre's *Fictional Truth*, mentioned at the end of Chapter 8, is also part of this endeavour. To focus on the 'rhetorical' nature of realist writing is to consider how such writing 'persuades' us of its realness, what particular rhetorical strategies it uses to convince us that what we are reading has a very close connection with the world we inhabit or believe to exist (or to have existed). With this in mind, we can turn to Barthes's seminal essay, 'The Reality Effect', which takes its cue from the rhetorical term *descriptio*. I will devote some considerable space to this structuralist/poststructuralist essay because it will allow us to bring together the work on language above and some of the theoretical material from Chapter 8, and I will take the opportunity to examine more critically some of the assumptions about realism by looking more widely at the issue of detail, which plays so prominent a part in our overall discussion of realism.

Barthes claims that until the middle of the nineteenth century there was a distinction made between 'realism' and 'verisimilitude'. What was 'real' was what in effect could be shown to have happened or to be a 'fact', and this was the domain of history. 'Verisimilitude', on the other hand, how 'life-like' something is, was a matter of public opinion and could alter over time: such things were always, in Classical phrasing, prefaced with 'Let there be, suppose ...'. Therefore, verisimilitude was always understood to deal with 'representation' rather than 'fact'. But for Barthes, this changes in the mid-nineteenth century and the distinction between realism and verisimilitude disappears. The distinction is lost because verisimilitude no longer admits to being representation, it acts as if it denotes 'the real' directly. But for Barthes, it does not actually *de*note anything, all it does is *con*note something we call 'the real', and it is this connoting which Barthes terms 'the reality effect'. This very much fits in with (and helped inaugurate) the argument that classic realism is illusionist, that is, it fools readers into believing that they have direct access to reality and makes them forget that what they have is a fictional representation.

Superfluous details

For Barthes, the collapse in the distinction between verisimilitude and realism – the reality effect – is a defining feature of modern realism. He uses Flaubert's novella, 'A Simple Heart', alongside the author's descriptions of Rouen in his novel *Madame Bovary*, to illustrate the move to modern realism. Barthes begins his piece 'The Reality Effect' thus:

> When Flaubert, describing the room occupied by Mme Aubain, Félicité's employer, tells us that 'an old piano supported, under a barometer, a pyramidal heap of boxes and cartons' ('A Simple Heart,' from *Three Tales*); when Michelet, recounting the death of Charlotte Corday and reporting that, before the executioner's arrival, she was visited in prison by an artist who painted her portrait, includes the detail that 'after an hour and a half, there was a gentle knock at a little door behind her' (*Histoire de France: La Révolution*) – these authors (among many others) are producing notations which structural analysis, concerned with identifying and systematizing the major articulations of narrative, usually and heretofore, has left out, either because its inventory omits all details that are 'superfluous' (in relation to structure) or because these same details are treated as 'filling' (catalyses), assigned an indirect functional value insofar as, cumulatively, they constitute some index of character or atmosphere and so can ultimately be recuperated by structure [...]

> If it is just possible to see in the notation of the piano an indication of its owner's bourgeois standing and in that of the cartons a sign of disorder and a kind of lapse in status likely to connote the atmosphere of the Aubain household, no purpose seems to justify reference to the barometer, an object neither incongruous nor significant, and therefore not participating, at first glance, in the order of the *notable*. (Barthes 1968: 141–2)

Barthes, therefore, acknowledges a possible metonymic function for the piano and the cartons – we can read class status and the nature of the owners from them – but the detail of the barometer is superfluous. Barthes then looks at the role of description in classic rhetoric and says that 'description' was once constrained generically and rhetorically by being part of the beautiful, that is, a type of rhetoric designed to 'excite the admiration of the audience' (1968: 143), but without any truth constraints (144). When we get to Flaubert, this aesthetic remains strong – his descriptions of Rouen in *Madame Bovary* are 'painterly' – but they are also constrained by realism, in that Flaubert is not at liberty to just put any old thing into his description of Rouen; it is necessary that it correlate with a Rouen that could have been observed at his time of writing. In Flaubert's use of Rouen, therefore, there is a double constraint. There is the aesthetic constraint of 'beautiful' description and the 'realistic' (that is, its denotative function), 'referential' constraint. Modern literature, starting with Flaubert, moves to make 'verisimilitude' and 'realism' identical, removing the distinction between 'representation' and 'fact'. In semiotic analysis, it would be said that the signifier gives direct access to the referent and the signified is excluded: the word 'barometer' appears to give us a (the) 'real' barometer: it is both 'life-like' and 'real' at the same time. To achieve this effect the detail of the barometer must hide its functioning as a 'sign', it must (a) hide the fact that it is just a representation, and not the real thing, and (b) it must hide the technique it uses to do this.

This may appear as politically-neutral linguistic 'structural analysis'. But what is at stake, both for Barthes and for wider discussion of realist literature, and perhaps realism itself as it pertains to philosophical realism, is clear on the last page of Barthes's essay when he gives us a slightly different term for 'the reality effect' and talks of 'the *referential illusion* in relation to the reality effect':

> The truth of this illusion is this: eliminated from the realist speech-act as a signified of denotation, the 'real' returns to it as a signified of connotation; for just when these details are reputed to *denote* the real directly, all that they do – without saying so – is *signify* it; Flaubert's barometer, Michelet's little door finally say nothing but

this: *we are the real*; it is the category of 'the real' (and not its contingent contents) which is then signified; in other words, the very absence of the signified, to the advantage of the referent alone, becomes the very signifier of realism: the *reality effect* is produced, the basis of that unavowed verisimilitude which forms the aesthetic of all the standard works of modernity. (1968: 148)

Barthes goes on to say how 'the sign' is degraded and how it disintegrates in the project of modernity, and words like 'regressive' and 'empty' enhance this negative judgement on what is happening. What is lost for Barthes is the understanding that writing and language are representations rather than the real itself, and that when writing and language are deemed to coincide with reality, when they are no longer understood as representation, we lose our ability to critique world affairs. The reality effect simply presents 'the real', and 'the real', thus offered, cannot be gainsaid. We accept the *effect* of the real, the *referential illusion*, as reality itself, and happy with the *form* of realism we do not enquire about its contents or workings. Hence, although not quite this explicit, the reality effect is part of the tool of bourgeois ideology and works to stop us questioning capitalism. What Barthes calls 'the reality effect' MacCabe calls 'pure representation': it is writing and language which gives the illusion of instant and unmediated access to the real. For Barthes it is a feature of modernity, and not located in a specific kind of writing. For MacCabe, it is a feature of the nineteenth-century realist novel. Nevertheless, MacCabe also says: 'Classic realism, however, exists in the present. To break with it is a contemporary struggle in which we must attend to those images from the past which are summoned in response to the dangers of conformism' (MacCabe 2003: 27). In other words, the problem of the reality effect, or of classic realism, is with us today, as Belsey also argues. If we do not deal with it we will succumb to the outrages of modernity and conformism.

Reality effects

Let us move on from Barthes's essay and trace the idea of super-fluous detail through to the present. Here is another barometer from another nineteenth-century French writer:

> The indestructible furniture which every other household throws out finds its way to the lodging-house, for the same reason that the human wreckage of civilization drifts to hospitals for the incurable. In this room you would find a barometer with a monk who appears when it is wet, execrable engravings bad enough to spoil your appetite and all framed in varnished black wood with gild beading, a clock with a tortoiseshell case inlaid with copper, a green stove, Argand lamps coated with dust and oil, a long table covered with oil-cloth so greasy that a facetious boarder can write his name on it with his finger-nail. (Balzac, *Old Goriot*: 32).

STOP and THINK

Can we take the opposite view to Barthes? We know that 'concrete detail' is an unmarked marker of realism, and that description of furniture is often a marker of literary realism, as far back as Defoe. How, then, can we have superfluous detail? Are not all these details both necessary for the effect of realism, but at the same time superfluous in that any list will do? Do you skip descriptions because they are the 'boring bits'? That may prove that Barthes is right – we skip these parts because all they do is connote the real, signal to the reader that they are reading a realist text, so that the actual furniture, the details themselves are unimportant; it is simply the fact that there *are* details that counts. What do readers miss if they skip that whole paragraph? What has anybody missed?

That reference to Argand lamps seems superfluous. Check out Argand lamps.

Here, I think, is one of the problems we find with discussion of literary realism. It tends to treat realism as a genre with fixed specific traits, that is, hierarchy of discourses, transparency of language, but also a number of other things, such as the presentation of three-dimensional characters, narrative closure, the philosophical belief that the world is mind-independent and accessible through language, that we share a common phenomenal world. Realism does not work like that. Writers in the tradition following the nineteenth-century Realists are capable of recognising those traits which may have become stale and then proceed to refresh them. Yes, they are interested in the illusion of reality, and some may write as if language is transparent, but other writers realise that – just as Virginia Woolf realised – the old techniques will not do any more, and that does not mean throwing out the barometer with the bathwater.

Here is an example where Chekhov appears to amuse himself at the contextual and generic levels with the idea of superfluous detail in the following description of a room in Act IV of *Uncle Vanya* (first published in 1897):

> VOITSKI'S bedroom, which is also his office. A table stands near the window; on it are ledgers, letter scales, and papers of every description. Near by stands a smaller table belonging to ASTROFF, with his paints and drawing materials. On the wall hangs a cage containing a starling. There is also a map of Africa on the wall, obviously of no use to anybody.

This is concrete reality, and obviously realised as such on the stage, except, that is, the superfluous comment about concrete detail: 'There is also a map of Africa on the wall, obviously of no use to anybody.' What does he mean by that? It is a purely textual joke, not transferable to the stage. Is he not also pointing out that he recognises that detail is 'superfluous', that pretty much any furnishing will do? He is telling the reader that he understands that superfluous details mark out realism, and having recognised it, he makes it visible. But this 'marking' of the previously unmarked does not signal the end of realism since, as we witnessed in Eliot and others, it is quite possible for realism to comment upon its own techniques.

To make the point about how realist writing, in the aftermath of Realism, continues to reinvent itself, I return to Ferris's novel. Detail continues to mark it out as realism, but it understands this both as a textual feature *and* as a feature of our experience of reality. This passage describes the leave-taking of the latest person to be fired:

> Marcia picked her way across the desk, the credenza, and the book-shelves, removing a clock, a figurine, a cluster of books. She unplugged her radio and wound the cord around its brown plastic body and placed it in a box. Then she went through the desk drawers one redundant item at a time, investigating every matchbook, business card, hairband, Band-Aid, aspirin container, lotion bottle, bendy straw, multivitamin, magazine, nail file, nail polish, lip balm, and cough drop that had languished in her desk for who knows how long ... Marcia's office reverted back to the anonymous – nothing on the desk but a computer and telephone. (Ferris 2007: 329–30)

These things are elsewhere in the novel called 'useless shit', the modern version of 'superfluous detail'. But Ferris is making a different point: the useless shit, these superfluous details which are arbitrary, are also necessary. They define our lives and our reality: as soon as they are gone, the person is gone, life is gone. Barthes argues that one of the problems of superfluous details is that they are presented as a reality which cannot be evaluated or gainsaid: these things 'just are' (Barthes 1968: 146–7). Ferris, in doing this, in detailing the furniture of office life, is both representing reality through detail – *con*noting it – but also *de*noting – it is not empty, its referential function is restored in a meaningful way. MacCabe's and Barthes's underlying left-wing critique of realism may still hold good – we are the dupes of capitalism – but that does not mean to say that realism is politically suspect in the way they argue, nor that realism has to operate in the same way and at all times. This is how Madame Aubain's life ends in 'A Simple Heart', the tale that Barthes uses for his discussion of the reality effect:

> Madame's arm-chair, her pedestal table, her foot-warmer, and the eight chairs had all gone. Yellow squares in the centre of the wall-panels showed where the pictures had hung. They had carried off the two cots with their mattresses, and no trace remained in the

cupboard of all Virginie's things. Félicité climbed the stairs to her
room, numbed with sadness. (Flaubert 1961: 51–2)

This is more Flaubertian detailing, details from the life of the
dead child, Virginie. These details, this furniture, undoubtedly
could be replaced with any other furniture, in order to get both the
reality effect and the pathos, whereas metaphoric language is not
so easily substitutable. Again, this partly accounts for the elevation
of poetic language as more 'artistic' and valuable than prose and
the prosaic. Nevertheless, this precise detailing is emotional and
the very stuff of existence in a way that metaphor is not.

Accessible language

One of the features common to ideas about realism is that the
language used is 'accessible' and 'readable', in the sense that any
literate person can readily understand what they are reading, as
opposed to, say, 'difficult', 'avant-garde' or 'experimental' literature, or, indeed, overly 'literary' literature. Roland Barthes used
the opposition *lisible* (readerly) and *scriptible* (writerly) as the
coordinates for these different types of writing. It is a typical
assumption that realist writing is *lisible*, and broadly speaking, this
is true. This is partly because there is a whole swathe of realist
writing that aims for a large audience, and to attract and sustain a
large audience an understandable requirement is that the language
used to render narrative, character, description, dialogue, and so
on, does not make the reader work too hard to figure out what is
being said, at least on the surface level.

And yet, when we come to look at the works themselves, how
true is this? It would be more accurate to say that the idea of readability is one of the mainstays of realist writing, both for its
readers and for its writers, but that it does not necessarily define
the language of realism, since accessible language is clearly available in other genres and modes (think of *Frankenstein* or *Nineteen
Eighty-Four*, although these texts have things to say about
language). Also, 'readability' has to be further understood as a
sliding scale. The prose of Trollope and Mrs Oliphant does not
place too many demands on the reader, whereas George Eliot has a
more involved style that I have known readers to find difficult.

Similarly, Dickens's style can seem quite 'ornate' – for example, the opening to *Bleak House* and its extended fog metaphor.

But there is more at stake than reaching a wide audience through readable writing. The assumption can take on a philosophical hue, and a social and political intent. We have seen that one of the reactions in the 1930s and after against the difficulties of modernist literature was precisely to 'revert' to a more transparent language, and this partly for political reasons. The sense of crisis, of social and political urgency, demanded a writing that spoke to all, not just an aesthetically select few. The underlying assumption is that readable literature, with its shared language, offers the possibility of dialogue, as if we are all in this together (whatever situation 'this' represents). Only by hitting upon the right shared language can there be genuine dialogue. The kinds of relationship developed between realist authors and their audience in the nineteenth century would seem to offer the model for this. A shared language suggests shared values. In closing her chapter on Gaskell's *Ruth* and *Mary Barton*, Amanda Anderson turns to the end of another Gaskell novel, *North and South*, in which the factory owner Thornton makes a plea for everyday contact and dialogue between masters and men. Anderson glosses it like this:

> A nonteleological everydayness derived from the domestic mode here constitutes not retreat but a protection against an overly rationalized reform. Gaskell thereby articulates a model of communicative practice aimed not merely at mutual understanding but at social transformation, and mediated not only by rational discourse but by a sympathetic, continually renewed, nonreified recognition of the other. (Anderson 1993: 140)

Viewed in this manner, an accessible, shared language is a prerequisite for realist fiction with a social and political aim. It is noticeable too that Pam Morris's book *Realism* ends by looking at the possible applications of Habermas's 'communicative reason' for similar aims. Similarly, Lukác's defence of realism against modernism is dependent upon a language that is commonly accessible. Again, while an accessible style might be fundamental to the aims of realism, it is a dynamic rather than a static feature, dependent upon fluctuations in what readers are stylistically familiar with and which carry the air of a shared communication rather than one open only to initiates.

The limits of language

We have already seen that Eliot, for one, was aware of the potential instability of language, since 'railway' could mean different things to different people. As part of the Realist aesthetic, and the broader realist impulse, however, this aspect needs to be managed in order that at the macro level there is a shared understanding. Although local usages of language in Realist writing might draw on those features which are antagonistic to a straightforward communication, such as ironic commentary, metaphoric discourse and symbolism, these are invariably subordinated to the idea of a shared language, and of dialogue. But there is (and always has been) considerable opposition to this view of language: it has been argued that the instabilities of language cannot be downplayed in this way, and to do so betrays the way in which language and its relationship with the world works; it too severely restrains artists whose chosen medium is prose (Dickens's implicit complaint in *Hard Times*, according to Kearns); it cannot represent what is exceptional or beyond the rational, at least not in a convincing or sympathetic manner.

Thomas Carlyle's *Sartor Resartus* (1831) – part novel, part social critique, part philosophy – offers a view of language (and narrative transmission) which is inimical to the Realist view of language and discourse. The philosophical idea running through *Sartor Resartus* ('The Tailor Tailored') is that the visible world is merely the invisible world 'clothed', and hence made visible through dress. This notion is carried over to language – since 'all visible things are emblems' then 'language' is nothing but 'Metaphors'. – 'An unmetaphorical style you shall in vain seek for: is not your very *Attention* a *Stretching-to?*' (Carlyle 1975: 54). The proposition that language is inherently metaphorical and so an 'unmetaphorical style' is unachievable is part of Carlyle's jeremiad against the materialism of the nineteenth century as a whole, but the logic of such a view is that language simply does not work in the way that Realists believe it works and want it to work. Language is therefore not a suitable medium for Realism.

Philip Davis in *The Victorians* detects a view of language in the sermons of Cardinal Newman in the nineteenth century that also casts doubt on the possibility of language being fit for Realist purpose:

> In particular in the *University Sermons* he delivered to theological students, Newman was insistent that words do not have a literal 1:1 relation to the thoughts they represent; that, likewise, thoughts, being immaterial, are not conterminous with the material beginnings and endings of the sentences in which they are lodged. Reason was never sufficient on its own. Even in discursive prose, arguably the most direct form of written language, no sentence could ever be exhaustively explicit or flatly self-explanatory: there was always something implicitly meaningful in the space behind or around it. Alternatively, the thoughts may seem as separate as the sentences that convey them, yet apparently separate propositions are 'ever formed in and round the idea itself (so to speak), and are in fact, one and all, only aspects of it'. Nor was the size of a thought, under pressure of time, necessarily proportionate to the number of sentences used to articulate it. Writing, concluded Newman, 'is the representation of an idea in a medium not native to it' (Sermon 15).
>
> For Newman as for Ruskin, it was precisely the imperfection of the medium that created the most powerful intimations of the meaning, *off* the page, to which it could only approximate on it. The characteristic Newman phrases 'so to speak', or 'as it were', were a sign that the act was always one of partial translation, tacitly calling for imaginative life to fulfil it. That was why discursive writing was still not an autonomous logical system but an act of personal trust, on the part of the writer, in seeking the recognition of a reader to complete the act of meaning ... In its mediated struggle for communication from person to person, writing was a deep, social act, in hope of a real if invisible society of fellow-believers. (Davis 2002: 447–8)

We can see here from Davis's understanding of this view of language – one that might seem oppositional to Realism's aims – that in fact it remains part of the contract between authors, prose discourse and readers. Hence, and this must be part of the shared world of understanding that the Realist novel depends upon, the writing is given over to the reader – it is precisely *not* self-contained, its meaning depends upon the agreement of the reader, that 'nodding in agreement' I suggested in the Introduction. Of course, difficulties arise the further removed the reader is from the time of writing and publication, unless the reader subscribes to Fielding's classical notion that there are universals holding good regardless of age and circumstance. The realist writer's ability to render a plausible world, however, arguably minimises the distance. Thus, even where there is a view that might hold that language is largely metaphorical, that it is not contiguous with the material world or thoughts, or that it completely lacks a 1:1 relationship with the things it refers to, it is still possible for the Realist aesthetic to work, at least within the relationship developed in nineteenth-century literary culture.

Case study: Mrs Oliphant's *Hester*

Again, as with metonymy, it is more fruitful to see Realism working within a particular framework in a complex manner than to argue that it has a relatively easily classifiable feature and consistent attitude towards that feature. For instance, how are such feelings as intimations of the sublime, or romantic love and erotic longings, meant to be conveyed by a prose that is prosaic, without somehow misrepresenting these common experiences? It is not that the writing necessarily has to 'mimic' the object – 'purple prose' would here be the correlate of heightened emotion – but that to use prose in a linguistic style that is consistently rational, measured, metonymic and discursive would seem to bear out all those complaints against the dullness of realism. This, I think, is a genuine problem, and I return to Mrs Oliphant's *Hester* to explore the matter since, on a number of occasions and in different ways, the medium of language is portrayed as inadequate in its ability to represent the world and in its ability to enable us to comprehend the world – two of the cornerstones of the Realist aesthetic.

In the novel, Edward's actions, and the feelings between Edward and Hester, are deemed to lie outside the established norms, and outside the establishment as represented by Redborough. Catherine Vernon, the novel's matriarch, has believed that she can read people's characters, but she has singularly failed to understand her son Edward's character. When she discovers that he has ruined the bank and intended to elope with Hester her whole world crumbles:

> She held up her face to the sky – an old face, with so many lines in it, suddenly smitten as with a death blow. Her eyes, under the curve of pain, which makes the eyelids quiver, looked up to the pale skies with what is the last appeal of humanity. For why? – for why? – an honest life, an honourable career, a soul that had shrunk from no labour or pain, a hand that never had been closed to human distress – and repaid with misery at the end! Is there no reason in it when God's creature lifts a face of anguish to His throne, and asks why? She paused on the threshold of her house, which was desolate, and made that mute appeal. It was beyond all words or crying, as it was beyond all reply. (Oliphant 1984: 453)

Her world has collapsed: she has no language to describe her anguish, she has no context within which to articulate her despair; reason itself has failed as the means with which to comprehend the world. There is also a suggestion that her life is a 'dialogue' with the world, for which she has no 'reply'. The discourse between self and world is therefore also at an end. Edward has destroyed the fabric of discourse upon which the world is represented, especially the one with which the novel begins, that Vernon's is as safe as the Bank of England. It is not just that her son has failed her, and that her belief in her metonymic access to Edward's inner world through his polite exterior is shown to be wholly wrong, but that language itself has failed. The failure of language at this point is itself indicative of all that is opposite to the Realist aesthetic: it suggests that the irrational and Romantic view of the world must triumph. That Catherine has no language also relates us to the way in which the Romantic rebel Edward wants to wrench himself free of 'stock phrases' (see below). It looks here as if language is indeed inadequate to render all of human experience. I will return to this after a digression.

Oliphant's attention to language as a medium occurs in another interesting, if curious, passage. Roland explains to Hester that it is possible to make money without spending any, and continues to talk about the stock market, using it as a 'vehicle for flirtation':

'I should like to buy you a quantity of Circassians, for instance, exactly at the right moment, neither too soon nor too late, and sell them next day, perhaps when the market had turned, and hand you over a thousand pounds or two which you should have made without, as I said, spending a penny. That would make the profession romantic, poetic, if one could conduct such operations for *you*.' [Hester asks him what Circassians are]. 'You must accept certain words as symbols, or we shall never make it clear. And my business is to watch the market for you, to catch the moment when the tide is turning.' (1984: 336)

Just as it appears possible to make money by not spending it, which for Hester goes against the law of political economy, so Roland says that words need to be taken for symbols. However, Roland is being duplicitous. His reference to Circassians must be to Circassian women, beautiful women who were traded as slaves. This would chime with a dominant theme in the book: that for women to get a husband is a business matter rather than an affair of the heart. Roland's reference to the Circassians as an example of how he could make money – the buying and selling of women as stock – would be deeply offensive to Hester if it were explained to her. However, he refuses to say what Circassians are, suggesting that they are mere symbols rather than actuality, and that it is only through symbols that things can be made clear. In fact, this turn to symbols completely obfuscates the matter, and since it is at this point in the book that Roland becomes ever more unsympathetic as a character in the eyes of the reader given his now-overt sexist attitude (he had once seemed a romantic possibility for Hester), his manipulation of how both language and the stock market work – as symbols, counters, things that are meant to remain 'mysteries' to Hester and women in general – the use of the symbolic, getting something for nothing, is discredited. In this way then, while acknowledging that there is a view of language as 'symbols', the very use of symbols is seen to be dishonest. Thus one of the tenets of the Realist aesthetic is here at least restored, just as it entertains the view that is counter to it.

This necessity for language to be communal and transparent, at the expense of being poetic, is nevertheless accepted by the novel as one which will necessarily line up realism (including its prag-

matic overtones) with dullness, and align poetic language with
what is dangerous. Here is a passage which interweaves these
elements. In this scene Edward suggests to Roland and Harry that
they should risk the bank's money on a speculation. Harry backs
up Roland's view:

> 'That's just what I say. We have others to consider besides
> ourselves,' said the steadfast Harry.
>
> Edward made no reply. He was outvoted for the moment by
> voices which, he said to himself, had no right to be heard on the
> question. The best thing was to end the discussion and judge for
> himself. And the contemplation of the step before him took away his
> breath; it took the words out of his mouth. There would be nothing
> to be said for it. In argument it would be an indefensible proceeding.
> It was a thing to do, not to think, much less talk about. No one
> would have a word to say if (as was all but absolutely certain) his
> operations were attended by success. In that event his coolness, his
> promptitude, his daring, would be the admiration of everybody; and
> Harry himself, the obstructive, would share the advantage, and
> nothing more would be heard of his stock phrase. Edward felt that in
> reality it was he who was considering others, who was working for
> everybody's benefit; but to form such a determination was enough
> to make the strongest head swim, and it was necessary that he
> should shake off all intrusion, and have time and solitude to think it
> over in private. (1984: 344–5)

This passage is full of ideas about the connections between
language, reality, discourse, public perspective, and the real.
Edward fully concedes that if this is a question of rational, discursive argument, there is no way he can win. However, if he moves
beyond the realm of thought and speech to action, if he moves
beyond representation, he will be successful and earn admiration
for his heroic deeds. And in winning he will alter the nature of the
way this world is perceived. To eliminate Harry's 'stock phrase'
will be to win out over ordinary, hackneyed, dull, prosaic,
language. (There is a further irony in that it is a *stock* phrase.)
Edward will establish an alternative way of looking at things that
makes his individualism more socially responsible than theirs:
'Edward felt that in reality it was he who was considering others.'
In relation to the narrative, the reader cannot know at this point if

Edward's attempt to replace the 'prosing' of Harry and Roland with an action that is beyond language will succeed.

Another derogatory comment is made by Edward on the language of the commonplace, which again associates the financial security of the family with the stability of language, when he says: 'That Vernon's should be as safe as the Bank of England was a family proverb which admitted of no doubt'. In attempting to change the way that the bank's finances are handled, he is breaking apart the linguistic foundations of its representation.

There is a parallel in the way that *Hester* treats the aptness of language when people are in love. Again, there is something at stake for Realism, for if it is inadequate for the purpose of describing this state of affairs, by extension, language must fail in its ability to give us the world in its total set of relations. The following is an exchange between Edward and Hester:

> Now he had spoken indeed – not in the conventional way, saying he loved her and asking her to marry him, as people did in books.
>
> They hadn't needed to speak before – their looks had always shown that they loved each other. Since the first day when they met on the common, she a child, he in the placidity of unawakened life, there had been nobody to each but the other. She knew and felt it clearly now – she had known it and felt it all along, she said to herself – but it had wanted that word to make it flash into the light. And how unlike ordinary love-making it was! (Oliphant 1984: 362)

The language of realism is here substituted by the non-language of sublimity – words are inadequate to the feeling of love. On a level outside of language Hester assumes that Edward has disclosed all to her, he has spoken but not spoken. The way the two are placed on the common, in the spaces outside of society, is more consistent with the management of space in *Wuthering Heights*, and there is something of the language of Heathcliff and Cathy in this. But just as Catherine fails to understand Edward, so Hester too fails to understand him, preferring instead to infer from looks that they are in love. By not resorting to language to clarify the situation, Hester cuts herself adrift from 'communicative reason' and, dull as this might seem even within the context of the novel, it is 'communicative reason' that wins out over the danger of language when it is comprised of symbols, and the 'non-language' of horror and love.

Works cited and further reading

I have not entered into the debate about 'literary language' that is frequent in discussions of the interface between language and literature, assuming instead that if you have read this far, you are interested in the idea of literary language. Good places to start to engage with stylistics are *The Language and Literature Reader*, edited by Ronald Carter and Peter Stockwell (Abingdon, Oxon: Routledge, 2008), and Paul Simpson's books *Language, Ideology and Point of View* (London: Routledge, 1993) and *Stylistics: A Resource Book for Students* (London: Routledge, 2004). Michael Toolan's *Narrative Stylistics* (2001) remains an excellent introduction, and the classic *Style in Fiction: A Linguistic Introduction to Fictional Prose* by Geoffrey Leech and Mick Short has specific work on realism and stylistics (London: Longman, 1981).

Anderson, Amanda (1993), *Tainted Souls and Painted Faces: The Rhetoric of Fallenness in Victorian Culture*. Ithaca: Cornell University Press.

Barthes, Roland (1986), 'The Reality Effect' in *The Rustle of Language*. Oxford: Basil Blackwell, 141–8. First published in *Communications*, 1968.

Carlyle, Thomas (1975), *Sartor Resartus*. London: Dent.

Chekhov, Anton (1991), *Uncle Vanya* in *Five Plays*. Oxford: Oxford University Press.

Disraeli, Benjamin (1980), *Sybil*. London: Penguin.

Eliot, George (1965), *Middlemarch*. London: Penguin.

Engels, Friedrich (1969), *The Condition of the Working Class in England*. London: Panther.

Flaubert, Gustav (1961) 'A Simple Heart', in *Three Tales*. Harmondsworth: Penguin.

Gilbert, W. S. (1909), *Charity* in *Original Plays by W. S Gilbert. First Series*. London: Chatto & Windus.

Jakobson, Roman (1971), 'Two Aspects of Language and Two Types of Aphasic Disturbances', in Roman Jakobson and Morris Halle, *Fundamentals of Language*. The Hague: Mouton, 67–96.

MacCabe, Colin (2003), *James Joyce and the Revolution of the Word*, second edition. Basingstoke: Palgrave Macmillan.

Miller, J. Hillis, (1971), 'The Fiction of Realism: *Sketches by Boz, Oliver Twist*, and Cruikshank's Illustrations', in *Dickens Centennial Essays*, ed. Ada Nisbet and Blake Nevius. Berkeley: University of California Press, 85–153.

Oliphant, Mrs (1984), *Hester: A Story of Contemporary Life*. London:
    Virago.
Oliphant, Mrs (1989), *Phoebe Junior*. London: Virago.
Spector, Stephen J. (1987), 'Monsters of Metonymy: *Hard Times* and
    Knowing the Working Class', in *Charles Dickens*, ed. Harold Bloom.
    New York: Chelsea House, 229–44.

10

Philosophy, science and the ends of Realism

Philosophy and the realist impulse: Aristotle and Plato

As consistently registered in this book, there has been an ever-present realist impulse in literature and art, and the argument has been that in the nineteenth century this combined with other factors to produce the self-conscious Realist aesthetic. Among those factors philosophical and scientific ideas played a large part, although we should also note that philosophy of art prior to this period also advocated versions of realism. However, it is worth pointing out that the term often taken as synonymous with the philosophy of art – aesthetics – was concerned with art as the representation of what was 'beautiful'. One of the charges laid against realism has always been that it contradicts this principle, concerned as it is (in principle) to represent the world as it is found and observed, rather than either selecting only what is beautiful, or idealising what is found according to presumed anterior essences. How 'the beautiful' is conveyed via art has changed considerably over the centuries, but nevertheless this remained a rule of thumb against which art could always be judged. This is not to say that what is deemed ugly – morally or visually – could not be treated, but that the form treating it should itself aspire to those attributes which contributed to the quality of beauty: harmony, unity and proportion, for instance.

One of the earliest philosophical statements on art in relation to realism is in Aristotle's *Poetics*. It is interesting to see that Aristotle begins his thesis by making mimesis the first principle. Although we have already given some thought to mimesis in relation to

realism, we need to consider it in more detail, for on first appearance it would seem that Aristotle is proposing nothing other than
a thoroughgoing realist aesthetic.

I think there are two things to observe. The first is the considerable problem of how exactly to translate the term 'mimesis'. In my
Penguin Classics copy (1996), the translator Malcolm Heath
prefers to use the term 'imitation' rather than the often-used
'representation'. The problem with 'representation' for Heath is
that it suggests the relationship between the artistic production
and the object referred to is purely conventional in the manner
that a symbol represents an object. For Heath this means that
'represent' is an inadequate translation of 'mimesis', because for
Aristotle it is a fundamental human activity to imitate things and
events in the world, partly as a cognitive exercise, and partly
because an audience takes pleasure in such recognition. However,
what follows this in *Poetics* are the rules which make for the best
kinds of tragedy, and these are elements such as 'completeness'
(beginning, middle and end) and 'unity'. The necessity to consider 'magnitude' also suggests that the aesthetic constraints on
mimesis take it some distance from what we regard as appropriate
to realism: 'Any beautiful object, whether a living organism or any
other entity composed of parts, must not only possess those parts
in proper order, but its *magnitude* also should not be arbitrary;
beauty consists in magnitude as well as order'. The assumption
here is that beauty is an overriding principle. Taken as a whole,
Poetics presents the reader with a mix of some elements that favour
a realist aesthetic and some elements that pay considerable attention to form and artistic decorum, the latter often based upon
particular views of character and the necessity to show 'good' and
'bad' appropriately. These non-realist elements, if we can call
them that, remained influential on ideas about art until about the
eighteenth century. As we have seen, it was necessary for Realism
to contend quite robustly with the idea of art as beholden to ideas
of beauty and artistic decorum.

An interesting corollary to Aristotle's view on imitation and art
is Plato's. People perhaps know Plato as the philosopher who
wished to banish the poets, and the grounds upon which this is
done brings us back once again to the role of mimesis or imitation.

In Books II and III of *The Republic* (1971) the propensity of poets to lie and be the representative of things that are not conducive to the orderly running of the republic is made evident. In Book III there is antagonism towards the speaker who imitates rather than narrates, that is, the narrator who takes on the voice of the character or characters. The dislike of this is partly because, logically, no man can properly render so many different characters accurately, but also because if the character imitated is a bad character, there is the danger that the poet (or speaker of the poem) may themselves become bad. Diegesis is therefore acceptable in poetry: (where the poet remains distinct from the characters portrayed he is in a position of being able to explain events and actions, but mimesis – imitative poetry – is ruled out.)

There is a return to the role of the poets in the republic in Book X, and a different argument against artists and imitation is mobilised. In essence, by the very position artists occupy in the order of things, they are some distance from the truth. The painter, for instance, is thrice removed from the true nature of 'bed' if he paints a picture of one. The original idea for 'bed' is God's, and the carpenter's rendering of the bed through his skills comes second to this. The carpenter's bed represents a falling away from the one ideal bed, but the carpenter understands well the nature of bed from his making of it. In painting the bed the artist is third in line: God knows the absolute truth about the (ideal) bed, the carpenter has a pretty good idea, whereas the painter has no intimate knowledge of the bed, and therefore his depiction is some distance from the original (God's) ideal form. This argument is then applied, by analogy, to the poets: they must be thrice removed from the truth.

Although it is difficult to ascertain Plato's final position on the worth of poets – he admires Homer, and *The Republic* is itself a fine work of art – taken together with Aristotle's views, it would certainly seem that despite the centrality of mimesis (imitation) to arguments about the nature of art and what was right for artists to be aiming for, there was nothing incumbent upon the artist to conceive of the work of art in the manner that we have seen the Realists do. Indeed, the necessity for beauty and moral elevation as criteria mitigated the development of a complete realist aesthetic for serious art and literature. Kant's substantial contribution in the eighteenth century to ideas about art in his *Critique of Judgement* in fact consolidated a view of art that made this realism less likely. He argued for the autonomy of art; the idea that art did not offer a means of understanding; the idea that beauty can be universally observed by those with good taste; the idea of genius as non-copyable inspiration; the idea that what is beautiful is also morally good. All of these ideas contributed to the Romanticism that Realism reacted against. In this light, I will jump back once more into the nineteenth century.

Philosophy and Realism

If philosophic and aesthetic principles do not wholly coincide with the realist impulse until the nineteenth century, we still might ask exactly how much does literary Realism depend upon philosophical realism, or versions of it? Becker, in *Documents of Modern Literary Realism*, identifies a philosophical underpinning as essential to a definition of realism:

> Romanticism must ultimately be found to rest on an idealist metaphysics and its view of art to be one that is consonant with that metaphysical position. Realism came into being in the ferment of scientific and positivist thinking which characterized the middle of the nineteenth century and was to become what Zola always spoke of as the major current of the age. Realism really did constitute a fresh start because it was based on a new set of assumptions about the universe. It denied that there was a reality of essences or forms which was not accessible to ordinary sense perception, insisting instead that reality be viewed as something immediately at hand, common to ordinary human experience, and open to observation. This attitude demanded that its readers and adherents abandon a host of preconceptions about human nature, about the purposes and mechanism of the universe, and above all about the role of art. (Becker 1963: 6)

For Becker, then, it is this philosophical view which motivates the Realist aesthetic and which differentiates Realism from other artistic modes and affinities. What counts as real in this philosophy is what is available to 'ordinary sense perception', that which is experienced by the majority of ordinary people and which is readily observable. It is important to stress that this is what counts as reality, or the real, as opposed to other ideas which contend that what we see is a shadow world behind which stands the true reality. The latter notion is rather like Carlyle's in which the material world is merely the visible emblem – the clothing – for a spiritual world which, in turn, is the real world. We have seen that the Realists gave much more credit to what was not visible than this characterisation of Realism might allow but, nevertheless, in broad outline Becker I think is correct. And this view of the world, in philosophical terms, is what is called 'common-sense realism'.

There are a number of directions in which we can take the relationship between literary realism and the philosophical position of common-sense realism. We could see how engaged the writers actually were with philosophy; we could evaluate the match between philosophical claims and artistic production; we could look at common-sense realism to see how it differs from other types of philosophical realisms (yes, there are philosophical realisms other than the common-sense one); we could see how philosophical realism fares now against the considerable body of criticisms which find it untenable, but also how it relates to a counter-current that defends the realist view of the universe. Part of this will be to draw together in one place some of the things already discussed, and part will be to give specific consideration to further thought about the philosophy of realism and the realist aesthetic.

Realist writers and philosophy

We have already covered much of this ground in discussion of the tenets of Realism, so I will not spend too much on this aspect. Zola drew heavily on positivism, and Eliot too was enamoured of this view and method, yet surely it is not necessary to have read about positivism or be a follower of Comte in order to write a Realist novel? There will always be a question as to the strength and necessity of the connection between the nineteenth-century philosophical/scientific outlook, the Realist aesthetic and Realist works of art, particularly when, as we have seen, there has always been the realist impulse evident throughout the history of art. Additionally, where a writer or artist does not specifically lay claim to any philosophy or aesthetic, but produces within the popular aesthetic of the time, as many did and continue to do so, there may be little reflection upon what philosophical system authorises the aesthetic mode that the writer has chosen. Many currents flowed into the belief that the observable everyday here and now, rendered realistically, should be the object of artistic endeavour.

For Eliot it was certainly a matter of principle that her writing should follow the tenets of positivist philosophy. As early as 1855 in a review of a book on German philosophy Eliot enthuses over the positivist viewpoint, where the emphasis is on investigation of the world as it is rather than investigation of it to confirm pre-existing structures. It is a move from the a priori ('before the fact') to a belief that the a posteriori ('after the fact') method of investigation is what is required. Behind this is actually a change in the status of philosophy: it is not there to build systems (or identify them), it is there to reveal the world as it might be observed. By shifting to 'investigation' and the 'a posteriori', and eschewing the system-building of philosophy, Eliot, here and elsewhere, makes the novel the foremost means of understanding human nature and the world. The Realist novel therefore usurps philosophy as the best tool for getting to grips with reality. Eliot concludes the review:

> These are rather abstruse subjects to enter on in a short space, but we have at least been able to present one point of interest to our readers, in the fact that a German professor of philosophy renounces the attempt to climb to heaven by the rainbow bridge of 'the high *priori* road', and is content humbly to use his muscles in treading the uphill *à posteriori* path which will lead, not indeed to heaven, but to an eminence whence we may see very bright and blessed things on earth. (in Pinney 1967: 153)

Although Eliot here praises the merits of positivist philosophy, the implication is that to reveal reality as it is experienced on earth, a dedicated humility to the here and now is in itself what the general viewpoint should be. Such an approach is open to everybody, in all spheres, no doubt, but the Realist novel form, and its medium of discursive prose, happened to be the most apt means for dealing with the things of earth rather than heaven.

Common-sense realism

It is time to move away from the historical specifics of Realism, and engage with the broader philosophical claims that might underlie realism as a whole after its nineteenth-century incarnation. It should be remembered that positivism held that empirical science was the only means of acquiring sure knowledge about the world, and the nineteenth-century Realists adopted this view for their own work. Science therefore (or philosophy of science) remained the dominant authority.

Nigel Warburton's chapter on 'The External World' in his book *Philosophy* makes this claim:

> Common-sense realism is a view held by most people who haven't studied philosophy. It assumes that there is a world of physical objects – houses, trees, cars, goldfish, teaspoons, footballs, human bodies, philosophy books, and so on – which we can learn about directly through our five senses. These physical objects continue to exist whether or not we are perceiving them. What is more, these objects are more or less as they appear to us: goldfish really are orange, and footballs really are spherical. This is because our organs of sense-perception – eyes, ears, tongue, skin, and nose – are generally reliable. They give us a realistic appreciation of what is actually out there. (Warburton 1995: 90)

The implication, borne out by Warburton's subsequent explanations of various philosophical views, is that common-sense realism will struggle to hold its own under the weight of philosophical scrutiny.

'Common-sense realism' is the view I put forward in the introduction, along the lines that there is a world out there which exists, and to which we belong, and which we can describe in a manner that accurately reflects the true nature of these things. Along the way, however, we have encountered many challenges to this view of the world, particularly ones which argue that 'reality' is a construct of some kind, a consequence of the way language works or a consequence of bourgeois ideology, or a simultaneous construct of both. Warburton lists other objections to common-sense realism, and I will just note these and then move on to see how all this relates to our understanding of literary realism. I would just ask you to bear in mind in particular one feature of Warburton's summary of common-sense realism, and that is the assertion it is the unthinking view of most people. In other words, the default position for the majority of people is common-sense realism when they have not taken the trouble to think about what the world is and how they know about it.

In Warburton's view of common-sense realism, our access to the world is through our sense perception, predominantly that of sight, and while we might make our merry way through the world thinking no more of this, as soon as we consider it more closely a number of sceptical challenges arise which make this view difficult to sustain. For instance, our senses often deceive us as to the nature of things. If this is so, just how reliable can we assume them to be, for example in altered states of consciousness? The answer to this could be that we can generally work out what is real and come to the right conclusion. To which the sceptic replies, 'but you could still be dreaming or hallucinating'. Another related argument in the battery of scepticism could point up the fallibility of logic in coming to 'correct' conclusions about reality (although this involves self-excepting on behalf of the sceptic). As to being certain of my own reality, the assertion 'I think therefore I am' tells me little about the nature of anything – world or self – and the 'I' could in any case be a linguistic convenience rather than self-evident proof of identity.

Warburton glosses some refinements to common-sense realism in response to these criticisms of it. 'Representative realism' suggests that rather than our senses giving direct access to the world, we measure sense data against representations of these things that we have in our heads. The problem with this idea is that if we have no direct access to the real, how can we actually make such a judgement? One response to this is Idealism, which follows the logic of representative realism through to a conclusion to suggest that in fact there is nothing outside of our perception of reality, and so if something is not perceived it does not exist. The argument against this, and the related idea of phenomenalism, is that it is in effect 'solipsism', that is, things only exist in my mind – the world is a projection of my consciousness, it does not refer to a world outside it. One argument against solipsism is that the judgements we make about perception and experience depend on a language which, logic asserts, only makes sense if it is public, and this in itself vouchsafes for a world and people outside of myself: there can be no such thing as private language here. The final type of philosophical realism that Warburton identifies is 'causal realism', a belief that 'the causes of our sense experience are physical objects in the external world' (1995: 105), and he finds this to be the 'the most satisfactory theory of perception to date' (1995: 106), even though it falls short on accounting for *qualia*, that is, sense perception as a qualitative experience rather than mere information gathering. It also retains the assumption fundamental to all realist-based philosophies, that there is a world that exists independently of our perception of it.

'Everyday realism' versus everything else

What I am going to do now is suggest that 'common-sense realism' is only a part of the type of philosophical position that underwrites both Realism and realism. Let me go back to the nineteenth century in order to make the argument that we in fact need a different term, what I will call 'everyday realism', in order to describe the kind of default realist position taken up by the majority of people and with which nineteenth-century Realism accords.

The subtitle of Engels's *The Condition of the Working Class in England* (1845) is: 'From Personal Observation and Authentic Sources'. Compare this with Disraeli's assurance from the same year at the front of *Sybil* that his books, designed to illustrate 'the Condition of the People', have the 'authority of his own observation' and 'the authentic evidence which has been received by Royal Commissions and Parliamentary Committees' ('Advertisement'). What's going on here? This is nineteenth-century realism, dependent both on an individual's sense-data (common-sense realism) *and* reliance on the evidence of other, external views, in this case Royal Commissions and Parliamentary Committees. This realism is thus a combination of sense perception (personal observation) *and* publicly-verified knowledge, and such a form of triangulation, I would suggest, is the philosophical underpinning of nineteenth-century Realism, with different degrees of emphasis certainly. But the necessity for triangulation is central to it – that is, the match between public and private perception, observation and knowledge. This also explains why Realist literature has to balance the public and the private and establish a correct ratio for it, a process which involves authors and audience working collaboratively. I would suggest that rather than 'common-sense realism' being the default position, this mix of individual perception, common knowledge, authoritative statements, application of reason, belief and tradition, represents the default position. Let me call this 'everyday realism'. This hardly amounts to a philosophy, since it is more a description of the general practical engagement of the world by people when 'not thinking' more consciously about that very engagement. Such a way of going about the world is unsystematic and hence not amenable to a philosophical validation. The advantage is that there is no great pressure on individuals to reconcile within themselves otherwise incompatible beliefs. Eliot's understanding that there are myriad influences on every action within the complexity of a social web is of this order, even if observation, from the novelist's point of view, suggests that systematic objectivity is feasible and desirable.

Everyday realism aside, the role of science in any contemporary realist view tends to remain problematic. The current difficulty is that the everyday realist view still continues to depend in some way on the belief that science is the most secure and authoritative method of giving us knowledge of the world, yet science is currently unable to tell us what the physical world consists of, and the philosophy of science cannot authoritatively state what science is able to deliver in terms of knowledge. This is partly because there is no agreed philosophical position as to how we might conceptualise the world, our relation to it, and the role of language and culture in this.

In surveying the current state of affairs, Brian Greene states: 'Space and time capture the imagination like no other scientific subject. For good reason. They form the arena of reality, the very fabric of the cosmos … Yet science is still struggling to understand what space and time actually are. Are they real physical entities or simply useful ideas?' (Green 2005: ix). The physical world that science describes at macro and micro levels is quite bizarre.

Superstring theory, for instance, posits that the basic units in the universe are not non-dimensional particles (points) but one-dimensional loops whose vibrations at different levels correspond to what we have previously designated 'particles'. And instead of the three dimensions plus time that we take as fundamental to our spatio-temporal world, string theory suggests that there are nine dimensions plus time. There has been no evidence to support string theory – it is purely speculative – yet it is a seriously considered contender for a theory that will explain the physical basis of the universe. String theory is part of the effort to reconcile the general theory of relativity, which deals with what is macro in the universe, and quantum theory, which deals with the micro. One of the necessities to unify these incompatible frameworks is that it will then reveal the constitution and process of the big bang, and thus the origins of the universe, and consequently the very nature of reality.

Yet in spite of this – and throughout the twentieth century the uncertainty principle as described in quantum physics has undermined the positivist belief that we can locate with certainty the position of all objects in space and time – the everyday realist view continues, unmindful of the precarious microworld beneath, the cosmos at large, and the fact that we do not know what makes up the physical world. Everyday realism does not have to answer to the problems of individual sense perception upon which common-sense realism and other realisms are exclusively founded, and hence seems a better description of the default realist position, both then (nineteenth century) and now.

Philosophy of science in the twentieth- and twenty-first centuries queries exactly what kind of knowledge science can give us, and what status it can have relative to other kinds of knowledge. Nevertheless, a strand of philosophy has emerged called 'critical realism'. This is most closely associated with the British philosopher Roy Bhaskar, and is a response to the relativism of postmodernism and poststructuralist critiques, for critical realism believes that we can improve our knowledge rather than just construct different views. It asserts that there is a mind-independent world, and suggests that what science has access to are certain activations of the structures inherent in that world, rather than believing we get the total picture, and that this knowledge is through our sense-perception. There may be other structures inherent in the physical world that are not activated. This approach, with some modifications, can also be applied to observations of the human world, although there is greater variability in the structures and the possibility of their activation, and humans are indeed capable of changing the structures themselves. Critical realism could, therefore, underpin a contemporary realist aesthetic if writers and artists chose for it to do so, in the manner that Eliot and Zola adopted positivist ideas.

STOP and THINK

Contemporary writers and artists do not seek the authority of critical realism for their projects – should they? Is everyday realism enough, even if it does not stand up to much scrutiny, even if, in fact, it is quite inaccurate or downright wrong? Put another way, everyday realism persists in the face of rather damning critical opposition. As soon as you start to think about it, everyday realism is not tenable if it has to answer to science and philosophy on the terms of those disciplines. Alternatively, though, as soon as you stop thinking about the philosophical and scientific premises that might underpin everyday realism, as a practical method for engagement with the world, everyday realism seems to be fit for purpose. Is it possible to think about everyday realism in this way, and having thought about it, hold on to it?

Well, possibly. You do not need a theory of everything to understand everything (see Greene 2005: 327), and neither do you need a theory of theories (philosophy) to understand how you might understand everything. You do not need a theory of language to communicate, or a theory of communication to realise that you have understood what you have discussed (as you do not have to understand the mechanics of the internal combustion engine in order to drive a car). Such theories may ultimately explain reality at the levels of science and philosophy, but the experience of reality may be said to continue to remain outside scientific and philosophical views of it, and so, in this sense – if realist art and literature are to re-present the shared experience of reality – everyday realism (as I have tentatively configured it) can still potentially stand behind a realist aesthetic as a viable philosophical viewpoint. The question then is, is the realist aesthetic itself still valuable?

Has the realist aesthetic had its day?

Just because we live our lives in the manner which suggests that the majority subscribe to everyday realism, it does not mean that art and literature are obliged to represent the world in this way. The opposite argument indeed might have more force, for if everyday realism is our unthinking, habitual mode of existence, art forms which challenge this can alert us to our somewhat uncritical state, showing alternative points of view, different kinds of perception, different kinds of knowledge, alternative views of linguistic usage and narrative construction, different cognitive approaches to the world and human behaviour. I do not think that any of this can be gainsaid: modernist and postmodernist aesthetics, and the philosophical and critical ideas that lie behind these artistic modes, have shown this. The gap between the Realists and ourselves – and the realists of the 1930s and 1950s – is that there was a social necessity to work from within the Realist aesthetic. Although arguments over accessible art continue to rage, and realism is seen as the primary aesthetic for popular art, 'realism' has few of the constraints of nineteenth-century Realism and tends to once more be conflated with mimesis and being adjudged 'realistic'. As long as things look like the things we know and behave in a plausible manner, in a spatio-temporal universe we believe to continue to exist, the art is acceptable. Such a realist aesthetic maintains some of the tenets of its nineteenth-century forbear, but lacks the self-conscious urgency and exploration of a new aesthetic and, indeed, does not feel the need to defend itself as an aesthetic.

Realist writers want to give us the real, and the more interesting ones understand that they cannot rely on hackneyed methods of representation. They are no doubt perfectly aware that language is not transparent, that it is a mediation, but that still does not accord with many people's psychological, cognitive and emotional experience of reality. Language and representation are the real, and it remains contentious to argue that modern realism deliberately, and rather sinisterly, conflates representation with realism. A novel such as Zadie Smith's *On Beauty* (published in 2005) is a contemporary novel in the realist tradition. It deals directly with many of the social problems of the contemporary world: the effects of global capitalism, the place of religion in the modern world, questions about class, gender, race, age, family relations, and the nature of representation. It knows its literary and critical theory, yet still presents all this within the realist mode of a belief in its ability to re-present a recognisable world in an accessible language. That is a lot of ground to cover. Nevertheless, unlike Joshua Ferris's novel, it is not aesthetically experimental, despite its knowingness, and is undoubtedly more typical of contemporary realist literature than Ferris.

Has the nature of reality changed?

One of the reasons readers found Darwin's argument for evolution in *The Origin of Species* so persuasive was that he was able to draw on processes observable in the world, the way gardeners or farmers were able to improve their stock, for instance, by controlling certain genetic aspects. These were the same processes at work in evolution, but over a much greater time period. Moving into the twentieth century, as argued above, the scientific understanding of the world begins to operate at a level which has little connection with what is observable, either with the naked eye, microscope or telescope. We are reliant on a mathematics which is beyond most informed understanding. Realism, as a mix of philosophical attitude and artistic project, has to contend with this along with new media, which intrinsically appear to be antithetical to realism. In addition, there are many other media which are better suited than literature for the mimetic component of realism.

Even as the novel was dominant in the nineteenth century, the invention of modern photography in the 1820s and advances in this technology in subsequent decades offered the means for recording and representing the real world which no other pictorial medium could achieve. Similarly, sound recording and reproduction following Edison's work in the 1870s meant that the reality of speech did not depend upon art's ability to represent it. If Realism was intent on mimesis, it was easily outdone by other technologies. However, as this book has consistently argued, Realism as unmediated access to the real world was never really part of its aesthetic, so in this sense these advances in technology in relation to the real did not necessarily affect the Realists to any great extent, even though they were aware of them.

Nevertheless, I do not think that this is quite satisfactory. If, as I have suggested, there has always been a realist impulse, itself part of our desire to be represented with the real, then technologies whose mimetic abilities have overtaken those of art must have some impact on the realist aesthetic. In addition, the nature of the contemporary world is increasingly marked by the condition of 'virtuality', relationships between people and groups which do not exist in 'the real world' but which are conducted within a space deemed to be 'virtual', that is, 'not real'. This could be anything from 'immersion' in computer games to the virtual lives people inhabit to various degrees on the internet. An argument against realism, then, is that its attachment is to a world that is characterised by not being 'real' at all but virtual to start with. If much of our lives is conducted in cyberspace, the aims and tenets of a realist aesthetic can no longer have much relevance.

I do not have anything profound to offer in response to this. The forms of 'bracketing out' from the real world may have changed, but in essence this is still 'bracketing out'. By this I mean that in any culture where there is a separation between an art that represents and a world that is represented, even an art whose aesthetic is dependent upon an appropriation of improved mimetic techniques (or different ones) is still ontologically separate from the world it mimics. The experience of virtuality – if we take it in the sense of 'virtual reality' – is just that: an experience of something that approximates to 'real' experience. So, just like dreams and hallucinations, while personal experience may tell us that we are experiencing 'the real', there is always a perspective which can place this in its true position. Although there is a slippage here between that kind of virtuality inherent in computer gaming and the like, and that kind of virtuality of electronic communication (virtual communities), they are still judged against the real 'real'. As long as these things continue to be set alongside the spatio-temporal world of everyday experience, there is an ontological distinction that lets us know when we are in a virtual world and when we are in the real world. This too must be part of the every-day realist position.

Summary conclusion

The Realism of the nineteenth century is beholden to certain prevalent scientific and philosophic views. Some of these views are themselves dependent upon an older empirical tradition, which itself was (as argued by Watt) part of the philosophical underpin-ning for the emergence of the modern novel and its realist aesthetic, and so there is certainly a continuity in the philosophical worldview which accords with Realism and the form of its main proponent, the novel. As we have already seen with modernism and postmodernism, many of the certainties about self, language, narrative and art that the Realists held as necessary were replaced by other ideas less conducive or antithetical to the Realist's enter-prise. The twentieth century has seen a full-scale onslaught on many of the tenets that enable both philosophical realism and a realist aesthetic to hold good. Nevertheless, as shown, something akin to what I have termed 'everyday realism' persists and is arguably viable in the face of hostile criticism, and this in turn underwrites an aesthetic which continues to retain some domin-ance as a popular mode for many different art forms, not just literary realism. Its very existence, whether stated explicitly or held to be implicit by its practitioners, presumes that the world exists in a particular way, and that we are involved in the world in this way, and that to render the world realistically, with all that entails in terms of a battery of realist techniques, is still a valuable enterprise.

Works cited and further reading

Archer, Margaret, Roy Bhaskar, Andrew Collier, Tony Lawson and Alan Norrie (1998), *Critical Realism*. London: Routledge.

Aristotle (1996), *Poetics*. Translation and Introduction by Malcolm Heath. London: Penguin.

Baudrillard, Jean (1988), 'Simulacra and Simulations', in *Jean Baudrillard. Selected Writings*, edited by Mark Poster. Cambridge: Polity Press.

Beaumont, Matthew (ed.) (2007), *Adventures in Realism*. Oxford: Blackwell.

Becker, G. J. (ed.) (1963), *Documents of Modern Literary Realism*. Princeton, New Jersey: Princeton University Press.

Bruck, Jan (1982), 'From Aristotelian Mimesis to Bourgeois Realism', *Poetics* 11.3: 189–202.

de Magalhães, Theresa Calvet (2003), 'Realism after the Linguistic–Pragmatic Turn', *Cognitio*, São Paulo, 4.2: 211–26.

Davies, David and Carl Matheson (2008), *Contemporary Readings in the Philosophy of Literature*. Toronto: Broadview Press.

Greene, Brian (2005), *The Fabric of the Cosmos*. London: Penguin.

Lister, Martin, Jon Dovey, Seth Giddings, Iain Grant and Kieran Kelly (2003), *New Media: A Critical Introduction*. London: Routledge.

López, José and Garry Potter (eds) (2006), *After Postmodernism: An Introduction to Critical Realism*. London: The Athlone Press.

Margolis, Joseph (2007), *Pragmatism without Foundations. Reconciling Realism and Relativism* (second edition). London: Continuum.

Nelson, Quee (2007), *The Slightest Philosophy*. Indianapolis: Dog Eared Publishing.

Penrose, Roger (2005), *The Road to Reality: A Complete Guide to the Laws of the Universe*. New York: A. A. Knopf.

Pinney, Thomas (ed.) (1967), *Essays of George Eliot*. London: Columbia University Press.

Plato (1971), *The Republic*. Oxford: Oxford University Press.

Ronen, Ruth (1995), 'Philosophical realism and postmodern antirealism', *Style*, 22 (June).

Ronen, Ruth (2002), *Representing the Real*. Amsterdam: Rodopi.

Rorty, Richard (1999), *Objectivity, Relativism and Truth*. Cambridge: Cambridge University Press.

Smith, Zadie (2006), *On Beauty*. London: Penguin.

Trigg, Roger (1980), *Reality at Risk: A Defence of Realism in Philosophy and the Sciences*. Sussex: The Harvester Press.

Warburton, Nigel (1995), *Philosophy. The Basics*. London: Routledge.

Index

400705